COLLECTED WHEEL PUBLICATIONS

VOLUME 20

NUMBERS 296 – 311

BPE

BPS Pariyatti Editions

BPS Pariyatti Editions
An imprint of Pariyatti Publishing
www.pariyatti.org

Copies of this book for sale in the Americas only. Although this is an American edition, we have left any British spelling of words unchanged.

First BPS Pariyatti Edition, 2025
ISBN: 978-1-68172-200-9 (Print)
ISBN: 978-1-68172-201-6 (PDF)
ISBN: 978-1-68172-202-3 (ePub)
ISBN: 978-1-68172-203-0 (Mobi)
LCCN: 2018940050

Contents

WH 296 & 297 The World's True Welfare
The Venerable Vīdāgama Maitreya 1

WH 298 to 300 Thoughts on the Dhamma
Venerable Mahāsi Sayādaw 45

WH 301 & 302 Investigation for Insight
Susan Elbaum 83

WH 303 & 304 Contemplation of Feelings
Nyanaponika Thera 133

WH 305 to 307 The Paccekabuddha: A Buddhist Ascetic
Ria Kloppenborg 169

WH 308 to 311 The Noble Eightfold Path
Bhikkhu Bodhi 235

Key to Abbreviations

A	Aṅguttara Nikāya	Nidd	Niddesa
Ap	Apadāna	Paṭis	Paṭisambhidāmagga
Bv	Buddhavaṃsa	Peṭ	Peṭakopadesa
Cp	Cariyāpiṭaka	S	Saṃyutta Nikāya
D	Dīgha Nikāya	Sn	Suttanipāta
Dhp	Dhammapada	Th	Theragāthā
Dhs	Dhammasaṅgaṇī	Thī	Therīgāthā
It	Itivuttaka	Ud	Udāna
Ja	Jātaka verses and commentary	Vibh	Vibhaṅga
Khp	Khuddakapāṭha	Vin	Vinayapiṭaka
M	Majjhima Nikāya	Vism	Visuddhimagga
Mil	Milindapañha	Vism-mhṭ	Visuddhimagga Sub-commentary
Nett	Nettipakaraṇa	Vv	Vimānavatthu

The above is the abbreviation scheme of *A Pali Text Society* (PTS) as given in the *Dictionary of Pāli* by Margaret Cone.

The commentaries, *aṭṭhakathā*, are abbreviated by using a hyphen and an "a" ("-a") following the abbreviation of the text, e.g., *Dīgha Nikāya Aṭṭhakathā* = D-a. Likewise the sub-commentaries are abbreviated by a "ṭ" ("-ṭ") following the abbreviation of the text.

The sutta reference abbreviation system for the four Nikāyas, as is used in Bhikkhu Bodhi's translations is:

AN	Aṅguttara Nikāya	DN	Dīgha Nikāya
MN	Majjhima Nikāya	Sn	Saṃyutta Nikāya
J	Jātaka story	Mv	Mahāvagga (Vinaya Piṭaka)
Cv	Cullavagga (Vinaya Piṭaka)	SVibh	Suttavibhaṅga (Vinaya Piṭaka)

The World's True Welfare

The Lōvāḍa Saṅgarāva
A Didactic Poem of the 15th Century from Sri Lanka

by

The Venerable Vīdāgama Maitreya

Translated from the Sinhalese by

F. M. Rajakaruna

Introduction by

Prof. Ānanda Kulasuriya

WHEEL PUBLICATION NO. 296/297

Translator's Preface

The idea of translating the *Lōväḍa Saṅgarāva* into English was born as a result of a discussion I had with two friends about eight years ago. They were both businessmen, but the subject discussed was not the markets, the foreign exchange or the next business deal, but was on education. Someone casually remarked on the small book of Sinhala verses, the *Sirith Mal Dama,* a code and guide to the small schoolgoers, how they had to conduct themselves at home, on the way to school and back, verses from which they had to recite at home and in class. Next came the withdrawal from school use in Sri Lanka, of the *Lōväḍa Saṅgarāva*, a book of verses used in higher grades, and verses from which were recited daily in one class or another.

I undertook to translate the *Lōväḍa Saṅgarāva* into English, so that we could put it into the hands of parents and adults and through them reach the younger generation. The following day I went in search of a copy of the book, but none of the large book-sellers in the city had a copy to sell. I scoured the pavement "book-stalls," where I found a mildewed, dust-covered copy. I drew on my memory, for I had known all the verses by heart and found confirmation in print.

For refreshing my memory of the verses, I have referred to the Venerable Devundara Vachissāra Thera's edition of the text, provided with a paraphrase in modern Sinhala (Colombo, 1966, M.D. Gunasena & Co.).

I wish to express my deep sense of indebtedness to the Venerable Nyanāponika Mahā Thera, who kindly took charge of the manuscript. But for his intervention and the tedious task of editing and revising the script, shared by his helpers, this work may never have reached the readers in the present form.

I wish to make a further reference to the two *kalyāṇa mitrayo* (benevolent friends) who gave me the idea and the encouragement to do this work, the late Mr. N. S. de S. Wickremasinghe, and Mr. B. Darsin de Silva both of Balapitiya. To the first named, no longer with us, I offer the wholesome benefits that may accrue to me by this good work, and to the second, my good wishes for prosperity here, and more opportunity to join in the service to the Dhamma.

Lastly, I wish to state that I undertook this task with one intention. The Venerable Author's wish was to bring knowledge of some of the simpler teachings of the Buddha to those who did not understand Pāli, the original language of the Buddhist canonical texts. It was now my own humble intention to take the Venerable Author's wishes a step further, by carrying his noble thoughts to a wider circle of readers who know neither Pāli nor the Sinhala language.

F. M. Rajakaruna
Colombo, Sri Lanka
January 1981

Introduction

Moral maxims find artistic expression in many literatures. Such sayings are widely prevalent in Oriental literature, so also in Pāli and in Sanskrit, where they were included in the category of *subhāsita* (lit. "well spoken," "good counsel") or *nīti* (lit. "right conduct" or "behaviour") literature. They also constitute a well-known element in Western classical literature and were known to the ancient Greeks as "*gnomes*" (a term derived from a word meaning "an opinion"). From this derives the practice of referring to such writings as gnomic literature. Sinhalese literature contains a fair number of such writings.

Literary works seeking to impart moral instruction or embodying the wisdom of the ages were arranged by the ancients in a metrical pattern for the better aid of the memory. The Greeks, who wrote gnomic verse in the 6th century B.C., adopted the elegiac couplet while Sanskrit poets, down the ages, composed their verses in the *śloka* metre. Sinhalese authors generally employed the rhymed quatrain or *sivupada* in preference to the unrhymed *gī* metre. The aim of this poetry was less to excite the hearer by passion or move him by pathos than to instruct the mind and improve his morals. For that reason, it was also known as didactic poetry (the adjective in this expression being derived from a Greek word meaning "apt for teaching"). The term was used to describe the class of poetical works which dealt exclusively or almost entirely with moral maxims. It thus included all poetry that dealt in a sententious way with questions of human morals. Such poetry often took the form of persuasive sayings or exhortations which advised people what they ought to and ought not to do. Brevity was of their essence. A moral maxim of the kind indicated above would accord with the definition of a gnomic expression given by the Elizabethan critic Henry Peacham as "a saying pertaining to the manners and common practices of men which declareth with an apt brevity, what in this our life ought to be done, or not done." That sums up adequately the basic characteristics of content, aim and literary form of this kind of writing.

The practice of introducing moral maxims into their poetical compositions was known to Sinhalese poets, who included them amidst descriptions and narratives. They doubtless drew their inspiration from classical writers. Lengthy passages of good counsel were sometimes incorporated into Sinhalese poems. The substance was drawn, in the majority of instances, from the Jātaka literature and sometimes from other collections of Buddhist stories. The advice to a young girl in the *Kāvya Sēkaraya* of Sri Rāhula, and the remarks on proper and improper conduct contained in the *Guttilaya* of Vḷttḷve are but two notable examples of such writings. Such instances may be found in almost any Sinhalese poem. But the *Lōväḍa Saṅgarāva* of Vīdāgama Maitreya Thera is one of the earliest, if not the earliest, Sinhalese poem dealing exclusively with moral instruction.[1]

The Author

The author of the *Lōväḍa Saṅgarāva* was Vīdāgama Maitreya Thera or, as he was known in his own writings, Vīdāgama Methimi. The name of Vīdāgama calls to mind at least two famous names in the literary history and politics of late mediaeval Sri Lanka. Two monks who came from the same village and resided in the same monastery, and who, each in his own way, played a prominent role in the affairs of the time, came to be known as Vīdāgama Theras.[2] Both names are associated with the history of the city of Jayavaddana/Kōṭṭē. The elder of the two lived before the foundation of the Kōṭṭē kingdom. He gave sanctuary to the young prince Parākrama whom one of the latter's rivals, Vīra Alakesvara, was interested in eliminating from the political arena. When the young prince came of age, the Venerable Thera took the initiative in confronting him with his rival. The Elder was later instrumental in setting him on the throne. Although he is known to have been the head of the monastic establishment at Vīdāgama, the Ñāṇānanda Pirivena, and according to tradition to have been the preceptor of the young prince, he was not an author.[3] He died

1. Thera = Elder Monk.
2. An undated collection of moral maxims, the *Dahamgätaya*, is sometimes cited as the oldest existing such work. See C. E. Godakumbura, *Sinhalese Literature.* Colombo, 1955, pp. 209-210.
3. The first Vīdāgama Thera's name is sometimes mentioned as the author

shortly after the prince ascended the throne as Sri Parākamabāhu VI of Kōṭṭē. He is also said to have held the office of Saṅgharāja.[4] The second monk who hailed from Vīdāgama is our author.

Little is known for certain about the author's early life. More information is available regarding his life and activities as a member of the Order. He is nowhere mentioned as a pupil of the Elder Vīdāgama, Parākramabāhu VI's teacher and mentor, although he had been his *protégé* in childhood. Since he resided in the same monastery as the Elder Vīdāgama, it is possible that he was a pupil of the latter.

It was not the practice of Sinhalese to disclose details of their personal life. Our author was no exception to the rule.

We are, however, fortunate in that the learned author's name and monastic residence are mentioned in his literary works. Having entered the Order, he took up residence at the Vīdāgama monastery near Rayigama, where he continued to live throughout his monastic career. He belonged to the Mahānetra-mūla (Mahānetra-prāsādamūla) fraternity. When he wrote his first work, his reputation as a literary figure was not very great. But by the time he composed his second work, he could say of himself that he was a scholar "well-versed in Sinhalese, Pāli and Sanskrit, who possessed a competent knowledge of other sciences as well."[5] When his third work was completed, he had become the chief monk of his monastery. He received the enthusiastic praise of scholars, versed in the arts of poetry and drama, prosody, grammar and poetics.

of one of the versions of the *Attanagalu Vaṃsaya*. This was the second of the two Sinhalese translations of the Pāli *Hatthavanagalla-vihāra-vaṃsa,* and is associated with the Vīdāgama fraternity. It is not impossible that the Elder Vīdāgama was its author, though it is more likely that it was written by a younger monk of the same fraternity.

4. JRASCB, Vol. XXII, No. 63 (1910) p. 39.

5. *Dat neka Sat helu saku magada ā risin.*

Literary Work

Four literary works are attributed to the author. In the order of composition in which they are customarily placed by scholars, they are:

1. *Lōväḍa Saṅgarāva*
2. *Haṃsa Sandesaya*
3. *Kav Lakunu Miṇimal*
4. *Buduguṇa Alaṅkāraya*

The *Haṇsa Sandesaya* is given the second place on the ground that the king whose praises are sung in the poem is considered to refer to Parākramabāhu VI of Kōṭṭē. But it is quite likely that the monarch was the eighth, who bore the name, Vīraparākramabāhu, in which case it would be the last of the author's works. Literary scholars have referred to the fact that this work displays a greater maturity and richness of composition than the *Buduguṇa Alaṅkāraya*.

Literary Period

The fifteenth century was a propitious period for Sinhalese literature. It displayed a vitality unprecedented in the history of the language. It was a period in which Sinhalese poetry burst into flower with poets producing literary creations in new metrical patterns. The seeds of this movement were sown in the latter half of the fourteenth century when a new literary genre arose in the form of the *sandesa* ("message") poems. This activity in the sphere of poetry took place after a lapse of about two centuries. The dominant literary figure of the period was the scholar-poet Śri Rāhula Sthavira of Toṭagamuwa, the author of several works, and a close associate of, and adviser to, the king. The king himself was a scholar in his own right and a great patron of the arts. Their combined efforts contributed, in no small measure, to the efflorescence that took place.

The poetry that emerged in the fourteenth century and flourished in the fifteenth was simpler in structure than the earlier type. This verse, known as *gī*, was unrhymed and its metres were based on *mātrās* or "syllabic instants," whereas the later verse belonged to the rhymed quatrain type and was intended to be recited to more or less fixed metrical schemes. This kind of poetry, though having affinities in vocabulary with that of the earlier period, adopted a language that was current and closer to popular usage and was therefore more readily intelligible than the *gī* poetry.

Apart from the *sandesas* or "message poems" which were of a similar character, the subject matter of poetry continued to be the Jātaka story in which the chief character, the *bodhisatta* or the Buddha-aspirant was identified with the Buddha in a previous life. Sometimes the compositions took the form of didactic verse, as in the present instance; or, as in the case of another work of our author, the subject matter was drawn from an incident in the life of the Buddha. This rhymed four-line verse, which came into prominence during the period under survey, continued to be the most popular metrical pattern until about the middle of the twentieth century. It has not lost favour with contemporary poets, among whose writings its influence is still perceptible.

Another side of the picture is represented by the secular poetry referred to earlier. The essence of such poetry of which the "message poem" was the model consists of sending a message to a deity or a religious dignitary through the agency of some non-human being; the latter in the case of Sinhalese poetry is always a bird. Five of the eight poems belonging to the first wave of such compositions fall within the period under review. It is possible that a sixth, namely the second in order of composition, was written in the same century.

The origins of this type of poetry are much earlier than the age in which Vīdāgama Thera flourished. Literary evidence of inspiration from Kālidāsa's classic *Meghadūta* ("The Cloud Messenger") is found among the earliest extant specimens of Sinhalese poetry, while a poem of the same genre is known to have existed in the *gī* period (8th–13th centuries C.E.). The Sinhalese *sandesa* poem of the late fourteenth and the fifteenth centuries follows the same conventional pattern. It provides examples of the poet's genuine appreciation of the beauties of nature as reflected in the charm of a flourishing rural countryside rather than the expression of romantic appeal of solitude.

The *Lōväḍa Saṅgarāva,* as its title indicates, is a collection of didactic verse for the World's Good. It consists of rhymed four-line stanzas written in easy and straightforward language, embodying the moral teachings of Buddhism. It is especially intended to explain to those unacquainted with the Pāli scriptures the fruits of actions (Sinh. *kam-pala*; Pāli *kamma-phala*). The workings of *kamma* or morally significant action are to be understood here in the threefold sense of mental, verbal and physical action. The author's avowed purpose is to lead his readers away from the path of evil to that of moral virtue. Evil deeds bring in their wake evil results while good ones bring good results.

The poem, which comprises 140 verses, an English translation of which here follows, has been inspired by a Pāli poem of similar content and inspiration, the *Saddhammopāyana,* composed by the Mahā Thera Ānanda of Abhayagiri. Some of the stanzas in the Sinhalese poem appear to be translations while others may be considered adaptations of verses occurring in the Pāli poem. The latter itself is based on Candragomi's *Śiṣyalekha,* a Sanskrit poem incorporating some of the basic teachings of Buddhism, intended for the education and edification of the faithful. It is useful to recall the fact, in order to note the continuity of a scholastic literary tradition, that there exists an early Sinhalese translation of the *Saddhammopāyana* by a monk named Ānanda. We find the work translated again into Eḷu (Sinhalese) by a Buddhist monk during the Buddhist revival of the eighteenth century. It is quite possible that our author had these sources at his disposal.

The most striking feature of the poem is its simplicity of diction and directness of appeal. The two elements in combination perhaps contribute to the powerful impact it makes on its readers or more correctly hearers. The choice of words in the original Sinhalese and the naturalness of their arrangement, together with the fast-moving metre of 16 syllabic instants (*mātrās*)[6] which facilitate memorisation and ready quotation, account for the popularity of the work.

A sense of urgency is conveyed through the poem as, for instance, when the reader is reminded constantly of the value of being born as a human. Human life is rare, difficult to obtain and too precious an opportunity to be lost. No time is to be wasted

6. Other metres of 26 and 18 syllabic instants are also used, though the majority of stanzas are composed in this metre.

for the performance of good deeds. There are eight woeful states where one cannot do good (V.8). This sentiment is sustained throughout the poem.

The appearance of a Buddha is indeed a rare phenomenon; and so is life as a human being. Both conditions are required for one to be freed from this woeful round of birth and death. "Why, good men, do you not exert yourselves?" asks the author (V.19). For "sooner shall the head of a (blind) turtle that comes up to the surface from the ocean's bed, once in a hundred years, find the single hole of a drifting yoke-pole, than a being who has been born in the lower realms gain birth in this world of men" (V.18).

Influence and Popularity of the Work

Since it was first composed, this little poem has exerted much influence on both young and old. It continues to be an important factor in the moulding of the character of young people and has remained a basic component of the curriculum. It is popular among the older generation, not only because of its forceful diction and directions of appeal, but because it creates in the minds of adult readers an awareness of the realities of life. A consideration of the intellectual and emotional climate of the times in which the author lived would help to understand better the influence and popularity of the poem.

At the time the poem was written in the fifteenth century and perhaps even earlier, many un-Buddhistic ideas and practices had crept into the social life of the people. Worship of the gods, a practice consciously fostered by brahmin priests from South India, some of whom had gained the king's confidence, had begun to exert a powerful influence on the royal court. This practice stemmed from an attitude of mind which placed greater reliance, in the face of problems, on some external agency such as a Hindu god or local divinity than on individual effort. In times of insecurity and social and political crises, people were encouraged to invoke the blessings of the gods and to seek their intercession in finding solutions to their difficulties.

The practice of worshipping gods of the Hindu pantheon, such as Siva, Brahma, Visnu and Agni, had become fairly widespread among the broad masses of the people, to judge from the utterances of our author himself. And if one were to read between the lines of Vīdāgama Maitreya Thera's *Buduguṇa-Alaṅkāraya,* it had begun to exert a dominant influence on their minds and hearts. Those divinities had undoubtedly gained many votaries. It is not unreasonable to think that the observance of the daily ritual of *ti-saraṇa* (three refuges) and *pañca-sīla* (five precepts) was being steadily undermined and relegated to the background. The worship of the Buddha, as guide and teacher, and the fostering of Buddhist modes of thinking in daily life were neglected, if not deliberately ignored. Intellectual and emotional attitudes which encouraged freedom of thought, self reliance and discipline based on the practice of Buddhist virtue were giving way to a fatalistic view of life, based on blind irrational faith in some unseen power. What was more, such practices received the approval, if not the encouragement, even of members of the Sangha.

In that context, the writings of Vīdāgama Maitreya were a protest against the prevailing practices, of which he disapproved. In another sense, his voice was a call to his audience to restore to its rightful place the worship of the Buddha, and to hear and put into practice his noble teachings. The author did not want brahmin practices and the worship of gods to contaminate Buddhist devotion. He expected no royal favours and thus indirectly condemned those of his fellow monks who sought them.

Although our author lived and wrote in an age when poetry thrived and poets received the unstinted patronage of kings, he was not concerned with practising the poetic art. There is no doubt that he would have shunned the title of "Poet." He exhorted his audience fervently to give themselves up to the Buddha, in the fullest devotion of their hearts. His declared aim, as it was remarked earlier, was to bring home to his numerous listeners the basic truths of Buddhism as exemplified in the workings of *kamma*. To achieve that end he chose the medium of verse.

In this task, the present poem has played a leading role. Its popularity remains undiminished. It brings the large audience to which it is addressed face to face with the realities of life. Such episodes as the one referred to above, drawn from traditional lore and expressed in colourful turns of phrase, serve to demonstrate truths valid not only for the author's time but for all time.

No originality is claimed for the ideas contained in the poem either by the author or his critics. But the manner of putting them across is uniquely the author's. Those ideas that he has taken from other sources he invests with a vigour of his own. If the reader feels that in these verses he hears the voice of the preacher and moralist rather than that of the poet and literary artist, he is correct in his judgement. For that is what the author really is, a preacher more than a poet. In that role his performance is commendable. The passage of time has not impaired the relevance of what he says.

Ānanda Kulasuriya

The World's True Welfare

Homage to the Exalted One, the Holy One, Fully Enlightened!

1. *Great ocean of virtue, thou, source of ultimate bliss,*
The physician, thou, to all the ills of beings,
The solar light, which night of false beliefs casts out,
Thou supreme sage, to thee in joy I obeisance make.

2. *To the Law, discovered in fullness by the Lord,*
But preached in a way to reach the grasp of all,
So that each, according to his gifts, can understand;
Which says: "Come and behold" in reverence I bow.

3. *With my hands held clasped on my brow,*
I salute the Order of well conducted monks,
That liveth in the lineage of Sariputt and Mogallan,
Whose feet have been adored by Brahma gods.

4. *My salutation offered in reverence deep*
To the blessed tamer of men, the Order and the Law,
In service to those that ignorant are
Of the ancient and archaic Pāli tongue

The results of actions good and bad
In lucid Sinhala I sing.

5. *In the past, not far remote,*
Some sixty monks they say,
Listened to Dhamma truth
Sung in Sinhala verse

On the nature unwholesome of aggregates all,
And earnestly did ponder and dwell
Thereon, and with misgivings naught,
Reached Nibbāna's bliss.

6. *Hence, treat it not lightly*
Though in Sinhala 'tis told.
If this glorious teaching, in joy

Is in its profound depths well absorbed,
With deference due, of aims sincere
And minds clean and intents pure,
Ensure it certainly will bring
Life in deva worlds and bliss supreme.

7. *Listen not to the Teaching,*
Being seated even low,
Where standing the preacher speaks;
Do not be perched on seat that's higher;
This above all: be not of confused mind.
Listened to with attentive mind,
The Law will to heaven or freedom lead.

8. *The exhortation of the Sage*
Ever was for man to be
Diligent in wholesome acts engaged:
The dissolver of worldly woes
in the cycle of births and rebirths,
The winner of emancipation, bliss;
But eight there be of states
Where these acts cannot be done.

9. *If born in the horror-giving states of woe*
One hundred and thirty-six as known,
In the nether world's long enduring woes
With horrors untold, and where
Opportunities never are
For any wholesome deeds.

10. *Or if born in animal worlds*
Resulting from previous actions bad,
Where fear, never-ending, rules
The passion-driven minds;
Calmness or serenity never hath place
In the lower animal mind.

How then can wholesome thoughts
Arise in such dire states?

11. *Those who indulge in unwholesome acts*
As clearly defined in the Law
Being born in states of lower beings
With no access to food of any kind,
Even body excretions, no water
To drink, unable to quench their parched throats
Though drowned in the deep celestial river
Such beings are debarred from wholesome acts.

12. *A man, though born to luxury,*
Enjoying fabulous wealth and every joy,
In regions where the Laws of the Sage
Are unknown, and never were heard,
Where wholesome actions never are done,
But bad, never can opportunity find
For actions wholesome, pure.

13. *Those beings, misled by ignorant guides*
Who omit all wholesome acts
But commit all evil actions dark,
When reborn in human form, deaf,
Dumb, and blind of eye,
"Behold, such beings for wholesome acts,
Even small, will miss all chance."

14. *Four Brahma worlds there be, of only mind*
And no form; and one of form,
No mind; these are planes,
Where good beings after death are born,
But chances of wholesome action offer never.

15. *To those followers of false beliefs;*
Which verily form the fortress strong
In saṃsāra's city; or like a stubborn stump
Of an ever-leafing parasitic evil's plant,
Like poisoned pikes in Nibbāna's path
And roads that lead to happy states,
Never to such, will joy of good results accrue.

16. *In times when no Buddhas on earth appear,*
All world-systems in the universe's expanse,

And saṃsāra, in darkness would be;
All beings wilt; of actions good and bad
In ignorance live, with higher planes
And Nibbāna's bliss ever closed to man.

17. *If you are not deaf, and listen with*
Understanding to the Buddha's Law,
Yet still abstain from acting well;
You do so, not because the time is wrong
For doing what will make you right,
But because you choose the other path.
You should make good effort now.
For there are only those eight occasions
Where merit cannot be acquired.[7]

18. *A turtle in the ocean expansive and deep,*
Surfacing once in a hundred years,
Does more chances have to pass his head
Through drifting floating yoke,
Than being released from states of woe
A chance of regaining birth as man.

19. *Between intervals of infinite length*
Do Buddhas on earth appear;
After much suffering doth one
A birth as human being achieve;
Conditions, essential two, these be,
To procure, realize Nibbāna's bliss;
Then wherefore, good people,
Do you not strive to achieve this end?

7. The eight wrong moments (*akkhaṇa*), or inopportune times, are: when a Buddha has appeared and his Teaching is taught but a person has been born (1) in hell, (2) as an animal, (3) as a ghost, (4) among long-lived deities, (5) among unintelligent barbarians, not visited by followers of the Buddha, monastic or lay; or though born in the middle countries, a person (6) has wrong views, or (7) is stupid and dull, or, though he may have favourable qualifications, no Buddha has appeared at that time, and his Teaching is not taught. The ninth opportune time is when the above personal and environmental obstacles are absent. See Aṅguttara Nikāya, The Eights, No. 29.

20. *Those that would commit*
The fivefold evil acts,
Suffer here on earth,
And worse, in realms of woe;
Hence acquire ye benefits
Of wholesome acts on earth,
Waste not this chance,
Of this rare human state.

21. *Like those that would relishingly eat*
Of mangoes poisonous and wild,
What use is there in pleasing the mind
In any measure, with pleasure of senses five?
For death stalks even now, behind:
Be diligent and skilful in wholesome acts.

22. *A surer way there never is, to end the woes,*
That never ending follow this cycle of births,
Than a life of diligence, aware every moment,
Devoted only to wholesome acts;
Even as the one, his head on fire,
Tarries not quick relief to find.

23. *Even as stone with effort skywards cast,*
Returns but to this earth, anon,
And remains not in space between,
Even so, to those who will not
With joyous mind, understanding, free,
Engage their time in wholesome acts,
No place deserving, more
Than the unwholesome realms of woe.

24. *Think not as permanent this body of yours,*
This aggregate of rotting unwholesome parts;
Its impermanence is paralleled be sure
By the swift lightning's flash.
Never allowing this body, the mind
To seek for evil, but strive for ever,
With diligence, wholesome acts to pursue.

25. *The archer poised, in darkness*
Shooting at a hair from far,
Would miss the aim, if ill-timed
With swift lightning's flashing glow;
Endowed with a body, impermanent
And evanescent as the lightning's flash,
Neglect to pursue the wholesome acts
And you'll miss in future the happy states,
And above all, Nibbāna's consummate bliss.

26. *Nowhere is any sanctuary found*
That's inaccessible to certain death;
Happiness here is but limited withal
By resulting energy of actions past—
What occasion, then, is there for man
For laughter, jesting, dancing and joy?
And forgetting the words of the Enlightened One—
The remover of worldly woes?

27. *For those abhorring saṃsāra's woes,*
There never can be a time as this, the present.
They that have the values realized
Of morality and giving, delay they never wilt
To them one hour's time-span
Is as good as a thousand years.

28. *Be daily aware of death's approach*
And hence be diligent in wholesome acts.
What proof is there—presumptuous thoughts—
That the morrow will not bring death?
Who can with death, of legions many,
Bargain with time and assurance give?
Why then does man, if things thus be,
Indolent refrain from wholesome acts in life?

29. *What need to gorge with food and drink*
This body, and bedeck it always in finery?
For, where can you from hence, this body take
But leave it here? Be not indolent,
Rather active in wholesome actions be,
For this alone can you from life's ocean save.

30. *If you wish that ferried you were*
Across dread saṃsāra's ocean deep,
And ensure the reaching at the shores
Of Nibbāna's steady strand and firm,
Avoid all evil acts and with diligence learn,
By listening to the dispensation of the Sage;
Strive hard, relenting never, engaged in acts
That wholesome be, with evil barred.

31. *Prepare thy mind always, for wholesome deeds alone;*
For is not such mind the ready field
For insight and truth to root, and light Nibbāna's way?
Why are words well-meant for spiritual gains
Never with awareness heard?
Waiting, are ye, for realization's light
To flash when born in states of woe?

32. *The birth of Buddha, giver of Nibbāna's bliss,*
Occurs on earth, in millions of years but once;
This period, the present, on earth,
Is one with such a Blessed One:
Fail to grasp the truth right now,
And chances of a possible next are slight.

33. *Think of service to self, and others too, alike,*
Let thoughts of loving-kindness embrace all beings;
Without this basic need, compassion,
saṃsāra's lengthy sojourn cannot end:
How then, can you Nibbāna's city e'er reach?

34. *The humble cur, that licks the bone,*
Cast oft, bloodless, without flesh,
Hath his hunger unappeased,
With no nutriment absorbed.
Think but likewise of sensual pleasures,
No abiding happiness is there,
Though obvious not, being illusion-veiled,
'Tis unwholesome withal, and begets but woe.

35. *A hawk on wing, meat tight held in beak,*
Would assuredly be killed by other hawks,

If meat he did not drop;
Those that would cling to pleasures
Of senses five with greed, likewise
Will for ever be visited and plagued,
By five-and-twenty horrors and woes.

36. *The Teaching of the Sage, we have it,*
Sweet of word and deep of sense;
With perfect hearing thou art blest, no deafness sore;
Nothing there is thou couldst not do,
By way of wholesome acts;
The thing that thou couldst ill-afford
Is to suffer pain in states of woe.

37. *Indulgence in evil deeds is honey-sweet in the act,*
But when resultant suffering comes
It is as painful as a scorching fire;
full well the way to repel evil, sin;
Seal for good the three great inlets—
of thought, of speech, of body—
which evil ingress allow.

38. *"It is better far for man to die*
Living a life of righteous deeds
Than live for a period long
A life unrighteous led."
Recall to mind the words of the Sage,
Live a life sincere, of wholesome deeds
And reach Nibbāna's goal.

39. *When one single being, grieving only*
On account of a mother bereaved,
Hath dropped such copious tears,
In innumerable births, that they exceed
The volume of waters of all oceans' aggregate;
How is it then, you still cling to saṃsāra's chains?

40. *Just as the crab in pot*
Over hearth now placed,
Sports in glee, in water cool,
Till the flames do rise,

Even so will it be with you,
If you wallow in sensual pleasures,
Not thinking what afterwards comes.

41. *The lighted torch of rushes,*
Held pointed windwards would
Assuredly burn the holder's hand,
Were it not soon dropped:
The ignorant who eagerly indulge
In pleasures five and praise them
Will suffer in the states of woe.

42. *You who are so proud*
Of this short span of life
Where happiness and joy
Are just the limited results
Of wholesome actions, in the past:
Do not thus court suffering in states of woe,
For you are like those bedecked in finery
Borrowed for a feast, and ever in debt
And in thraldom held by those that loaned.

43. *Like unto the robber to torture led,*
With blood-red garlands decked,
And with music of the beating drums,
Hemmed in by ruthless guards—
Thus are ye who, endowed with wealth,
Would cling to it and not to charity part;
In cases both: a mockery, a jest,
Devised by Māra, the evil one.

44. *The robber from hilltop, pushed to death,*
Fanned by cool breeze, in his swift descent,
For body heat and sweat, no comfort finds.
You, who by virtue of some wealth, ever did
Commit only evil acts, now passing through:
Decay and heading to certain death,
What avails you such happiness from wealth?

45. *Seek for yourself and realize within*
The evil results of sensual pleasures five,

Which so unrelenting allure the mind of man;
Go forth to ascetic life, in able-bodied youth,
For would the man atop the tree, eating
its sweet luscious fruits, remain,
Not descent, till the roots below are hewn?

46. *Teachings of the Enlightened One*
Have ever been true; never of fallacies found.
Learn from these, that the body is not lasting;
That life itself is as a dewdrop hung
Pendent on a grass blade's tip.
Hence wholesome actions should
With no delay be done.

47. *Harken unto these my words,*
Productive of weal in this life and the next:
If living in happiness, misnamed as such,
You commit but only evil acts,
And resulting, are born as ghost
Or demon or even lower form,
No chance will you have for wholesome acts,
But shall in hunger ever roam.

48. *Those beings, who with greedy minds*
Did unwholesome acts commit,
Would arraigned before Yama
Be in public audience charged:
Thence can you never live
In leisure and in ease,
But suffer torture in the states of woe.

49. *Those who in constant pleasure and luxury live,*
Though advised by the wise to lead a righteous life:
And who themselves have seen with eyes thereon,
The difference in men who only did
Wholesome acts, and those that unwholesome do,
Yet would not believe and turn to good:
To them the reward: endless suffering
If fallen into states of woe.

50. *Not knowing wholesome actions good,*
From unwholesome ones being folly-driven,
Some kill the living beasts.
"Tis delicious," eating the flesh they say;
Such pleasers of palate, such gourmets,
Can never the states of woe evade.
Hence forsake, right now,
This relish for animal flesh.

51. *Feeding on delicious foods,*
Flavoured to epicure's gluttonous needs;
Sweet balms and unguents
Of fragrant sandal, rubbed on skin;
The body bedecked in finery,
With ornaments worn to taste;
Men but act the part of puppets:
Now on stage; next, tossed aside.

52. *Search but for Truth, with wisdom thine own,*
On what hath been said, over and over again,
Of the non-lasting nature of the body and form;
In no-wise wholesome, in firmness the least,
An aggregate of rotting two-and-thirty parts;
Thought wisdom clear, thou canst this discern:
Futile would birth in this human world be,
If wholesome actions were not fulfilled;
Realization full, will come too late,
If born in hopeless realms of woe
Totalling one hundred and thirty-six.

53. *Though born together now in this world,*
As wished in previous births, long past,
Knitted together in affection and love,
And living as one, in association close
life departs, in utter loneliness engulfed,
Deserted by the very household, one would be;
All bonds of affection, love, so far professed,
Would fall apart shattered, cast away:
Only the results of wholesome actions done
Would constant company keep, and assure future weal.

54. *Endowed with a body careless and foul,*
They play about, carousing and dancing oft.
Though a man live attached to his spouse,
Enjoying the pleasures of married life,
When dreaded death, knowing his time, comes around,
To claim him as his, and to take him along,
Can vows or promises defer the date
And keep him here on earth a little more?
Therefore it behoves us all, everyone, to do
Wholesome actions, that good results accrue.

55. *Why wouldst thou not in Buddha take refuge,*
And diligent be, in wholesome actions pure?
Dost thou await time at which death comes,
To be escorted by Yama to the realms of woe?
Were it not better far, in wisdom, to live a virtuous life,
And fulfil wholesome actions all the while?
Oh relatives, that would weep for parting loved one,
Can greater folly there be? Can weeping, Death prevent?

56. *Though ye should weep, be overcome with grief,*
No more shall ye see the departed one;
Why not prepare the mind, to actions wholesome, the while?
Than rather wealth accumulate and hoard in vain?
Why use this rotting body, you'll leave behind,
Only for gaining pleasures, sensual, of the flesh?
Oh harken to my words, be cleanser of defilements,
Be victor and win the citadel of bliss.

57. *Being impaled on, and suspended from,*
The bait-hook of saṃsāra are living beings;
The bodily pleasures you eke out,
Subject to certain decay all the while,
Which hover around you and oppresses,
Are like a dance-show seen performed
Spotlighted by the transient lightning's flash:
This truth well-grasped, delay not in actions good.

58. *Think never as beyond possibility's range,*
Performance of action wholesome and good.
All charity, antidote to grasping, giving away,

Partake with equal joy and with others share
Results of wholesome acts by others done;
Good results accrue in equal measure
As much to you as to the doer do,
Good deeds can lead you, too,
To divine states and finally Nibbāna's bliss.

59. *Food in various flavours dressed*
Is eaten but hunger to appease;
Sweet smelling unguents on body rubbed
Do but bad odours and stinks dispel;
Medicines these are to fight the ills
The human body is heir to—
How then can you name them ever
"happiness" or "pleasures," when they are not?

60. *Thinking of your comforts as the highest*
You often swell with pride;
But illusions are they, as empty, as void
As sweet perfumes rubbed in a dream;
Practise charity in spirit and deed;
And in virtue and morality live;
Unrighteous living leads man
From happiness, "light," to "darkness," woe.

61. *The log of wood, set ablaze,*
Is thereafter called a fire, not wood;
Even so did the great Sage speak,
In reference to this human form,
As the fountainhead of all suffering and of pain.
Hence know this as fact you all:
Not a body, is this, but just a mass of suffering.

62. *If one lives long, this body*
Through decay will finally break up.
If not long lived, one will drift soon
To the cavernous mouth of death.
A pleasure found between a slow
And certain death, to call that
Real happiness, who would dare?

63. *News of robbers' attack, nearby home*
Would keep one awake, on vigil,
In fear and doubt, to save his own.
Seeing that all living beings
As a matter of course are claimed by death,
Whatever withholds you now
From performing wholesome deeds?

64. *The greedy crow, lured by taste of flesh,*
Perched on putrid elephant's carcass adrift
On river, did himself die, marooned on ocean's expanse;
If ye would likewise cling with greed
To wealth and luxury you've amassed,
Then hopeless are you to cross,
saṃsāra's fathomless fear-filled seas.

65. *Ye that wouldst run deserting wife and child,*
To hide in jungles remote and wild,
On news of foreign invaders' march,
Seeing that horrid decay and death
With no uncertain trend advance on you
Why wouldst thou delay in doing actions pure?

66. *Like unto the man caught in swirling current,*
Drifting down-river with fear and sorrow overcome
But would not board the rescuing boat
To pick him up that's to him rowed—
Why wouldst thou not to the bliss-giving Law adhere
Instead of heading for the realms of woe and suffering?

67. *Behold the suffering that men undergo,*
For a petty pittance, for a livelihood,
As soldiers trained in archery
And the battle-arts of armed men;
If one would lead a righteous life
Trained in morality, with joyous devoted mind,
He assuredly can, for millions of years to come,
Pleasures in celestial spheres enjoy.

68. *Overcome by decay, the time will come*
When thou can'st not with ease erect stand,

Or from standing, change such pose to sit;
Then frail of limb, there will no longer be
Beauty nor looks in this form;
Hence to wholesome deeds and charity
Shouldst thou this time devote.

69. *Your children and your wife*
Thought of as your own
Are born and live, just as results
Of actions in the past performed,
And the same kamma keeps them here,
Whether for long a time or short;
But for you, only the clinging thoughts
Remain: "They are my own."

70. *Not devoting time to disciplining self,*
You are engrossed in showering attention
And love, and fondling your children dear
And darling wife: but what are they?
Shells and toys for play in childhood used.

71. *It is an occurrence, common seen on earth,*
For mortal beings struggling hard
To earn and accumulate riches and wealth,
And then to states of woe depart;
Provide, care for, and maintain withal
Wife and offspring—all sorrows cause;
But never are diligent in nor devoted to
The practice of morality, which emancipation brings.

72. *Though you be without a morsel,*
The pangs of hunger to appease,
Or without one wrap of clothing,
Your bare nudity to cover;
Think of the suffering in states of woe unmeasured;
Then dally not any longer, but diligent be,
Hesitant not in wholesome deeds and pure.

73. *If thou must ever destroy and kill*
Let your victims be mind-defiling thoughts
Of clinging, hate and ignorance;

And choose to live environed by
Men who in virtue happiness find.
Speak then only words of advice
That should enlightenment sure award;
If thou should'st listen, listen then,
To words from the Law, propounded by the Sage.

74. *If you would ever eulogize at all,*
Praise then, the virtues of the Enlightened One;
If development you wish, then let it be
The developing of the mind, from evil freed;
If giving you would do, to charity give away,
And share with others results of good deeds done,
If conqueror or victor you'd wish to be,
Then conquer and assure the type of life
You wish in future births to come.

75. *However much you listen to the Dhamma*
No wrong is done by doing so.
If complete renunciation is your wish,
First you should renounce your evil ways.
If you would wish to purify your mind,
You should perfect and keep secure your virtue,
If you would understand these facts,
The time to do so is just now.

76. *This tree, saṃsāra, many branches has,*
Which in turn bear many a poisonous fruit,
Being the sorrows and suffering that life entails:
The branches are the many hundreds
Of evil acts that challenge living beings;
Which, if not overcome, but weakly yielded to,
Produce results of severe sufferings, grave:
Hence, give ear, with serenity and joy,
With mind composed and wavering never
To results of the ten unrighteous acts men do.

77. *Learn this Law, the Enlightened One has taught,*
Thereby bring up the mind to calm and peace,
And forsake all actions despicable, base;
Those that take the lives of other beings,

Whatever the mode employed be,
Will suffer unending pains and sorrow,
In the four great states of woe.

78. *Frogs who become a prey in snakes' mouths,*
Relishingly eat of wriggling worms:
Behold those mortals trembling with fear
In the mouth of certain decay and death,
They still take lives of other beings!

79. *Whether it be by force*
Or by deceitful action,
Be it with one's own hands,
Or by your instructions given—
What belongs to another,
Ungiven, is by theft acquired.
The resultant force of this evil act,
From one state of woe to another he takes.

80. *Innumerable are examples of the suffering of men*
Who for greed and pleasure committed theft.
If seeing such suffering here on earth
One would not yet from theft desist,
When comes that time again
For him, to live in happiness and peace?

81. *The adulterer caught in the act,*
Or proven as such, no mercy receives;
And if tortured and done to death,
No questions are asked, nor justice claimed;
Hence think not as light nor trivial treat,
The evil results of the adulterous acts:
The sweet-rosy path of adultery
Leads but to the states of woe.

82. *Hearken with clarity of mind*
To the words that I speak;
The utterance of falsehood,
Be it but for only once,
Is to seal off and barricade
The path to happy states;

Escape one never will,
Without suffering in states of woe.

83. *The utterance of words in rashness done,*
Not pre-thought, in ignorance of evil and good,
Is like a string of weapons sharp,
Round one's neck in vanity worn;
Speech that aims to man from man divide,
Are words: the evil results of which
Can never be known in present birth.

84. *Harsh, unpleasant words that offend,*
Like iron spikes in listeners' ears, avoid;
With joy of mind, pleasant words
And sweet speech employ, if you must speak.
A heinous crime it is, to use harsh speech;
The venom of its resultant evil effects
Leaves not till future suffering absolves.

85. *From the remotest time of civilized man,*
The wisest have deplored and avoided use
Of frivolous talk, productive never,
But surest procurer of evil and woe;
Not in fun though it be, should one
Indulge in such profitless talk;
A pleasant royal highway it is,
That lures one to states of woe.

86. *If at sight of opulence and wealth*
In other beings, thoughts, greed-based,
Thus arise, "To him it should not be,
Why may it not to me accrue?"
The resulting evil force potent,
Of this one thought itself is enough
In after-births to cause to suffer.

87. *To think of those you do not like,*
And wish them dead is hatred sore;
Such wishes but drag you low, are feet
That lead you on to states of woe.
Never, never permit such thoughts
To rise in your mind, but dispel.

88. *Two and sixty there be of views*
That differ much from the path
To Nibbāna's eternal bliss,
As by the great Sage proclaimed:
Followers of any such teaching false,
False-believers are, to hold them true:
They form the seeds of poisonous fruits
Which cause and perpetuate saṃsāra's woes.

89. *Those that follow such false beliefs*
That teach not the disciplining of self,
Will burn in the conflagration's blaze
Which will the universe to ashes turn.
Having gone through suffering sore,
In the eight great states of woe,
Released, yet suffer again they will,
In realms uncharted, in outer universe.

90. *A margosa seed planted in soil*
Pregnant with all earth's nutriments sweet,
Negating earth's natural sweetness will bear
But fruits of bitter taste;
Likewise what words are said
And whatever actions that be done
By those that cling to false beliefs
Are productive of evil, and never of good.

91. *Those that would commit be it even one*
Of the ten unwholesome actions listed above
Or cause such actions to be done
By order, advice or instruction giv'n,
Or even by word approval grant
And endorse in thought, by agreement shown
In the commission of such evil act
Will at no distant far off date
Suffer the results thereof in states of woe.

92. *These ten impure unwholesome acts,*
Which bring in their wake sure sorrow and pain—
You escape by committing them never.
And if in this human world you lead a life

Undisciplined and defiant of the Law—
Like one falling from top of Mount Meru;
With never a stop or pause between—
You needs must fall and be submerged
In the bottomless sea of woes.

93. *Even the all-knowing Omniscient One*
Did not in full define, the hundred
And six and thirty realms of woe,
Consisting of eight major ones
With eight and twenty smaller others,
So great in suffering and pain
That even thoughts thereof doth terror bring.

94. *The incessant pain and sorrow*
A man in a day would suffer here on earth,
Whose body with spears sharp
Three hundred times wounded through,
Would be but one second's pain suffered,
In the untold tortures in woeful states;
Computed thus, would not the Himalayan range
Equal only the size of a mustard seed?

95. *Ages ago, a woman but killed a goat,*
The neck being cut and severed clean;
Reborn in realms of woes she suffered,
With flames of fire her body entwined,
Decapitations, too, as many times
As hairs on slaughtered goat she faced;
So it shall be for all wrongdoers:
The inexorable law of cause and effects.

96. *Once, in fun, a man did steal*
His friend's attire and did conceal,
But later confessed the same,
And the clothes to him restored.
Later born as a deva in celestial abode
This "joker practical" was without attire.
Hence, in fun though it be
Take not what's not yours, unoffered.

97. *A man who adultery relished*
And oft indulged in it through life,
Being born in "region of woe of molten lead"
In bubbling, boiling, molten lava immersed
He now comes out for breath of air,
In thirty thousand years but once.
Ye wise, who would of your welfare think,
Avoid such unwholesome deeds.

98. *Once a king, who with great enjoyment*
Did utter a lie, wittingly, pre-thought,
Did therefore lose his iddhi powers,
And in this human form itself,
Did find himself in realms of woe,
And condemned there to suffer long.
Know ye, therefore, what evil results ensue
From utterance of falsehood, words untrue.

99. *A man, who by tale-bearing did*
Two monks divide, who were close friends,
Suffered aeons on end in realms of woe;
Was born thereafter in ghostly form,
With a face that was ever-rotting putrid flesh,
And doth still suffer in that form.
Hence, from now speak not words
That would one man from another divide.

100. *A monk, a follower of the Enlightened Sage,*
Yet did abuse the Order of holy ones,
In words that were harsh and unkind too,
He was born in the realms of woe, suffered there,
For such a long time, lamenting still,
Now born in ghost form so he doth suffer.
Hence, oh beings, abuse not another being,
Nor use in speech, unpleasant words and harsh.

101. *Frivolous speech that's unproductive, vain,*
Leads one but to states of woe:
After periods of suffering or torture and horrors,
If perchance, he be born on earth as man,
His words, by hearers in human society,

Will never for a moment credited be,
E'en though the words he speaks be true.

102. *Those who, in envy, wish for themselves*
That which to others rightfully belongs,
Will suffer, being born in realms of woe;
If chance permits his birth again on earth,
Ne'er will his wishing-thoughts bear fruit;
Hence, never, ever from this time on
Permit such thoughts entry to thy mind.

103. *Bear not thoughts of hatred to others,*
Such thoughts unfeeling and harsh,
Beget no good, are evil withal,
Leading to suffering in states of woe,
Of diverse forms and repeated in turns,
And resulting in later births on earth,
To illness and bodily pains to be subjected.

104. *Spurn false beliefs as poison, hence;*
For believers in such are born
In states of woe, and after suffering there,
If reborn on earth will subject ever be,
To bodily illness, and deformity
With a mind obtuse, from wisdom divorced,
And where only impure thoughts arise.

105. *Knowing patently with no doubts attached,*
How birth after birth, defilements of the mind
Cause suffering without end to mankind here,
The Sage supreme did disclose the way,
To emancipation gain from saṃsāra's woes;
Which in accordance with, here I set forth,
The wholesome acts, as means thereto:
Hearken oh beings, for your weal it shall be.

106. *Without ordering others to give*
(Too lazy to offer the gifts yourself),
You yourself should make the offerings.
Your aim in giving only this should be:
The beneficent act and its resultant good;
Happy before giving, while giving, and thereafter too.

(The requisite states three, of the donor mind.)
Wherever born in after-life you be,
Will find yourself endowed with untold wealth.

107. *In a house on fire burning within,*
With flames blazing all around,
Only the household goods thrown out
Will ever, in future, useful be;
This lesson, ye bear well in mind,
And in charity give, never miserly be:
For this cause alone can assurance make,
Of happy results in future lives.

108. *If you possess not anything more*
But the morsel of food held in hand,
About to reach the lips and feed yourself—
Give it as alms to the calling beggar,
Never will hunger's pangs you feel,
And never will feel future suffering's pain
For the thought, "I have much, I'll keep enough,
The rest as alms in charity I'll give,"
Will never, never arise in the mind
Of him who looks to future bliss.

109. *Believe not the words of those evil ones,*
Who wholesome actions never do;
Cleanse well your mind of the defilements three—
Of desire, of ignorance and of hate.
Daily, in practice, observe the precepts five,
And weekly the eight, in happy frame of mind;
Thus can you enter the city of bliss,
And emancipation gain, all obstacles razed.

110. *Strive always to eradicate*
All thoughts of clinging, desire and greed,
With a mind alert, aware and wisdom-based.
Retain the morality of mind unsullied,
Even as the pure moonbeams clear.
Safeguard it e'en as the yak its tail:
Resulting from such moral living,
Emancipation in no long time attain.

111. *The most wholesome action man can do,*
The noblest, the Buddha has proclaimed,
Is the mental force generated through
Thoughts of loving-kindness spread
By wishing all living beings to be free
Of sorrow and grief, and from illness.
Immunity full, good health, ne'er pain,
Lives of amity here, next—Nibbāna's bliss.

112. *Behold ye how men on earth*
Of benevolent things would not even think:
With mind enraged in anger and hate,
Pain they would on each other deal.
Meditate, thoughts of loving-kindness
Project around on all living beings:
Surest means this will prove to be,
Of reaching happy planes and Nibbāna's bliss.

113. *Like money-lenders who loan their gold*
To patrons known, in trust, and usury gain—
Invite other beings to share of good results
Of wholesome actions that you perform.
The results of such deeds—wishing to share—
Return to the giver double- or triple-fold,
Depending on how oft 'tis done:
Hence omit not this wish to share.

114. *Learn well yourself this Law*
That the Blessed One has taught;
Teach it to others in compassionate love
By the results of skilful act performed.
Bar for ever the roads to realms of woe
And assure life in realms of endless joy;
Next achieve the final goal of Nibbāna's bliss.

115. *Raise your hands in joy, and salute,*
As if you the living Buddha saw,
At sight of those who know his teaching well;
Hearken well with attention and love
To every word uttered, line by line,
And close the entrances to realms of woe.

116. *The worshipping of the Buddha at sight*
With respectful veneration unmixed,
From the time he comes within vision's range,
With complete lack of hauteur of mind,
The offering of food and offerings floral.
And lights, all result in reaching
Happy abodes and Nibbāna's bliss.

117. *Wild flowers of the forests bloom*
On every day, and everywhere;
Wherever you may be, offer them
In the name of the Blessed One.
For him it shall be, for him alone,
And productive of results wholesome be.
If one can't this afford to do,
This simple little act,
Whatever more can you do
To escape deep saṃsāra's woes?

118. *The wise man a wholesome act performs*
By a simple little ruse:
The wise surveying all beings on earth
And proclaiming the virtues of virtuous ones,
Discriminating not with prejudice base,
Whether to them he be partial or not.

119. *Those that provide for and serve*
The Buddha's Order of holy monks,
Their parents, and their teacher-guides,
Those who are well advanced in years,
The elders too of the family group;
Others stricken by illness sore
And others yet, that live the ascetic life
Will be happy here and in the heavenly world.

120. *If one would but value in his mind,*
The virtues of the holy Triple Gem,
Which can rescue the worldly beings
Struggling in saṃsāra's endless-seeming sea;
And place them on the safe terrain
Of Nibbāna's shores, by happy thought thereof—

Never would again subjected be
To the sorrows and pains of repeated birth.

121. *No help, can such as relatives give;*
Nothing in reality matters, except the results
Of wholesome actions that you perform;
Nothing can they give that one can own,
Or use in a future birth that follows this;
But if one would trust in a future to be,
Recollect and always recall to mind
The virtues and values of the threefold gem,
This alone would qualify one for birth
In realms of happiness, with no other good acts done.

122. *Greater by far in consequence is*
The resulting effects in refuge sought,
In Buddha, and following his way of life,
Than covering the earth with precious gems,
And building thereon a mansion vast,
Equalling in size over all the brahma worlds,
Decked with pennons of beaten gold,
With arches and domes of precious stones.

123. *You, who cannot grasp the law proclaimed*
By the Buddha taught, and in accordance live
A life of morality simple, a life austere,
That provides endless, varied happiness to man,
And allows not birth in realms of woe;
To such as you, then, the only hope
For escaping saṃsāra's sorrows and pains,
Will be the threefold aid, no other;
The Teacher, his Teaching and Order of holy monks.

124. *Having learnt the Law, propounded so well,*
Practise, and consummation reach
In performing wholesome acts;
The defilements of the mind and causes thereof,
Eradicate for ever; prevent their arising too;
And thus ensure a future life
In happy abodes, and gain Nibbāna's bliss
And repel any chance of future woe.

125. *A beggar on the streets, begging around,*
Long time ago, met Anuruddha, the saint,
Who at mealtime was on his begging round,
And offered him one spoonful of the food
That he had gathered for his meal;
Resulting on this wholesome deed,
Was he born a deva chief, Indaka by name.
Oh, you wise! Know now, the results of giving away,
Give of your wealth in alms, in charity give.

126. *She was a lady of noble birth*
Who ages ago but for one short day
The eight precepts well kept;
Born she was in deva abodes
And of beauty without peer,
Enjoying a life of heavenly pleasures untold,
In the company of Sakka the deva king;
Therefore protect this virtue with a firm resolve
And live not for a moment void of good.

127. *Of all the wholesome acts that one can do*
The noblest, effective most, can meditation be:
It alone can mind's defilements clean,
And mind's strength and culture raise.
Surest cause it is to ensure birth
In happier planes, and brahma abodes to gain.
Conquer the legions of the evil one,
And win freedom's bliss which is hard to gain.

128. *Transferring of results of wholesome deeds,*
By you performed, with unmixed joy of mind
Is like unto a golden stairway
Leading to the sixfold heavenly abodes;
It's the full moon bright, with its cooling beams,
That allays the heat of fearsome woeful states.
Hence share the results of wholesome deeds
That you perform with all you meet.

129. *On the day that the monastery of Jeta Park*
Was gifted as offering to the supreme Sage,
A poor man present, overcome with joy,

Fully approving and endorsing in mind
This wholesome act, wished its results to share:
And acquire did he, the wholesome results in greater measure
Than did the guild-master[8] himself, that donor rare.
What matters hence, whether the doer of the deed
Does not or does, wish others the benefits share?

130. *Once when the Lord to an audience preached,*
A humble frog entranced by the music of his voice,
Sat with mind composed and never moved,
When a stake, unwitting driven, his poor heart
Did penetrate, killing him there transfixed.
He was reborn in deva abodes with luxury and joy.

131. *A poor man once, in great devotion,*
To the supreme Sage offered at a relic shrine
But one common flower of a humble weed;
Five hundred lives was he born on earth,
And ruled as "universal monarch of the wheel."

132. *A man who saw the Buddha Vessabhū,*
And to him obeisance paid but once,
For one-and-thirty aeons able was he
To avoid birth in states of woe,
And enjoy affluence and joy on earth,
And happiness in turn in deva abodes.
Oh beings, what debars you from such
Simple wholesome acts, let alone other greater ones?

133. *If you would preach, explaining the Law,*
Defining clearly the evil and the good,
Expecting not any material gains or gifts
For service such, but the compassionate mind:
"My aim in this shall only be
To guide my listeners in their assay
To overcome the woes of saṃsāra's deep"—
The happiness you gain in consequence of this
Will be great beyond all measures.

8. Anāthapiṇḍika, the donor of the Jetavana monastery.

134. *If one attends on those disciplined,*
Those homeless ones and ascetics in morality pure—
Others that see, will always him befriend.
The wise by attending on the holy ones
Do reap the benefits of these wholesome acts;
Those who would know the good from the bad,
Would realize this as a noble wholesome act.

135. *If those that in wholesome deeds engage,*
Would joyfully speak of their values to others,
The merit thereof would be multiplied;
Whenever such beings are born on earth
Their fame would spread far and wide
Like the risen full moon: know this as fact.

136. *A man who sought refuge in the Triple Gem*
For thirty-one aeons the realms of woe escaped,
Was born to much prosperity and wealth on earth
And finally reached certain emancipation's bliss.
Why dost thou not the Three Refuges seek?
Why suffer the sorrows and pangs on earth?

137. *It is only through delusion and ignorance*
That you think not of the virtues of the Blessed One,
The only refuge to you without hope.
If with mind calm and serene you think
On his virtues, doubt not
Happiness in various forms results.

138. *If all beings would bear in mind*
The many great virtues of the Blessed One,
The noblest being of the threefold world,
And recall with wisdom clear, these thoughts—
saṃsāra's ills never harshly fall on them,
And all blessings will to them accrue.

139. *By the great good effects of this effort,*
This presenting of the collection of thoughts
That I have writ for the benefit of the world
For beings ignorant of evil and good:
May all beings keep the happiness they gain
And reach Nibbāna, the eternal bliss.

140. *May this book of verses composed*
In joyous and compassionate mind
To guide the readers to Nibbāna's light
By Thera Maitriya of Vīdāgama,
In the ancient Vīdāgama monastic halls,
Last for long years to come.
And illume the minds of men!

Thoughts on the Dhamma

by

Venerable Mahāsi Sayādaw

Selected from His Discourses

WHEEL PUBLICATION NO. 298/299/300

Preface

While the present book was in preparation, its author, the Venerable Mahāsi Sayādaw of Burma, passed away at the age of 78. Thus, unexpectedly—as death so often comes—this publication has turned out to be a memorial issue in honour of one of the outstanding contemporary teachers of Theravada Buddhism, especially in the field of insight meditation (*vipassanā*). It was not long before he passed away that the Venerable Sayādaw had conveyed his consent to a compilation of his thoughts and observations, chiefly on insight meditation.

The selections here presented have been taken from sermons of the Venerable Mahāsi Sayādaw dealing with various Suttas (Discourses of the Buddha). The sermons had been delivered in the Burmese language and were translated into English by various hands. A set of seven books containing these English translations was published in 1980 by the Buddha Sāsana Nuggaha Organisation of Rangoon ("Sāsana Yeiktha"), which gave its kind permission for extracts from these books to be reproduced in the present anthology. These selections have been slightly edited, and references to their sources are given after each extract. A short biography of the Venerable Author is also included here.

In issuing this anthology, it is hoped that the sayings will be found instructive and inspiring, and that they will stimulate the reader to take up earnestly the threefold cultivation of morality, meditation, and wisdom, reaching their culmination in liberating insight wisdom.

It was a direct approach to that liberating insight (*vipassanā*) which the Venerable Mahāsi Sayādaw taught for many decades to a very large number of meditators from East and West. Based on the "Foundations of Mindfulness" (*satipaṭṭhāna*), he devised an effective method of meditative practise, partly derived from tradition and his own teachers, and partly evolved by himself. This method certainly demanded, or led to, a high degree of mental concentration, but did not require the prior attainment of full meditative absorption, the *jhānas*. Yet, as some of the extracts in this book will show, the Venerable Mahāsi Sayādaw was fully aware of the great significance of full concentration of mind in the *jhānas*, and he neither discouraged their cultivation nor belittled their value. But as a wise and compassionate teacher, he wanted to help those who, for psychological or environmental reasons, would have been faced with a long and frustrating struggle in their attempts to gain jhānic concentration.

For such a person, the method of direct insight practise could open an access to the core of the Teaching by direct meditative experience. In the course of the diligent practise of that method, there would follow a natural growth of mindfulness and concentration, of inner firmness and calm, which would place the meditator in a better position to attain to the *jhānas*.

In conclusion, the undersigned wishes to express his humble respect to the late Venerable Mahāsi Sayādaw, and his deep-felt gratitude for the guidance and inspiration he received from him.

Nyanaponika Thera
Forest Hermitage
Kandy, Sri Lanka
September 1982

The Venerable Mahāsi Sayādaw

The Venerable U Sobhana Mahāthera, better known as Mahāsi Sayādaw,[1] was born on 29 July 1904 to the peasant proprietors, U Kan Htaw and Daw Shwe Ok at Seikkhun Village, which is about seven miles to the west of the town of Shwebo in Upper Burma, once the capital of the founder of the last Burmese dynasty.

At the age of six he began his studies at a monastic school in his village, and at the age of twelve he was ordained a *samanera* (novice), receiving the name of Sobhana. On reaching the age of twenty, he was ordained a bhikkhu on 26 November 1923. He passed the Government Pāli Examinations in all the three classes (lower, middle, and highest) in the following three successive years.

In the fourth year of his bhikkhu ordination, he proceeded to Mandalay, noted for its pre-eminence in Buddhist studies, where he continued his further education under various monks of high scholastic fame. In the fifth year he went to Moulmein, where he took up the work of teaching the Buddhist scriptures at a monastery known as Taung-waing-galay Taik Kyaung.

In the eighth year after his bhikkhu ordination, he and another monk left Moulmein equipped with the bare necessities of a bhikkhu (i.e., alms-bowl, a set of three robes, etc.), and went in search of a clear and effective method in the practice of meditation. At Thaton he met the well-known meditation teacher, the Venerable U Nārada, who is also known as Mingun Jetawun Sayādaw the First. He then placed himself under the guidance of the Sayādaw and at once proceeded with an intensive course of meditation.

He had progressed so well in his practice that he was able to teach the method effectively to his first three disciples in Seikkhun while he was on a visit there in 1938. These three lay disciples, too, made remarkable progress. Inspired by the example of these three, gradually as many as fifty villagers joined the courses of intensive practise.

---

1. The Burmese word *Sayādaw,* meaning "Venerable Teacher," is an honorific term and way of address given to senior or eminent monks.

The Venerable Mahāsi could not stay with the Venerable Mingun Sayādaw as long as he wanted as he was urgently asked to return to the Moulmein monastery. Its aged head monk was gravely ill and passed away not long after the Venerable Mahāsi's return. The Venerable Mahāsi was then asked to take charge of the monastery and to resume teaching the resident monks. During this time he sat for the Pāli Lectureship Examination on its first introduction by the Government of Burma. Passing this examination on the first attempt, in 1941 he was awarded the title of Sāsanadhaja Sri Pavara Dhammacariya.

On the event of the Japanese invasion, the authorities gave an evacuation order to those living near Moulmein at the Taung-waing-galay Taik Monastery and its neighbourhood. These places were close to an airfield and hence exposed to air attacks. For the Sayādaw this was a welcome opportunity to return to his native Seikkhun and to devote himself wholeheartedly to his own practise of *vipassanā*-meditation and to the teaching of it to others.

He took residence at a monastery known as Mahā-Si-Kyaung, which was thus called because a drum (Burmese: *si*) of an unusually large (*mahā*) size was housed there. From that monastery, the Sayādaw's popular name, Mahāsi Sayādaw, is derived.

It was during this period, in 1945, that the Sayādaw wrote his great work, *Manual of Vipassanā Meditation,* a comprehensive and authoritative treatise expounding both the doctrinal and the practical aspects of the Satipaṭṭhāna method of meditation. This work of two volumes, comprising 858 pages in print, was written by him in just seven months, while the neighbouring town of Shwebo was at times subjected to almost daily air attacks. So far, only one chapter of this work, the fifth, has been translated into English and is published under the title *Practical Insight Meditation: Basic and Progressive Stages* (Buddhist Publication Society).

It did not take long before the reputation of Mahāsi Sayādaw as an able teacher of insight meditation (*vipassanā*) had spread throughout the Shwebo-Sagaing region and attracted the attention of a prominent and very devout Buddhist layman, Sir U Thwin, who was regarded as Burma's Elder Statesman. It was his wish to promote the inner strength of Buddhism in Burma by setting up a meditation centre to be guided by a meditation teacher of proven virtue and ability. After meeting Mahāsi Sayādaw and listening to a discourse given by him and to the meditation instructions given to nuns in Sagaing, Sir U Thwin was in no doubt that he had found the ideal person he was looking for.

In 1947 the Buddha Sāsana Nuggaha Organisation[2] was founded in Rangoon with Sir U Thwin as its first President and with its object the furthering of the study (*pariyatti*) and practise (*paṭipatti*) of Buddhism. In 1948 Sir U Thwin donated five acres of land at Kokine, Rangoon, to the organisation for the erection of a meditation centre. It is on this site that the present *Thathana* (or *Sāsana*) *Yeiktha,* i.e., "Buddhist Retreat," is situated, which now, however, covers an area of twenty acres, with a large number of buildings.

In 1949, the then Prime Minister of Burma, U Nu, and Sir U Thwin requested that the Venerable Mahāsi Sayādaw come to Rangoon and give training in meditation practice. On 4 December 1949, the Sayādaw introduced the first group of 25 meditators into the methodical practice of *vipassanā*-meditation. Within a few years of the Sayādaw's arrival in Rangoon, similar meditation centres sprang up all over Burma, until they numbered over one hundred. In neighbouring Theravada countries like Thailand and Sri Lanka such centres were also established in which the same method was taught and practised. According to a 1972 census, the total number of meditators trained at all these centres (both in Burma and abroad) had passed the figure of seven hundred thousand. In the East and in several Western countries as well, *vipassanā*-courses continue to be conducted.

At the historic Sixth Buddhist Council (Chaṭṭha Saṅgāyana) held at Rangoon for two years, culminating in the year 2500 Buddhist Era (1956), the Venerable Mahāsi Sayādaw had an important role. He was one of the final editors of the canonical texts, which were recited and thereby approved, in the sessions of the council. Further, he was the questioner (*pucchaka*)—that is, he had to ask the questions concerning the respective canonical texts that were to be recited. They were then answered by an erudite monk with a phenomenal power of memory, by the name of Venerable Vicittasārabhivaṃsa. To appreciate fully the importance of these roles, it may be mentioned that at the

2. That is, Organisation for Promoting the Buddhist Religion.

First Council, held one hundred days after the passing away of the Buddha, it was the Venerable Mahā Kassapa who put forth those introductory questions which were then answered by the Venerable Upāli and the Venerable Ānanda.

After the recital of the canonical scriptures, the Tipiṭaka, had been completed at the Sixth Council, it was decided to continue with a rehearsal of the ancient commentaries and sub-commentaries, preceded by critical editing and scrutiny. In that large task, too, the Sayādaw took prominent part.

In the midst of all of these tasks, he was also a prolific and scholarly writer. He authored more than 70 writings and translations, mostly in Burmese, with a few in the Pāli language. One of these deserves to be singled out: his Burmese translation of the commentary to the *Visuddhimagga* (*Visuddhimagga Mahā-Ṭīkā*), which, in two large volumes of the Pāli original, is even more voluminous than the work commented upon, and presents many difficulties, linguistically and in its contents. In 1957 Mahāsi Sayādaw was awarded the title of Agga-Mahā-Paṇḍita.

Yet even all of this did not exhaust the Sayādaw's remarkable capacity for work in the cause of the Buddha-Dhamma. He undertook several travels abroad. The first two of his tours were in preparation for the Sixth Council, but were likewise used for preaching and teaching:

Thailand, Cambodia, and Vietnam (1952); India and Sri Lanka (1953, 1959); Japan (1957); Indonesia (1959); America, Hawaii, England, Continental Europe (1979); England, Sri Lanka, Singapore, Malaysia, Thailand (1980); Nepal, India (1981).

In the midst of all these manifold and strenuous activities, he never neglected his own meditative life, which had enabled him to give wise guidance to those instructed by him. His outstanding vigour of body and mind and his deep dedication to the Dhamma sustained him through a life of 78 years.

On 14 August 1982, the Venerable Mahāsi Sayādaw succumbed to a sudden and severe heart attack which he had suffered the night before. Yet on the evening of the 13th, he had still given an introductory explanation to a group of new meditators.

The Venerable Mahāsi Sayādaw was one of the very rare personalities in whom there was a balanced and high development of both profound erudition linked with a keen intellect, and deep and advanced meditative experience. He was also able to teach effectively both Buddhist thought and Buddhist practise.

His long career of teaching through the spoken and printed word had a beneficial impact on many hundreds of thousands in the East and in the West. His personal stature and his life's work rank him among the great figures of contemporary Buddhism.

Writings of the Venerable Mahāsi Sayādaw in English Translation (Selection):

The Progress of Insight through the Stages of Purification, with the Pāli Text (1)
Practical Insight Meditation: Basic and Progressive Stages (1)
Practical Vipassanā Meditational Exercises (2)
Purpose of Practising Kammaṭṭhāna Meditation (2)
The Wheel of Dhamma (Dhammacakkappavattana Sutta) (2)

(1) Buddhist Publication Society, Kandy, Sri Lanka.
(2) Buddha Sāsana Nuggaha Organisation, 16 Sāsana Yeiktha Road, Rangoon, Burma.

The Dhamma

One Truth

Indeed, truth must be one and indivisible. This must be borne in mind. Nowadays, when Buddha-dhamma is being disseminated, there should be only one basis of teaching relating to the Middle Way or the Eightfold Path: the practice of morality, concentration, and acquisition of profound knowledge, and the Four Noble Truths. But if one were preaching that the aims and objects of Buddhism can be achieved without recourse to the actual practice of the Dhamma, we should understand that such a one has strayed from the Path.

Discourse on "To Nibbāna via the Noble Eightfold Path"

The Need for Practise

In these days there have cropped up misstatements running counter to what the Buddha actually taught. Knowledge, it is said, is accomplishment; and there is no need for anyone to practise Dhamma once knowledge has been attained. Such a statement virtually amounts to the rejection of the practice of the Dhamma, to the exclusion of the Noble Eightfold Path. But in point of fact, the Noble Eightfold Path is to be constantly practised, for it is a set of disciplines to be cultivated (*bhāvetabba*) which can generate the power to gain insight into the nature of the Path. Without effort, nothing comes up naturally. And yet there is a school of thought which wrongly suggests that making an effort itself is *dukkha* or unsatisfactoriness, and that therefore, it should not be indulged in. In the face of such dogma who will be prepared to take the trouble of meditating upon the Noble Eightfold Path and practise its tenets? If there is no one to practise this Dhamma, how can its light shine within him? And in the absence of any insight into the nature of the Path, how can one eliminate defilements and attain Nibbānic peace?

Discourse on "To Nibbāna via the Noble Eightfold Path"

The Path in Three Stages

Good Buddhists are in the habit of wishing for realisation and attainment of Nibbāna whenever they accomplish any meritorious deed. The *summum bonum* will not, of course, be attained immediately by their mere wishing. It will be attained only in one of the higher planes which they will reach by virtue of their good deeds; and then only if they actually practise developing the Eightfold Path. So, why wait till a future existence? Why not start now and work for liberation in this very life?

Discourse on "The Wheel of Dhamma"

Putting Knowledge into Practise

According to the Buddha, knowledge relating to the Noble Path transports one to the stage where all suffering or unsatisfactoriness ceases. But it must always be borne in mind that the Path offers salvation only to those who actually practise it.

In your travels a vehicle takes you to your destination while those who stand by it are left behind. Knowledge about the Noble Path is like that vehicle. If you ride in it, you will be conveyed to your destination; and if you merely stand by it, you will be left behind. Those who desire to be liberated from all sufferings should use that vehicle. That is to say they should use knowledge they gained for practical purposes. The most important task for you while you are born into this Buddha Sāsana is to practise Dhamma so that you reach Nibbāna, where all sufferings cease.

Discourse on "To Nibbāna via the Noble Eightfold Path"

The True Faith

The theory of rejection of *kamma* is gradually gaining more favourable attention because people's greed (*lobha*) is increasing and their hankering after sensual pleasures is making a corresponding increase. Nowadays, there are some who are of the opinion that if one avoids evil deeds, one will not achieve any useful purpose. That view leads people to these false faiths.

The ignorance of *kamma* and its effect that is becoming rife now is the result of overwhelming greed (*lobha*) superimposed by delusion (*moha*).

The Buddha himself realised this and so he urged people to make efforts to reduce the volume of greed and delusion. Faithful disciples will follow the Buddha's directions and try to reach realisation through meditation practise, and thus free themselves from these false faiths. They come to realise that the *kamma* of the previous existences had made them what they are in the present existence, and the *kamma* of the present existence, if not yet free of craving (*taṇhā*), will determine the state of the next existence. Thus, they confirm their belief in the true faith.

Discourse on the Hemavata Sutta

The Deities' Dissatisfaction

Do not have the impression that if one becomes a celestial being owing to one's good deeds, one gets to a place where every wish is fulfilled and one does not need to have any more wishes; that is, one would be satisfied to the full. No being is ever satisfied with what has been given, and will always ask for more. To get more, further efforts have to be made, and suffering ensues from these efforts.

Discourse on the Hemavata Sutta

The Great Pity

Men are just living their lives without being actually aware of the slow and gradual deterioration of their bodies and the onset of disease of one kind or another till at the last moment when nothing can be done to cure the disease, death is at hand. Then only do they realise the sad fact.

The same pattern applies to man's next existence; the gradual deterioration of the body, the onset of old age and disease, and the eventual death. This the Buddha perceived. He surveyed millions of ailing beings and dying beings, and the sorrows of those who are near and dear to them, and a great pity arose in him. "Millions upon millions" is the current term, but in reality the number is countless. If the history of a being's existences were to be illustrated pictorially, the pictures so depicted would fill the entire surface of the earth, and more space would be needed. The pictures of the being's birth, old age, illness, and death were perceived by the Buddha, who felt a great pity for that being; that was how the great pity, or *mahā karuṇā,* arose in him.

Discourse on the Hemavata Sutta

Slavery

The Buddha saw that all beings were slaves of lust and greed, and that moved him to great pity. Living beings serve their lust and greed even at the risk of their lives. They go out in search of the things their lust or greed urges them, and risk their lives to get them. They have to work daily for all their lives to satisfy their lust and greed, and after death, and in the next existence, too, they remain slaves of the same master, craving (*taṇhā*). There is no period of rest for them.

In this world a slave may remain a slave only during his lifetime, but a slave of lust has an unending term of servitude till the time of salvation when he becomes an Arahat and thus ends his wandering through *saṃsāra.*

Discourse on the Hemavata Sutta

Listening to the Dhamma

To attain realisation of the Dhamma while listening to a sermon, one must have a settled mind, for it is only through concentrated attention with a settled mind that one can attain *samādhi* (concentration), and only *samādhi* can still the mind for insight. If the mind wanders during the sermon over domestic, economic, and other secular affairs, *samādhi* will not be attained. If anxiety sets in, it is all for the worse. If distraction and anxiety crop up, the essence of the Dhamma will slip, and as *samādhi* is lacking, there will be no insight, and if one cannot attain insight for *vipassanā,* how can one attain realisation of the Dhamma Concentrated attention while listening to a sermon is, therefore, an important factor.

The listener must listen carefully, with full mental involvement, and the words of the Dhamma must be adhered to in practise. If one attends to a sermon in this way, one's mind will be calm and absorbed in the sermon; one will be free from interference, and thus attain purity of mind.

Discourse on the Hemavata Sutta

Self

There are three different views of the ego or self. The first is the belief in self as the soul-entity. The second is the view of self based on conceit and pride. The third is the self as a conventional term for the first person singular as distinct from other persons. The self or "I" implicit in "I walk" has nothing to do with illusion or conceit. It is a term of common usage that is to be found in the sayings of the Buddha and Arahats.

Discourse on the Ariyāvāsa Sutta

The Burden of the Aggregates

The Burden

What is the heavy burden? The *khandhas*[3] are the heavy burden.
Who accepts the heavy burden? *Taṇhā,* craving, accepts the heavy burden.
What is meant by throwing down the burden? Annihilation of *taṇhā* is throwing down the burden.
Heavy is the burden of the five *khandhas.*
Acceptance of the burden is suffering; rejection of the burden is conducive to happiness.
When craving is uprooted from its very foundation, no desires arise. An old burden having been laid aside, no new burden can be imposed.
Then, one enters Nibbāna, the abode of eternal peace.

Discourse on the Bhara Sutta

How Heavy the Burden Is!

How heavy the burden is! When a man is conceived in his mother's womb, the five aggregates appertaining to him have to be cared for. The mother has to give him all necessary protection so that he may be safely born to develop well into a human being. She has to be careful in her daily pursuits, in her diet, in her sleep, etc. If the mother happens to be a Buddhist, she will perform meritorious deeds on behalf of the child to be born.

When the child is at last born, it cannot take care of itself. It is looked after by its mother and the elders. It has to be fed with mother's milk. It has to be bathed, cleansed, and clothed. It has to be carried from place to place. It takes at least two or three persons to look after and bring up this tiny burden of the five *khandhas.*

---

3. *Khandha:* The five "groups (of existence)" or "groups of clinging"; alternative renderings: aggregates, categories of clinging's objects. The five are: the material body, feeling, perception, mental formations (including volitions), and consciousness.

When a man comes of age, he will have to look after himself. He will have to feed himself two or three times a day. If he likes good food, he will have to make special efforts to get it. He must make himself clean, bathe himself, clothe himself. To tone up his body, he will have to do some daily exercise. He must do everything himself. When he feels hot, he cools himself and when he feels cold, he warms himself up. He has to be careful to keep up his health and well-being. When he takes a walk, he sees that he does not stumble. When he travels, he sees that he meets no danger. In spite of all these precautions, he may fall sick at times, and will have to take medicinal treatment. It is a great burden to tend to the welfare of his *khandhas,* the five aggregates of psycho-physical phenomena.

The greatest burden for a living being is to fend for itself. In the case of human beings, some have to work for a living starting from the age of twelve or thirteen, and for that purpose they have to be educated. Some can get only an elementary schooling and so they can get employment only as menials. Those who can get a good education are profitably employed in higher positions; but then they have to work day in and day out without any break.

But those who were born into this world with past good *kamma* do not feel the burden. A man born with the best *kamma* has been fed and clothed since childhood by his parents who gave him the best education as he came of age. Even when he grows to be a man they continue to give him all support to raise him up into a man of position who can fulfil his desires and wants. Such a fortunate man may not know how heavy the burden of life is.

Those whose past *kamma* is not good never know affluence. As children they know only hunger, not being able to eat what they would like to eat or dress in a way that they would like to dress. Now that they have grown up, they are just trying to keep their body and soul together. Some do not even have their daily quota of rice ready for the table. Some have to get up early to pound rice for cooking. Some do not even have that rice; and so they have to borrow some from their neighbours. If you want to know more about this life, go to poor men's quarters and make enquiries yourself.

Discourse on the Bhara Sutta

Carrying the Heavy Burden

This body, one of the *khandhas,* is a heavy burden. Serving it means carrying the heavy burden. When we feed and clothe it, we are carrying the burden. That means we are servants to the aggregate of matter (*rūpakkhandha*). Having fed and clothed the body, we must also see to it that it is sound and happy both in the physical and psychological sense. This is serving the aggregate of feeling (*vedanākkhandha*). Again, we must see that this body experiences good sights and sounds. This is concerned with consciousness. Therefore we are serving the aggregate of consciousness (*viññāṇakkhandha*).

These three burdens are quite obvious. *Rūpakkhandha* says: "Feed me well. Give me what I like to eat; if not, I shall make myself ill or weak. Or, worse still, I shall make myself die!" Then we shall have to try to please it.

Then *vedanākkhandha* also says: "Give me pleasurable sensations; if not, I shall make myself painful and regretful. Or, worse still, I shall make myself die!" Then we shall have to hanker after pleasurable sensations to serve its needs.

Then *viññāṇakkhandha* also says: "Give me good sights. Give me good sounds. I want pleasant sense-objects. Find them for me; if not, I shall make myself unhappy and frightful. Eventually I shall make myself die!" Then we shall have to do its biddings.

It is as if all these three *khandhas* are perpetually threatening us. So we cannot help complying with their demands; and this compliance is a great burden on us.

The aggregate of volitional activities (*saṅkhārakkhandha*) is another burden. Life demands that we satisfy our daily needs and desires and for that satisfaction we have to be active. We must be working all the time. This round of human activities gets encouragement from our volition prompted by desire. These activities make threatening demands on us daily, indicating that, if they are not met, trouble and even death would ensue. When human desires remain unfulfilled, they resort to crime. How heavy the burden of the *saṅkhāras* rests upon us! It is because we cannot carry this load well upon our shoulders that we get demoralised into committing sin that brings shame upon us. Criminal offences are committed mostly because we cannot carry the burden of *saṅkhārakkhandha* well. When criminals die, they may fall into the nether world of intense suffering or they may be reborn as hungry ghosts or animals. Even when they are reborn as human beings, their evil actions will follow in their wake and punish them. They may be short-lived; they may be oppressed with disease all the time; they may face poverty and starvation; they may be friendless; they may be always living in danger or in troublesome surroundings.

The aggregate of perception (*saññākkhandha*) is also a great burden; because it is with perception that you train your faculties like memory to be able to retain knowledge and wisdom which can discern good from bad and reject from your mind unwholesome things produced by unpleasant sense-objects. If the demands of the mind for pleasant sense-objects are not met, it will take up only evil, which does nobody any good. Regrets and anxieties arise because we cannot shoulder the burden of *saññākkhandha* well.

For all these reasons the Buddha declared the five aggregates of clinging (*upādānakkhandha*) a heavy burden.

We carry the burden of our *khandhas* not for a short time, not for a minute, not for an hour, not for a day, not for a year, not for one life, not for one world, not for one aeon. We carry the burden from the beginning of *saṃsāra*, the round of rebirths, which is infinite. It has no beginning. And there is no way of knowing when it will end. Its finality can be reached only with the extermination of the defilements of the mind (*kilesa*), as we get to the stage of the Path of the Noble Ones (*arahatta magga*).

Discourse on the Bhara Sutta

Ethics

The Light of Dhamma

Virtue, concentration, and wisdom (*sīla, samādhi, and paññā*) can lead one to the Path. Yet some assert that it is not necessary to observe the rules of morality if they are convinced of the teachings. It is often put forward by such protagonists that they have invented simplified or easy methods for their followers. How strange! It cannot be denied that, in Buddha's times, there were instances of intelligent and mature individuals who at once saw the light of Dhamma the moment they heard the Buddha's sermons. Of course geniuses exist like the *ugghaṭitaññū* who can at once grasp the meaning of the Four Noble Truths after a brief exposition, or the *vipañcitaññū* who can realise the Truth after a wider exposition. In Buddha's times such individuals gained the light of knowledge while listening to the Buddha's teachings without appreciable endeavour. But when it comes to an ordinary *neyya* individual who has to be guided for the gradual realisation of Truth, even the Buddha may not be able to let him see the light of Dhamma all at once. So, the following verse of the canonical Dhammapada, stanza 276, as taught by Buddha, should serve one as a reminder. In an expanded paraphrase:

You should strive for the annihilation of all potentials of defilements. Tathāgatas can only show you the way. You yourself must practise meditation on the objects for *samatha* (concentration) and *vipassanā* (meditation). Only then will you be liberated from the bonds of defilements that destroy what is wholesome and moral.

Discourse on "To Nibbāna via the Noble Eightfold Path"

Keeping the Precepts

Noble Ones who have attained the first stage of sainthood, the *ariyas*, adore the five precepts. They do not want to break them; they are always anxious not to break the *sīla*. They observe the precepts not because they are afraid that others would censure them, but because they want to keep their minds in purity, and purity of mind can be achieved only by observance of the five precepts. Not only during this life, but in all future existences they do not want to fail in keeping the precepts. They may not know that they have become stream-enterers (*sotāpanna*) in their previous existence, but they do know that they must observe the five precepts fully and with no fault.

Sometimes one comes across a person who has never since his infancy done any evil deed such as killing or stealing. He was not given any particular instructions by his parents, but he knows by himself what is an evil deed and refrains from it. He has kept his virtue pure since his childhood. Maybe he had achieved a special insight of the Dhamma in his previous existence. There are also instances of persons who, though born of non-Buddhist parents have come to the East to practise meditation. Maybe such persons have had some practise of observance of the Buddha's Dhamma in their previous existences. These are interesting instances, and their cases must be evaluated in accord with the extent and depth of their study and practise of the Dhamma.

Discourse on the Hemavata Sutta

On Kindness and Charity

All human behaviour resulting from the practice, in deed, in word, and in thought, of loving kindness shall be rendered memorable throughout one's life.

Where love, compassion, and respect pervade human society, there shall one find enduring unity.

Acts of charity inspired by loving kindness live long in human memory, generating love and respect among mankind, thus laying foundations for the unity of the whole world.

Discourse on "To Nibbāna via the Noble Eightfold Path"

Ill-will

Ill-will (*vyāpāda*) is one of the five hindrances on the holy path. It is like a disease that creates distaste for good food and makes the sick man listless and apathetic. Ill-will makes us irritable, bad-tempered, and suspicious. We do not trust even our friend who is on good terms with the man we dislike. A man who has ill-will should regard himself as suffering from a disease. Unless it is treated promptly, it may gain ground and lead to death. Likewise, the effect of unrestrained ill-will may be disastrous, as is evident in the newspaper reports of violent crimes.

Discourse on the Ariyāvāsa Sutta

Killing in Self-defence

Once, a writer said in one of the journals that a stream-enterer (*sotāpanna*) will not kill others, but if anyone comes to kill him, he will kill his attacker. That writer declared that he made that statement after a research of the nature of the human mind.

That is ridiculous. I just wonder whose mind he had made a research of, and how he could do that. He must have made a research of his own mind. He might have thought he was a *sotāpanna*. He might have asked himself if he would allow the attacker to kill him when he had an effective weapon to return the attack by way of defence, and it might have been his own answer that he would attack the attacker first. From his personal attitude he obtained the conclusions which he expressed in his article. According to the tenets of Buddhism, this is a ridiculous statement.

The very fact that one thinks one can and should retaliate if attacked proves that one is not a stream-enterer, for, according to Buddhist tenets, the person entertaining such a notion is a mere *puthujjana*, an ordinary worldling, definitely not a stream-enterer. A real *sotāpanna* would not kill even a flea or a bug, not to say a human being. This fact must be remembered once and for all.

Discourse on the Hemavata Sutta

Concentration

The Need for Concentration

There are some teachers who instruct their audience to keep their minds free and relaxed instead of concentrating on meditation points because concentration, they say, restricts the mind. This is in contravention of the Buddha's instructions, although it assumes an appearance of the Buddha's teachings. If, according to these teachers, the mind is set free, it will surely indulge in fond thoughts and may even revel in sensual pleasures.

Discourse on the Hemavata Sutta

Samādhi

Some are saying that *samādhi*—concentration of mind—is not necessary, that if one just ponders upon the two wisdom factors of the Eightfold Path, namely, Right Understanding (*sammādiṭṭhi*) and Right Thought (*sammāsaṅkappa*), there is no need to make a note of arising and vanishing. This is a skipping of the area of *samādhi*. *Jhāna-samādhi* is indeed the best to attain, but failing that, one should acquire momentary concentration (*khaṇika samādhi*), which is equivalent to access-concentration. Otherwise, it is not real insight-wisdom. So said the Buddha:

"Bhikkhus, try to acquire *samādhi*. A bhikkhu who has a stable mind knows the truth. What is 'knowing the truth'? It is knowing that the eye (*cakkhu*) is non-permanent, that visual form (*rūpa*) is non-permanent, and that visual consciousness (*cakkhuviññāṇa*) is non-permanent."

So it is clear that without *samādhi* one cannot acquire *vipassanā*-knowledge and attain the knowledge of the supramundane Paths and Fruits (*maggaphala-ñāṇa*). One can, therefore, decide that knowledge outside of *samādhi* is not *vipassanā*-knowledge, and that without *vipassanā*-knowledge one cannot attain Nibbāna.

Discourse on the Hemavata Sutta

Becoming and Dissolution

A bubble bursts soon after it has been formed. A mirage conjures up an image of reality which disappears on close examination. There is absolutely no substance in either of them. This is common knowledge. As we know their true nature, so also must we know the true nature of the phenomena. When a meditator acquires knowledge of concentration through the observance of the dissolution of the aggregates (*khandha*), he will discover that the known object and the knowing mind are all in a state of flux, now appearing, now vanishing. They are transitory. There is no essence or substance worthy to be named "mine" in them. They signify only the processes of becoming and dissolution.

Discourse on the Bhara Sutta

Meditation

Instructions to the Meditator

To develop mindfulness and gain insight-knowledge, the following points must be borne in mind:

Recognise correctly all physical behaviour as it arises.
Recognise correctly all mental behaviour as it arises.
Recognise every feeling, pleasant, unpleasant, or indifferent, as it arises.
Know, with an analytical mind, every mental object as it arises.

Discourse on "To Nibbāna via the Noble Eightfold Path"

Knowledge Deepens Through Practise

If the Path is practised to gain direct personal experience, it is usual that knowledge deepens as time goes on.

Discourse "on The Wheel of Dhamma"

Initial Doubt

Some people who have never meditated may have some doubt, and no wonder! For only seeing is believing, and their scepticism is due to their lack of experience. I myself was a sceptic at one time. I did not then like the Satipaṭṭhāna method as it makes no mention of *nāma, rūpa, anicca, anattā,* and so forth. But the Sayādaw who taught the method was a learned monk, and so I decided to give it a trial. At first I made little progress because I still had a lingering doubt about the method which, in my view, had nothing to do with ultimate reality.

It was only later on when I had followed the method seriously that its significance dawned on me. I realised then that it is the best method of meditation since it calls for attentiveness to everything that is to be known, leaving no room for absent-mindedness. So the Buddha describes the Satipaṭṭhāna method as the only way: *Ekāyano-maggo.*

Discourse on the Ariyāvāsa Sutta

A Very Effective Remedy

If you suffer from ill health or disease, and if you have no other remedy to alleviate the pain and suffering, the meditation practise upon the suffering of illness can give at least some relief if it cannot give you a complete cure. If the pain and suffering remain in your body, the meditation practice can render relief to your mind. But if you are angry or irritated by the physical suffering, your mind will suffer, too. The Buddha compared this dual suffering to being pierced by two thorns at the same time.

Let us say a man has a thorn in his flesh, and he tries to extract the thorn by piercing another thorn into his flesh. The second thorn breaks into the flesh without being able to extract the first thorn. Then the man suffers the pain from two thorns at the same time. So also, the person who cannot make a note of the physical pain in a meditation manner suffers both physical and mental pain. But if he can ponder well upon the physical pain, he will suffer only that pain, and will not suffer mental pain.

This kind of suffering—only physical pain—is like that suffered by the Buddha and Arahats, for they, too, suffer physical pain. They suffer from ill-effects of heat and cold, insect bites, and other kinds of discomfort. Though they suffer from the physical *dukkha,* their minds remain stable, so they do not suffer mental pain. The meditation method is a very effective remedy for physical pain and suffering.

Discourse on Lokadhammā

Depression

We should keep in mind the law of *kamma*—the Buddha's teaching that everything happens according to one's actions—and bear our misfortunes calmly. The best remedy in a crisis is the practice of *samatha* or *vipassanā.* If sorrow, grief, or depression afflicts us, during meditation hours such unwholesome states of consciousness must be noted and removed. The Buddha describes the Satipaṭṭhāna method as the only way to get over grief and end all suffering. So long as we keep ourselves mindful according to Satipaṭṭhāna teaching, we never feel depressed, and if depression arises, it passes away when we focus our attention on it.

Discourse on the Sakkapañha Sutta

Despair

Some meditators are disheartened because of their weak concentration at the outset, but as a result, some redouble their effort and attain unusual insights. So the meditator may benefit by his despair at this stage. According to the commentaries, we should welcome the despair that results from non-fulfilment of desire in connection with renunciation, meditation, reflection, and *jhāna.*

Sorrow is wholesome when it arises from frustration over any effort to promote one's spiritual life, such as the effort to join the holy order, the effort to attain insight, and so forth. We should welcome such sorrow for it may spur effort and lead to progress on the Path. It is not, however, to be sought deliberately. The best thing is to have wholesome joy in the search for enlightenment.

Discourse on the Sakkapañha Sutta

Strenuous Effort

Strenuous, relentless efforts in meditation practices for achievement of concentration and insight should not be misconceived as a form of self-torture. Leaving aside meditation practices, even the keeping of the moral precepts which may entail some physical discomfort and abstention, is not to be regarded as a practice of self-mortification.

In the practise of concentration and insight meditation, patience and self-control (*khanti-saṃvara*) play an important role; they are important factors for the successful practice of both. Therefore unpleasant physical discomfort should be borne with patience. The self-control practised thus is not self-mortification, inasmuch as its goal is not the afflicting and enduring of pain but one's progress in virtue, concentration, and wisdom (*sīla, samādhi, paññā*) as enjoined by the Buddha.

Discourse on "The Wheel of Dhamma"

How to Avoid the Two Extremes

Of the five sense objects—namely, sight, sound, smell, taste, and touch—those objects which would not violate observance of the precepts or which would be helpful to the practice of Dhamma may be made use of. Eating food which should be normally eaten, wearing clothes which should be normally worn, contributes to easeful practice of Dhamma, thus avoiding the extreme austerity of self-mortification.

Necessary material goods such as food, clothing, medicine, and shelter should be used, accompanied either by reflective contemplation or the practice of concentration or insight-meditation. Every time contact is made with the five sense objects, they should be noted as objects of insight-meditation. By adopting a reflective mood or by noting these sense objects as objects of insight-meditation, partaking of necessary food, clothing, etc., does not develop into enjoying them with delight or pleasure, thereby avoiding the other extreme of indulgence in sensuous pleasures. The Blessed One declared, therefore, that "Having avoided these two extremes (parts, practices), I have come to understand the Middle Path."

Discourse on "The Wheel of Dhamma"

Purity of Mind

You have purity of mind when you are mindful. It is a mistake to think that one can attain it only when one enters meditative absorption (*jhāna*). Purity of mind based on *jhāna* is due to the continuous stream of *jhānic* consciousness. Purity of mind through *vipassanā* is the purity that emerges at the moment of attaining insight. Both kinds of consciousness are alike in respect to purity of mind and freedom from hindrances.

Discourse on the Ariyāvāsa Sutta

Insight Meditation

Insight Knowledge

Insight knowledge (*vipassanā ñāṇa*) is attained by observing the actions of mind-and-body (*nāma-rūpa*) in the state of impermanence (*anicca*), suffering (*dukkha*), and no-self (*anattā*). It is not attained simply by casual observation, but by in-depth observation of the actions as they are happening, without leaving any one of them unobserved. Thus the observation should be on all actions such as seeing, hearing, smelling, eating, etc., as they are happening and without failing to observe any single action.

Discourse on the Hemavata Sutta

A Flash of Lightning

Watch a flash of lightning. If you watch it at the moment lightning strikes, you will see it for yourself. If you are imagining in your mind as to how lightning strikes before or after the event, you may not be regarded as having seen the flash of lightning. So try to know things for yourself by actual observation of things as they happen.

Discourse on "To Nibbāna via the Noble Eightfold Path"

No Ordinary Teaching

Beware of those who assert that *vipassanā* (insight-meditation) is unnecessary or superfluous. Such statements are not conducive to the practice of insight-meditation, without which our Buddhasāsana would be like any ordinary teaching.

Discourse on "To Nibbāna via the Noble Eightfold Path"

The Qualities for Success

It is impossible to do anything without faith or conviction. You will practise mindfulness only if you believe that it will help to develop insight-knowledge. But faith in itself will not do. You need, too, a strong will and unrelenting effort to attain the Path and Nibbāna. Possession of these qualities is essential to success in the practice of mindfulness and for gaining security in the abode of the Noble.

Discourse on the Ariyāvāsa Sutta

The Three Feelings in Vipassanā

The main object of *vipassanā* practice is to seek and cultivate the equanimity that is bound up with "equanimity about formations" (*saṅkhārupekkhā*) insight. To this end we should avoid sensuous joy and seek wholesome joy in good deeds and contemplation. Likewise we should welcome wholesome sorrow stemming from frustration on the holy Path and avoid unwholesome sorrow. In the same way we should avoid unwholesome equanimity of the sensual world and seek wholesome equanimity of the holy Path.

We should concentrate on wholesome joy, wholesome sorrow, and wholesome equanimity. For the cultivation of these wholesome states of consciousness means the elimination of their negative, unwholesome counterparts.

We should also eliminate wholesome sorrow through wholesome joy. This means that if we are depressed because of the failure to make much progress on the holy Path, we must overcome the depression by exerting effort for *vipassanā* insight. Likewise, wholesome joy must be rejected through wholesome equanimity.

Thus "equanimity about formations" (*saṅkhārupekkhā*) insight with joy or with equanimity is only a step removed from the holy Path and fruition.

Discourse on the Sakkapañha Sutta

Intrinsic Knowledge

Here we are not concerned with mere perception but with insight-knowledge, which can be gained only through actual practise. When you personally watch people going through a gate, you will notice for yourself their goings and comings; you need not depend on others to know at second-hand that they are going in and out of the gate. In the same way if you yourself watch and note the six sense-doors, the eye-door, the ear-door, etc., you will actually see how *nāma* and *rūpa* arise and pass away without resorting to the process of reflecting.

Take another example. Place a mirror at the roadside. All pedestrians and vehicles will be reflected in the mirror in their true nature. If you watch and note them, you will see them as they really are. In the same way if you watch and note with mindfulness all that appears at the six sense-doors, you will notice the sense-objects (which have no consciousness) arising while the mind (the subject that possesses the consciousness) is taking cognizance of such arising. Then both the object and the subject pass away. Then this process is renewed. The meditator will then come to realise that this is the phenomenon of *nāma* and *rūpa* arising and passing away. Consciousness and corporeality are, after all, not everlasting. They are not permanent. They are suffering. They are unsubstantial.

When you note the working of *nāma* and *rūpa,* you will come to know their true nature. Having known their true nature, what remains there to be thought of and considered? So one does not get at the nature of things by merely thinking about *nāma* and *rūpa,* without actually noting how they arise and pass away. Having come face to face with them, are you going to argue their existence? And it does not stand to reason if one merely recites, "Arising! Passing away!" without actually noting the actual process. The knowledge acquired by this method of thinking or reciting is not intrinsic but mere second-hand knowledge gained through books.

The essence of insight-meditation, therefore, is to note personally all *dhammas* and phenomena as they occur.

Discourse on the Bhara Sutta

The Knower and the Known

When a *vipassanā* meditator's insight-meditation becomes strengthened, Right Thoughts direct his mind to the realities of the sense-objects on which he concentrates; eventually he will get Right Views. All this happens in this way. As one begins to reach the stage of mindfulness and subsequently of purity of mind, one will be able to distinguish the knowing mind from the object known. For instance, when one is meditating on the rising and falling of the abdominal wall, one may be able to distinguish the phenomenon of rising and falling from the mind that knows it.

In much the same way, in the process of walking, one may notice that the act of raising the foot, extending forward, and putting it down is different from the mind motivating the movement. In this way *nāma*, the knower, can be distinguished from *rūpa*, the known. This can be effected without any preconception. One recognises the phenomena without giving any thought to them. In other words, recognition is spontaneous.

As the power of concentration of the meditator gains strength, and his wisdom gets sharpened thereby, he will come to realise the fact that his knees bend because he wishes them to bend. He walks because he wants to. He sees because he has eyes to see, and the object to be seen is there. He hears because he has ears to hear, and the object to be heard is there. He enjoys life because his *kamma* is favourable. In this way he is enabled to distinguish between cause and effect with reference to every phenomenon that takes place.

Discourse on "To Nibbāna via the Noble Eightfold Path"

Empirical Knowledge

Our main object is to attain insight-knowledge, which is accessible only through an empirical approach. Through experience, the meditator observes the distinction between mind and matter, and he realises the impermanence of everything. Experience may be followed by explanation on the part of the teacher, but not the other way around. For real knowledge has nothing to do with preconceived notions but is based on personal experience. The empirical knowledge acquired by the meditator is distinct and clear. In the course of his practise he comes to see nothing except the vanishing of everything. This is called *bhaṅga-ñāṇa*, knowledge of dissolution, which he learns to understand neither from scriptures nor a teacher, but from experience. As he keeps on meditating, he becomes more and more mindful until his mindfulness becomes perfect at the last stage on the Noble Path.

Discourse on the Ariyāvāsa Sutta

Conviction in Anicca

When the realities of *nāma* and *rūpa* are known, the meditator will realise that things come into being only to pass away. "*Hutvā abhāvato aniccaṃ,*" the Commentaries say. "Having become, things cease to exist; and that is impermanence." Only when he can appreciate the realities of this nature of origination and cessation will he gain conviction as to the impermanence of existence.

Discourse on "To Nibbāna via the Noble Eightfold Path"

The Law of Impermanence

Once you are convinced of the law of impermanence, your mind will be detached from the idea of permanence. When you reach that stage, ignorance will be dispelled from your mind. Then you will be able to get away from *saṅkhāra,* or volitional formations, which constitute *kamma* that produces rebirth. Now you see a flash of Nibbāna.

Discourse on "To Nibbāna via the Noble Eightfold Path"

Ego-Belief

Believers in the Dhamma who have acquired some knowledge about the fundamentals relating to *nāma, rūpa, anicca* (impermanence), *dukkha* (unsatisfactoriness), and *anattā* (egolessness, insubstantiality), should take up the practice of insight-meditation. It involves noting mind and matter in a state of flux at the six sense-doors in accordance with instructions relating to the establishment of mindfulness, *satipaṭṭhāna.* Note what the eyes see; note what the ears hear; note what the nose smells; note what the tongue tastes; note what the body contacts; note what the mind thinks; and then you will come to know all that is to be known in accordance with the degree of perfection you have acquired.

As a meditator practises mindfulness, his power of concentration will become strengthened and his mind purified. Then he will be able to distinguish the *nāma,* or the mind that knows, and the *rūpa,* or the body that is known. Then he will come to realise the absence of the thing called *atta* or self, or "I." Repeated noting will lead him on to the knowledge of the causes and effects of *nāma* and *rūpa.* In the end, the idea of self will be utterly destroyed. Before the practice of mindfulness he might be wondering if a self existed in the past, and is still existing at the present moment, and will exist in the future. After the *vipassanā-*

practice all such doubts will be resolved as the true nature of the phenomena is understood.

As the meditator continues noting, he will find that the sense-objects, together with the consciousness directed at them, vanish. They are all impermanent. They just arise and pass away of their own accord. What is not permanent is not satisfactory. Nothing is substantial. Then, what is there to cling to as "I" or "mine"? All phenomena are in a state of flux, now arising, now passing away. Contemplating on these matters, one can, by the conviction of one's own experience, do away with the idea of *attā*.

Some would like to think that noting merely the arising and passing away of *nāma* or *rūpa* is not enough. They would prefer to speculate at some length on what *nāma* or *rūpa* or the phenomena are. Such speculations are not based on self-acquired knowledge gained through actual practise, but on hearsay or book-knowledge. Insight-knowledge is perceptual and not intellectual.

Discourse on the Bhara Sutta

Self-discovery

The five aggregates of grasping must be learned well. You do not learn them by rote. You learn them by actual experience and practise. You must try to realise yourself the phenomena of arising and passing away of mind (*nāma*) and body (*rūpa*). *Vipassanā* means the insight you gain through your own inquiry and effort. Only after self-discovery as a result of meditation will all doubts about the non-existence of self or ego be dispelled. Then only can it be said with certainty that there is none which can be called an entity, and that what appears to be an entity is, after all, an aggregate of mental and bodily processes. As you become illumined with this realisation, you will come to understand the law of cause and effect. As you continue to meditate on this causality, you will encounter the state of flux, or the constant arising and passing away of mind (*nāma*) and body (*rūpa*), which, after all, are not permanent.

Discourse on "To Nibbāna via the Noble Eightfold Path"

The Path Factors in Vipassanā

A meditator has to note and observe every object that appears to him via the six sense-doors. This he does with an effort; and that is the Right Effort. Then he has to keep his mind on what he has noted so as to be aware of it. And that is the Right Mindfulness. As he has to be mindful, his mind will have to be fixed or concentrated on the object. And that is the Right Concentration. These three constituents of the Path (*magga*)—Right Effort, Right Mindfulness, and Right Concentration—are grouped under the heading of concentration (*samādhi*); they are the *samādhi-magga*. Then there is the process of thinking out what existence really is, which is classified as Right Thinking or Right Thought. As a result of this right thinking, we have the Right View. These two are grouped under the heading of wisdom (*paññā*); they are the *paññā-magga*. All these five in the *samādhi* and *paññā* sections are together classified as *kāraka-magga*, or the activators, which combine their efforts in the process of simultaneously noting and knowing.

Right Speech, Right Action, and Right Livelihood constitute the section on virtue; they are the *sīla-magga*, which may generally be deemed to have been fulfilled before the meditator takes up insight-meditation. During the period of meditation, these three *sīla-magga* (path-factors of virtue) remain unpolluted; in fact they get more and more purified as time goes on. With these three in this group added to the five in the previous groups, we have the eight Path factors as appearing in *vipassanā* (and hence called *vipassanā-magga*) on which we are to meditate.

Again, in the development of insight meditation, basic qualities of the elementary Path (*mūla-magga*) must be fulfilled. Of them, the first and foremost is the firm conviction that beings are the responsible "owners of their actions" (*kammasakata-sammādiṭṭhi*), a view well established in the law of *kamma*. Only when a meditator has absolute faith in this law of action and its consequences can he practise *vipassanā*. He must believe that the result of carrying out *vipassanā* or meditation exercises can lead him to the Path, to its fruition, and finally to Nibbāna. It is only with this faith that he will be able to exert Right Effort.

Discourse on "To Nibbāna via the Noble Eightfold Path"

Mindful Perception Leads to Detachment

"In the seen there should be only the seen; in the heard only the heard; in the sensed only the sensed; in the cognised only the cognised." This was the Buddha's instruction to Māluṅkyaputta and Bāhiya.[4]

One must note what is seen as seen and no more. That is the general idea. For meditation practice, however, one must note the beginning of any object or sense as it is in the process of happening. If one could concentrate on each phenomenon distinctly and separately, one would not feel any attachment or desire, and thus craving (*taṇhā*) is gotten rid of.

Discourse on the Hemavata Sutta

The Unseen and the Seen

When the Buddha was about to give instructions to Māluṅkyaputta Bhikkhu, he asked:

"Māluṅkyaputta, do you have any desire for the appearances that you have never seen, or those that you are not in the act of seeing, or those that you never expect to see?"

"No, sir, that is impossible," replied the bhikkhu.[5]

Now if I were to ask you the same question as the Buddha put to Māluṅkyaputta Bhikkhu, you would give the same answer as he did. You would not have any feeling of love or hatred for a person whom you never expect to see, would you? Now there are many such people in so many villages, towns, cities, and countries, and you would never have any feeling of love or of hatred for them. You wouldn't have any attachment, desire, or lust for them.

Defilements do not arise from the unperceived. This point should be noted.

As for the things seen, however, defilements arise both in the act of seeing and after having seen because a mental picture is retained in the memory and on reflection or recall, defilements would recur. These cherished memories are stored up in the

4. Saḷāyatana Saṃyutta, SN 35:95; Udāna I, 10.
5. Saḷāyatana Saṃyutta, SN 35:95.

archives of the latent tendencies (*anusaya*), as deeply rooted memories. It is necessary to root these out by means of *vipassanā*.

Discourse on the Hemavata Sutta

Warning

When the knowledge of investigating the aggregates as composite, and thus as unsubstantial, works, the meditator becomes fully convinced of the truth of the Dhamma relating to the three marks of *anicca, dukkha,* and *anattā,* on the contemplation of which he can further follow the trend of knowledge about the arising and passing away of *nāma* and *rūpa.* This is the stage when he attains *udayabbaya-ñāṇa,* the knowledge of arising and passing away. At this stage he will see a radiance in his mind. He will feel highly exultant. His awareness will be extraordinary. There will be nothing of which he fails to take notice. His mind is sharpened, and his memory becomes clear. Strong faith will be established. He will be joyous both physically and spiritually. This state surpasses description. But, if at this stage one becomes attached to such pleasurable mental states, they will become precursors to defilements of the mind, and be obstacles to further mental development. Joy, in a way, is no doubt a support to the meditator in his efforts to gain more strength and determination to strive further for higher goals until he reaches his destination, namely, mature *vipassanā*-knowledge. So he is warned just to note the mental state of joy as it occurs, and then to dismiss it altogether to gain insight.

Discourse on "To Nibbāna via the Noble Eightfold Path"

Eliminating the Unwanted

Every moment of mindfulness means the gradual destruction of latent defilements. It is somewhat like cutting away a piece of wood with a small axe, every stroke helping to get rid of the unwanted fragments of wood.

Discourse on the Ariyāvāsa Sutta

Penetrative Insight

Nāma and *rūpa*, or the truth of suffering, are seen as impermanent, as suffering, or as non-self. Every time they are seen thus, there is no chance for craving to make their appearance. Thus there is liberation from craving and clinging. It is called knowing the Truth of Origination by abandonment (*pahānabhisamaya*), though not by realisation.

Every time *rūpa* and *nāma* become subjected to his awareness, the meditator is free from ignorance (*avijjā*) that could lead him to the wrong path. Being thus free from *avijjā*, he is free from the ills of *saṅkhāra-viññāṇa*. This is a temporary cessation of ills (*tadaṅga-nirodha-sacca*). This temporary cessation of ills is realised by *vipassanā* at every instance of noting, but not as its object of contemplation.

Things hidden behind heavy curtains or thick walls become visible when these barriers are shattered asunder or windows are opened out. Likewise the Four Noble Truths are kept hidden behind *avijjā*, which takes note of that which is wrong but covers up that which is right. By developing the Eightfold Path through meditation exercises, Truths which were not known before become apparent through *vipassanā*-knowledge, the knowledge of the Noble Path. *Avijjā* has been penetrated, and the Noble Truths become known by means of penetrative insight.

Discourse on "The Wheel of Dhamma"

Investigation for Insight

by

Susan Elbaum

WHEEL PUBLICATION NO. 301/302

Preface

We have come into this world at a remarkable time, one of those brief periods when the teachings of a Buddha are readily available. There is his Noble Eightfold Path of wisdom, morality and concentration and specifically the technique of *vipassanā* meditation by means of which we can train our minds to see the ultimate nature of all phenomena of the world, their transience, unsatisfactoriness and essencelessness. With the development of this detached wisdom, our minds gradually lose their tensions, anguish and lust, and so real peace and happiness can develop.

This article is written in all humility by one who has just begun to walk on the Path, in the spirit of "*ehipassiko*," the characteristic of the Dhamma that invites all to come and see and try it. There is yet a long way to travel, but there is no doubt whatsoever that the Path leads to the Goal and so this article is an expression of the mind's wish to encourage and urge others to undertake for themselves this profoundly beneficial task of eliminating ignorance and craving and so end all suffering.

Susan Elbaum

Introduction

All the teachings of the Buddha had one goal—the elimination of all suffering, all grief, misery, pain and anguish. All the kinds of meditation he explained were designed to train the mind of the student to become detached from all the phenomena of the world, within and outside of himself. This is the aim of Buddhist meditation because detachment is the opposite of *taṇhā* or craving and it is this *taṇhā* that is the source of all the sorts of suffering experienced by sentient beings. This desire is very deeply ingrained in our minds because of our ignorance about the real nature of the phenomena of the world. So, *vipassanā*, insight-meditation techniques of the Buddha, are designed to enable us to penetrate our illusions about the nature of reality which are perpetuated by our inaccurate perception of the world and ourselves. Insight has to be gained into the impermanent, unsatisfactory and essenceless nature of all conditioned phenomena, of everything mental and physical, all of which is the effect of certain causes. Insight is often conceived of as a magical experience suddenly just happening and instantly making all things clear. But, by and large, insight develops slowly and gradually through the careful process of observation, investigation and analysis of phenomena until the ultimate nature that lies behind their apparent, conventional truth is distinctly and indubitably perceived. It is this process known in Pāli as *dhammavicaya* (investigation of Dhamma) and also the closely related one of *yoniso-manasikāra* (systematic attention) which will be examined here. Ledi Sayādaw in his *Bodhipakkhiya Dīpanī*[1] defines *dhammavicaya* as identical with *paññā* (wisdom) and *Sammā Diṭṭhi* (Right Understanding or View) and then describes the investigative process with the simile: "Just as cotton seeds are milled, carded, etc., so as to produce cotton wool, the process of repeatedly viewing the five *khandhas* (our personal aggregates of body, perception, feeling, volitions and consciousness) with the functions of *insight knowledge* (*vipassanā ñāṇa*) is called *dhammavicaya.*" First the subjects to be investigated, or the contents of the investigation for insight leading to liberation,

1. Translated as *Requisites of Enlightenment* in The Wheel No. 171/174.

will be examined. Then the role of *dhammavicaya* specifically as a part of *vipassanā* meditation will be discussed. Then will come the role of systematic attention in preventing the arising of the mental hindrances which can block progress in meditation and as one of the basic factors conducive to the growth of wisdom. Finally the way to use investigation of Dhamma with the other Factors of Enlightenment and then with the elements of the Noble Eightfold Path are shown. A well-trained, well-controlled mind is a powerful tool capable of rationally thinking through and continually comprehending the ultimate truths of existence. By developing the mind's ability to penetratingly and objectively investigate, we are working to free ourselves of all ignorance, and thus of all craving and its resultant suffering.

Contents of Investigation

Investigation of Dhamma is one of the key factors the development of which can lead us to liberation from all suffering. The Buddha defines this *dhammavicaya* as "searching, investigation, scrutinizing, for insight into one's own personal conditions... and... externals." *Dhammavicaya* is one of the Seven *Bojjhaṅgas* or Factors of Enlightenment and is usually translated[2] as "Investigation of Dhamma." The word "*Dhamma*" has two quite distinct uses and so investigation of it implies both analysis of *the Dhamma*—the essential truths of existence as taught by the Buddha—and analysis of *dhammas*—all things whatsoever. Investigation of the Dhamma must include careful thought leading to a thorough understanding of at least these teachings: the Four Noble Truths, the Three Salient Characteristics of Existence, and the Doctrine of Dependent Origination, and some idea of the workings of *kamma*. When we study the *dhammas*, we are primarily concerned with determining for ourselves the ultimate nature of our own Five Aggregates, the mind-and-matter phenomenon, with its six sense organs, and of the six respective classes of sense objects which are the basis of all consciousness, contact, feeling, perception and mental activities.

2. *Kindred Sayings* (translation of Saṃyutta Nikāya), 5 Vols. Pāli Text Society, London, (quoted as:) K. S., V, p. 93.

When we investigate the Dhamma, we are trying to thoroughly understand and grasp the significance of the Teachings of the Buddha. These truths are things which he discovered for himself and therefore knew with total certainty. For us to just accept them on faith alone will not be of too much benefit. In the well-known discourse the Buddha gave to the Kālāmas, he said, "Be ye not misled by report or tradition or hearsay... Nor out of respect of the recluse (who holds it). But Kālāmas, when you know for yourselves: 'These things are unprofitable, these things are blameworthy,'... then indeed do ye reject them... But if at any time ye know for yourselves: 'These things... when performed and undertaken conduce to profit and happiness,'—then Kālāmas, do ye, having undertaken them, abide therein."[3] And he intended that the Kālāmas treat his words just like those of any other teacher. We must explore the teachings of the Buddha thoroughly, carefully and rationally for ourselves by taking the Four Noble Truths, the Three Salient Characteristics and the Doctrine of Dependent Origination (including *kamma*) as working hypotheses which are to be understood and demonstrated to the satisfaction of our own minds. Even if on first contact with these ideas we cannot understand them, we must not for that reason alone reject them out of hand—this kind of attitude will block and prevent all our progress on the Path. After all, it is quite reasonable to assume that there have been people in the world wiser than ourselves and that the Buddha was one of them. Once we have worked even a little on the Path and gained some benefit from it, we know that the Buddha was far wiser than we are, as it was he who first taught this means of liberation. So we willingly keep our minds open to explore what he says even if it does not initially make much sense to our limited way of thinking. On the basis of full comprehension of these Truths gained by this balance between an open mind and confidence, liberating wisdom automatically must grow.

3. *Gradual Sayings* (translation of Aṅguttara Nikāya), 5 Vols., Pāli Text Society, London, I, p. 173.

1. The Four Noble Truths

The first aspect of the Dhamma to deal with is the Four Noble Truths: Suffering, its Origin, its Cessation and the way leading to the Cessation of Suffering, the central teaching of the Buddha, because "It is through not understanding, not penetrating the Four Noble Truths that we have run on, wandered on, this long, long road" of *saṃsāra* (K.S., V, p. 365).

We must carefully consider the nature of life to determine for ourselves whether it is essentially happy or unhappy, satisfactory or unsatisfactory, full of joy or woe. No matter what we look at—our body, our mind, the external world—if we penetrate the apparent superficial truth of it, we are bound to find that *dukkha* (suffering) predominates vastly over *sukha* (happiness) because all the seemingly pleasant experiences and aspects of life are doomed to fade away and leave behind them the same state of unsatisfiedness that was there before the momentary respite given by the sensual pleasure. If we think about the nature of the body, obviously it *has* to grow old, get sick and ultimately die and at almost no moment from the time of birth do we find ourselves in perfect health; and from then on it is all a downhill battle since death is the only possible outcome of life. If we keep this in mind, how can we say there is lasting satisfaction or happiness in life? Ledi Sayādaw puts it this way in the *Maggaṅga Dīpanīi*:[4] "From the time of conception there is not a single moment... when there is no liability to destruction. When actual destruction comes, manifold is the suffering that is experienced." If we examine our minds, there, too, we see that the vast majority of the time they are in some unhappy state—ranging from mild dissatisfaction through anxiety to downright despair. Only rarely are there moments of joy and to these we react by attempting to cling to them, and that state of desiring, too, is *dukkha*. If we look to the external world that we learn about through our senses and realize how many people are in agony with dread disease; how many sentient beings are preying on one another for food, for sport, for power; how many are dying lonely and helpless—at this very moment—we cannot doubt that *dukkha* predominates. The Buddha summarizes

4. Translated as *The Noble Eightfold Path and Its Factors Explained* in The Wheel No. 245/247.

the First Noble Truth saying, "Birth is suffering, death is suffering, sorrow is suffering; not to get what one desires is suffering; in short all the five groups of existence are suffering" (Dīgha Nikāya 22). We have to investigate and see just how it is that all existence is *dukkha,* and one way to do this is to ponder over the "sights" of suffering seen by the Buddha before his Enlightenment, which caused him to leave home and seek the ultimate liberation for Suffering. We would do well to consider an old being, a seriously ill person and a corpse. Such attention to these will teach us a great deal about both internal and external *dukkha.*

In order to find our way out of all this suffering, we have to be very clear about its cause, and as the Buddha saw it, *taṇhā* (clinging, craving, desire, lust, etc.) is the basic cause of *dukkha.* "From craving springs grief, from craving springs fear," from all kinds of craving unhappiness comes; from endearment, affection, attachment, lust (as well as from the negative side of it: hatred, aversion, ill-will) (Dhp 216). Craving is in itself *dukkha,* and it inevitably leads to more ill in this and in future existences.

To realize how this is true, so that we are convinced of the necessity of giving up absolutely all craving, we have to examine the workings of our own mind thoroughly. We must observe how our mind is virtually always engaged in some form of craving or desire—either positively reaching out for some object or obversely trying to push something away—whether the object is gross or subtle. While we are actually craving for some object—be it something as mundane as food or as lofty as rebirth among the Brahma gods—we are in a state of mind that is unsatisfied, that is incomplete and longing for completion—this lack of satisfaction, of completeness, is *dukkha.* Then, if we should attain the object, our *taṇhā* does not disappear; it is actually reinforced and more *dukkha* results. Getting what we want may lead to a new object for desire, or to modify the original one to avoid boredom. But satisfying *one* craving does nothing to eliminate the basic mental process of *taṇhā;* in fact more fuel is simply added to its fires when we obtain what is wanted. If the desired state, experience or thing is unobtainable, then a more acute form of *dukkha* results—frustration. And if we consider the feelings associated with the negative form of *taṇhā,* aversion, they are always clearly unhappy, *dukkha.* Thus we can determine for ourselves how *taṇhā* causes all our suffering in this lifetime.

Craving (*taṇhā*) is also the cause of rebirth, and once there is a new life the whole chain of *dukkha* inevitably culminating in death automatically comes into play. Most of us cannot know the phenomenon of rebirth directly for ourselves as the Buddha did, but we certainly see the logic in it. All kinds of craving, if looked at carefully, turn out to be just different forms or manifestations of the underlying desire to perpetuate our existence. The great power of this force pushing for life does not just vanish at the time of death, but these urgings for renewed existence (*bhava saṅkhāras*) become the cause of rebirth in the appropriate place. Most of these forces in sentient beings are not wholesome, so when most beings die and the life continua take a new form, it is in the Realms of Woe. Thus we can see how *taṇhā* produces a new life with all the *dukkha* that comes along with it. Seeing how much suffering is experienced, all because of craving, surely is strong motivation for us to figure out how to eliminate this *taṇhā.*

The Third Noble Truth says that there *is* a cessation of suffering; and suffering will and must cease when the cause (*taṇhā*) is eliminated. "For who is wholly free from craving there is no grief, whence fear?" (Dhp 216). Any phenomena which arise due to causes and conditions have to pass away when those causes cease to operate. So, if we ponder on it, we must conclude that the vital task for us is to root out all our tendencies to crave; all our desires and aversions irrespective of their objects must be given up if we are to be liberated of *dukkha.* To become utterly detached from every thing, state of mind or experience on any plane of existence, to see that absolutely nothing is worth clinging to: this is the wisdom that must be cultivated by investigating all such phenomena. The insight thus gained will necessarily eliminate all desires and so all *dukkha.*

The Noble Eightfold Path was the means given by the Buddha to gain this liberating wisdom. It is by clearly understanding and following the steps of the Path that we gain the insight that there is nothing worth craving for. As this insight deepens through more and more thought on the subject, *taṇhā* decreases and eventually must disappear, and so we free ourselves of all suffering. The Path is divided into three sections: morality (*sīla*), concentration (*samādhi*) and wisdom (*paññā*). It is through the practice of *sīla* that *samādhi* can develop and through *samādhi, paññā.* The eight steps of the Path are all actually to be developed, not consecutively, but at any opportune time as they feed into one another at every stage. (For a detailed discussion of the Path, please see the final section of this paper.) There is a well-known analogy which describes the respective roles of morality, concentration and wisdom, and if we examine the simile carefully, we will come to understand how we must proceed in order to eliminate our *taṇhā.* A thirsty man comes to a pond overgrown with weeds and he wishes to drink the water in the pool. If he pushes the weeds aside with his hands and quickly gets a sip or two from in between them, it is like practicing virtue (*sīla*), restraining the gross verbal and bodily actions by very temporary means. If the man somehow fences off a small area of the pond keeping all the weeds outside the fence, this is like meditative concentration (*samādhi*) where even unwholesome thoughts disappear for a time, but they are only suppressed and can reappear if the fence breaks down. But if the man uproots every single weed in the pond leaving the water really pure and potable, this is like wisdom (*paññā*). It actually is only through wisdom, through constantly seeing things as they really are—changing, unsatisfactory, essenceless—that the subconscious, latent tendencies to craving are totally rooted out, never again to return. By means of careful investigation we can thus understand how the Fourth Noble Truth, the Noble Eightfold Path, operates, how "Right View, Right Aim, Right Speech, Right Action, Right Livelihood, Right Effort, Right Mindfulness, Right Concentration if cultivated and made much of, ends in the restraint of lust, ends in the restraint of hatred, ends in the restraint of illusion" (K.S., V, p. 5). Having thoroughly investigated, understood and penetrated these Four Noble Truths, we are bound to eventually put an end to our wanderings in *saṃsāra* and to all our suffering.

2. The Three Signata (*ti-lakkhaṇa*)

Investigation of Dhamma for full liberation also must include, in addition to the Four Noble Truths, a study of the Three Universal Characteristics or Signata of Existence (*ti-lakkhaṇa*): *anicca*—impermanence, *dukkha*—suffering and *anattā*—essencelessness. Everything in the universe, mental or physical, inside or outside of us, real or imaginary, that comes into being due to causes and conditions, has these three traits as its nature. And since there is nothing that exists without depending on other things, there is absolutely nothing which we can determine to be permanent, full of happiness only or having any real substance. We must examine these three truths very carefully to know how thoroughly and totally they apply in all cases. Once there is this deep insight into the nature of reality, detachment and thereby liberation follow.

The first of these to be investigated and in some ways the characteristic that underlies the other two is *anicca*—the utterly transitory, ephemeral, unstable nature of all mental and physical phenomena. On the level of the apparent truth, we know quite well that things change but we have to train ourselves to see how the process of change is going on continually at every instant in everything. How else could the gross conventional alterations like maturing and aging actually come about? We have to carefully examine all the evidence we can find to comprehend the profundity of the *anicca*-nature of existence. There is nothing which we can think of that would be as we know it conventionally if things were permanently stable. Change is synonymous with life—our bodies could not exist, let alone function, if the elements of which they are made remained constant or unchanged for even a brief time. Our minds could neither feel nor think nor perceive nor be conscious, if the mind were unalterable in nature. Likewise in inanimate objects, change is essential, although sometimes less apparent. We must thoroughly investigate this universal trait so that we can get beyond the limited scope of our usual perception which mistakenly takes apparent form for ultimate reality. Because of the incredible rapidity with which both mind and matter alter, we can only occasionally notice that a particular change has come about; we are never able to perceive the continual ongoing process of change which actually makes up existence. Everything is just in a state of flux, always becoming something else, never really stopping to *be* something; all *nāma* (mind) and all *rūpa* (matter) are just a continual series of risings and vanishings following very rapidly one after the other. The ultimate reality of everything is just these vibrations. The importance of really knowing *anicca* is described by the Buddha with the simile of a farmer plowing his field. "In the autumn season a plowman plowing with a great plowshare cuts through the spreading roots as he plows, even so, brethren, the perceiving of impermanence, if practiced and enlarged, wears out all sensual lust, wears out all ignorance, wears out, tears out all conceit of 'I am'... Just as, brethren, in the autumn season (after the monsoon rains) when the sky is opened up and cleared of clouds, the sun, leaping forth up into the firmament, drives away all darkness from the heavens, and shines and burns and flashes forth; even so, brethren, the perceiving of impermanence, if practiced and enlarged, wears out all sensual lust, wears out all lust for the body, all desire for rebirth, all ignorance, wears out, tears out all conceit of 'I am'" (K.S., III, pp. 132–33).

The characteristic of *dukkha* has been dealt with on the grosser level as the First Noble Truth, in which the suffering of illness, of age, of separation from the desired and association with the undesired, in our own minds and bodies and in the external world were considered. But there are many subtle ways in which we can see how life is—and must be—unsatisfying. It has been seen how life is inseparable from change, how without the perpetual process of development and disintegration there would and could be no existence at all. And yet there is the very profound contradiction between this *anicca*-nature of life and our constant desire and wish for stability, for security, for lasting happiness. If a situation is pleasant, we always hope that it will last and try our utmost to make it do so; but all experiences of life are doomed to pass away as everything on which they are based is completely impermanent, changing at every moment. So all our desires (and we are almost never without some form of *taṇhā* in our minds) are bound to be frustrated in the long run; we can never find the durable satisfaction we seek in this world of mind and matter. There is nothing in this universe of *anicca* that has even the potential capability of giving any real happiness because each and every thing is so completely unstable. We have to give careful attention to all the apparently pleasant and happy experiences that come in through the six sense doors (five physical ones and the mind as the sixth), to see whether they really can bring us satisfaction. The Buddha warns: "In him, brethren, who contemplates the enjoyment that there is in all that makes for grasping (in all the sense pleasures), craving grows... Such is the uprising of this entire mass of ill." If we analyze how we ourselves develop strong *taṇhā*—and in inevitable consequence *dukkha*—when we think about and dwell on our pleasurable experiences, we can come to see how this fearful irony of pain caused by considering pleasure unwisely is all too true. With this understanding, then, we will instead contemplate *dukkha* in these same phenomena because, "In him, brethren, who contemplates the misery that there is in all that makes for grasping, craving ceases... Such is the ceasing of this entire mass of ill" (K.S., II, p. 59). As we are able to comprehend this *dukkha*-nature of everything more and more, naturally the mind will cease to long for that which it knows cannot bring happiness. And so the mind grows detached and moves toward liberation.

The third universal characteristic, *anattā*—essencelessness, soullessness, egolessness—is the teaching unique to the Buddhas; it does not appear in any other religious or philosophical tradition. A complete understanding of *anattā* for and in oneself must be developed before liberation is possible. The Buddha explained this doctrine, so alien to our conventional way of thinking, in many discourses beginning with the second discourse after his Enlightenment.

> "Body... feeling... perception, the activities and consciousness (the five aggregates that make up everything there is in a 'being') are not self. If consciousness, etc., brethren, were self the consciousness would not be involved in sickness and one could say of consciousness, etc.: 'Thus let my consciousness be, thus let my consciousness not be'; but inasmuch as consciousness is not the self, that is why consciousness is involved in sickness. That is why one cannot (so) say of consciousness.
>
> "Now what think ye, brethren. Is body permanent or impermanent?"
>
> "Impermanent, Lord."
>
> "And what is impermanent, is that weal or woe?" "Woe, Lord."
>
> "Then what is impermanent, woeful, unstable by nature, is it fitting to regard it thus: 'This is mine; I am this; this is the self of me'?"
>
> "Surely not, Lord."
>
> "... Therefore, brethren, ... every consciousness, etc., whatever it be, past, future or present, be it inward or outward, gross or subtle, low or high, far or near—every consciousness, I say, must be regarded as it really is by right insight: 'This is not mine; this I am not; this is not the self of me.'

> "So seeing, brethren, the well-taught Ariyan disciple feels disgust for body, etc. So feeling disgust he is repelled, being repelled he is freed... so that he knows 'destroyed is rebirth... done is my task.'"
>
> —K.S., III, pp. 56–60

To develop insight in order to fully comprehend the implications of *anattā* takes a great deal of careful, systematic thought in combination with direct meditative experience. We must try to see that this thing we have habitually for an immeasurably long time called "I" actually has no real existence. This word can only be accurately used as a term of reference for the five aggregates—each of which is constantly changing—that go to make up this so-called "being." Only by investigating all the five *khandhas* in depth and finding them to be void of any essence or substance at all which might correctly be called one's "self" can we come to fully understand *anattā*.

There are two main ways to come to grips with this doctrine: via *anicca* and via *dukkha*. These two signata are to some extent manifest as apparent truths as well as being ultimate realities, while *anattā* is the complete opposite of the apparent truth. When we think of ourselves and use "I" or "me" or "man," etc., there is the inherent implication that these words refer to some constant, ongoing being. But we have previously seen that if we carefully investigate—intellectually and by direct observation in *vipassanā* meditation—all the five groups that comprise what we customarily consider "I" and all the physical and mental sense organs that are taken as "mine," that there is no trace of anything even slightly durable in any of them. Ledi Sayādaw explains the relationship between *anicca* and *anattā* by showing how people with untrained minds assume that there is some on-going core or stable essence somewhere in the five *khandhas* and take this substance to be their *attā*, their self or soul. "Those beings who are not able to discern the momentary arisings and dissolutions of the physical and mental phenomena of the five constituent groups of existence and thus are not able to realize the characteristic of *anicca* maintain: 'the corporeality-group (or sensation, perception, activities or consciousness-group) is the essence and therefore the *attā* of beings.'"[5] If we wish to take any of these groups as our substance, then we must admit that "I" "decay, die and am reborn every moment"; but such an ephemeral "I" is very far from our usual conception of ourselves. If we have carefully considered *anicca* as it exists in everything internal that could be considered "I," then we must come to the conclusion that this "I" is nothing but a mistaken idea that has grown from inaccurate perception which has been habitually reinforced for a long, long time. As the truth of *anattā* becomes clearer, we gradually let go of this "I" and so are closer and closer to Enlightenment, where not the slightest shadow of a trace of this misconception can remain.

If we discern all the mental and physical *dukkha* we have to undergo in life, we learn about *anattā* from a different angle. This *nāma-rūpa* phenomenon is constantly subject to this pain and that anguish, and yet we foolishly insist on calling the body and mind "mine" and assuming that they belong to "me." But the very idea of possession means that the owner has control of the property; so "I" should be able to keep my body and mind as I want them to be, naturally healthy and happy. As the Buddha stated in the quotation at the start of this section, "Let my body be thus; let it not be thus." But obviously and undeniably, suffering is felt and cannot be prevented by mere exertion of will or wishing. So, in reality, we have to come to the conclusion that there is no "I" who controls this *nāma-rūpa*; mind and body are in no way fit to be called "mine." "The arising of the five constituent groups do not yield to the wishes of anyone" (SDD, p. 93). Phenomena which are dependent upon specific causes which operate strictly according to their nature from moment to moment cannot be subject to control by any "being" and as we explore it thoroughly, we come to understand how this Five Aggregate phenomenon which we wrongly tend to consider "I" is just such a conditioned and dependent process. And suffering (or pleasure, for that matter) likewise comes about because of certain conditions, chief amongst them being *taṇhā*. There is no "being" who controls what ultimately happens to these five aggregates.

---

5. *Manuals of Buddhism*, Ledi Sayādaw. Union of Burma Buddha Sasana Council, Rangoon, *"Sammā-Diṭṭhi Dīpanī"*, p. 91.

Being caught in personality-belief (*sakkāya-diṭṭhi*)—the inability to comprehend *anattā*—causes tremendous *dukkha* to creatures on all the planes of existence from the lowest hell to the highest Brahmā worlds. This great source of suffering must be carefully examined and its workings understood if we are to escape from its powerful, deep-rooted grasp. "Ego-delusion is the foremost of the unwholesome *kamma* of old and accompanies beings incessantly. As long as personality-belief exists these old unwholesome actions are fiery and full of strength... those beings who harbor within themselves this personality-belief are continually under pressure to descend or directly fall towards the worlds of woe"[6] (A of A, p. 50). By thoroughly rooting out, seeing through and letting go of this mistaken conception that there is a real substantial "I," "all wrong views, evil mental factors and evil kammas which would lead... to the lower worlds will disappear" (SDD, p. 87). Thus if we can really know our *anattā*-nature totally, there is no longer any possibility of the extreme *dukkha* of rebirth in the lower realms of existence and the life continuum will "always remain within the fold of the Buddha's Dispensation wherever... reborn" (A of A, p. 52). But if one does not understand the impersonal nature of this five aggregate phenomenon, he will "undoubtedly have to preserve his soul (or self) by entertaining evil thoughts and evil actions as the occasion arises" (SDD, p. 50). We can see that if we act on the assumption that there is an "I" we are always in the position of attempting to protect and preserve this "self" and thus very much prone to commit unwholesome thoughts, words and deeds in relation to other "beings." "People are generally concerned with what they consider to be themselves or their own... and their bodily, verbal and mental acts are based on and are conditioned by that concern. So the root of all vice for the foolish concern is 'self' and one's 'own.'" Ledi Sayādaw explains how the belief that there is an "I" causes this continual rebirth with a strong downward tendency with the analogy of a string of beads:

"In a string of beads where a great number of beads are strung together by a strong silk thread, if one bead is pulled all the others

6. "The Advantages of Realising the Doctrine of Anattā" by Ledi Sayādaw in *The Three Facts of Existence: III Egolessness*, The Wheel No. 202/204, p. 50. Henceforth: A of A.

will follow the one that is pulled. But if the silk thread is cut or removed, pulling one of the beads will not disturb the other beads because there is no longer any attachment between them.

"Similarly, a being that possesses personality-belief harbors a strong attachment to the series of aggregates arisen during past existences... and transforms them into an ego... It is thus that the innumerable unwholesome karmic actions of the past existences which have not yet produced resultants will accompany that being wherever he may be reborn. These unwholesome actions of the past resemble beads that are strung and bound together by a strong thread.

"Beings, however, who clearly perceive the characteristic of not-self and have rid themselves of personality-belief will perceive that the bodily and mental aggregates that arise and disappear even within the short period of one sitting, do so as separate phenomena and not as a closely interlinked continuum. The concept of 'my self' which is like the thread, is no longer present. Those bodily and mental processes appear to them like the beads from which the thread has been removed."

—A of A, pp. 53–54

Thus the dispelling of personality-belief removes all the mental factors which might cause one to behave in such a way that would lead to rebirth in the realms of woe as well as cutting off the link of attachment to an "ego" that has kept us connected to all our evil deeds of the past. Even in this present life it is clear if we think about it that *sakkāya-diṭṭhi* (personality-belief) causes us great suffering and its elimination would be of great benefit. For example, "When external or internal dangers are encountered or disease and ailments occur, beings attach themselves to them through such thoughts as, 'I feel pain, I feel hurt,' thus taking a possessive attitude towards them. This becomes an act of bondage that later may obstruct beings from ridding themselves of those diseases... though they are so greatly oppressive" (A of A, p. 56).

However, understanding that it is this erroneous personality-belief that keeps us thinking that there is some ongoing essence or substance in this five aggregate phenomenon that can rightly be called "I" will not immediately or automatically prevent the thought of "I" from coming up in the mind as it is a very deeply rooted *saṅkhāra* that has been built up over a long period of time. Whenever a thought related to "I" does appear, we must mindfully apply the wisdom of *anattā* we have already gained and realize that "I" is nothing but an idea originating from an incorrect perception of reality. Whenever we notice ourselves thinking of an "I" as one of the aggregates or as related to one of them, we have to consider carefully the thought and reinforce our understanding that "Whatsoever material object... whatsoever feeling, whatsoever perception, whatsoever activities, whatsoever consciousness... (must be rightly regarded as) 'This is not mine, this I am not; this is not the self of me.'" This process of seeing the ignorance arise and repeatedly applying the Right View to it gradually wears away even the thoughts of "I," "myself" and "mine." This total elimination of "I"-consciousness which is nothing but a subtle form of conceit, and of this concept of "mine" which is a subtle form of *taṇhā*, does not happen until arhantship is reached. But our task is to deepen the comprehension and investigation of *anattā* to greater and greater depths of insight by means of *vipassanā* meditation.

A group of monks once questioned the Venerable Khemaka about *anattā* and inquired whether he had attained Arhantship. He replied that he was not yet fully liberated because he still had subtle remnants of "I am" in his mind. He said to them:

> I see that in these five grasping groups I have got the idea of "I am" yet I do not think that I am this "I am." Though (one is a non-returner)... yet there remains in him a subtle remnant of the I-am-conceit, of the I-am-desire, of the lurking tendency to think "I am" still not removed from him. Later on he lives contemplating the rise and fall of the five grasping groups, seeing thus: "Such is the body, such is the arising of body, such is the ceasing of it. Such is feeling... perception... the activities... consciousness."
>
> In this way... the subtle remnant of the I-am-conceit, of the I-am-desire, that lurking tendency to think "I am" which was still not removed from him—that is now removed.
>
> —K.S., III, p. 110

This explanation of Khemaka's was so clear and profound that, as a direct result of his discourse, all the monks who listened to it and Khemaka himself as well were fully liberated—with no remnants of "I am" remaining. So we would do well to carefully study what this wise monk said about the development of *anattā* so that we can come to understand how by means of this process of carefully observing, clearly experiencing and thoroughly investigating the rise and fall of the five *khandhas* we gradually eliminate the gross layers of *sakkāya-diṭṭhi* and by the same means, more and more refined, ultimately root out even the latent, subconscious tendency to think "I am."

Investigation into the Three Universal Characteristics—*anicca, dukkha,* and *anattā*—is a fundamental requirement for the growth of liberating insight. Once we have thoroughly analyzed our own *nāma-rūpa* and also the phenomena of the external world, and completely understood how everything we can conceive of—real or imaginary, mental or physical, internal or external—is totally unstable, incapable of bringing real durable happiness and without any actual substance, detachment must follow and with it freedom from the *dukkha* of existence. The process of gradually overcoming ignorance with wisdom comes through the direct bodily experience of the unsatisfactoriness and essencelessness of this *nāma-rūpa* in *vipassanā* meditation, combined with careful thought, so that these "experiences" have their full impact on the mind. Once again, it is by investigation in meditation that detachment from the "all" is won—and so too the ultimate peace free from all desire.

3. Dependent Origination (*Paṭiccasamuppāda*)

The doctrine of Dependent Origination (*paṭiccasamuppāda*) is one of the most profound and far-reaching teachings of the Buddha and as such this law of causality requires very thorough investigation and comprehension by anyone seeking liberation. Without clearly knowing the causal law, the Three Signata and the Four Noble Truths cannot be fully understood with the full insight that leads to dispassion, to Nibbāna. All of these are included within *paṭiccasamuppāda,* which demonstrates their relation with each other. The Buddha himself pointed out the great significance of this teaching to Ānanda when Ānanda said that he found the causal law quite plain. The Buddha admonished him saying, "Say not so, Ānanda, say not so! Deep indeed is this causal law, and deep indeed it appears. It is through not knowing, not understanding, not penetrating, that doctrine, that this generation has become entangled like a ball of string... unable to overpass the doom of the Waste, the Woeful Way, the Downfall, the Constant Faring on" (K.S., II, p. 64). And elsewhere Sāriputta quotes the Exalted One as saying, "Whoever sees conditioned genesis sees the Dhamma, whoever see the Dhamma sees conditioned genesis" (M., I, p. 237).

The general all-encompassing form of the law of Dependent Origination is a very simple statement of cause and effect but is something to which the meditator must give "his mind thoroughly and systematically"; succinctly it states "this being that comes to be; from the arising of this, that arises; from the ceasing of this that ceases" (K.S., II, p. 45). This is really just another more abstract formulation of the Second and Third Noble Truths—the cause of and the cessation of suffering. The full twelve-link formula of the *paṭiccasamuppāda* is an expansion of these two middle Truths, a full explanation of the process by which suffering is generated and how, by the removal of the causes, suffering also comes to cease. Thus in order to understand completely the Four Noble Truths, one must have contemplated on and gained insight into Dependent Origination as well. Another very important aspect of this doctrine to be understood is how its description of the process of life, the process of becoming, clearly demonstrates how it is a totally impersonal manifestation of certain causes, with no "I" or "being" in any way involved in or related to it, *anattā*. Finally, this doctrine enables us to discern just how *kamma* operates in generating the causes of rebirth.

The list of twelve links in direct order explaining the arising of suffering is usually described as beginning with the past life, going on to the present life and then to future life (or potential lives). *Avijjā-paccayā saṅkhārā*—ignorance conditions mental volitions. It is due to the root cause of ignorance (about the ultimate nature of reality) that the mind generates desires, *saṅkhāras, kamma. Saṅkhāra-paccayā viññāṇaṃ*—these mental volitions, this *kamma* of the past, gives rise to the rebirth-linking consciousness which is the first mind moment of the new (present) birth. Note there is no "thing" transmigrating from one life to another, only a process of cause and effect goes on. *Viññāṇa-paccayā nāma-rūpaṃ*—the mind and matter phenomenon (five aggregates) of the present life come to be due to the existence of this rebirth-linking consciousness. Conception has taken place and this *nāma-rūpa* phenomenon continues its processes until death intervenes. *Nāma-rūpa-paccayā saḷāyatanaṃ*—through mind and matter, the six sense bases are conditioned; with this very start of the new life the five physical sense organs and mind as the sixth come into being. *Saḷāyatana-paccayā phasso*—throughout the life these six senses are the condition for the arising of contact (with their appropriate objects) which occurs from moment to moment. *Phassa-paccayā vedanā*—feeling (pleasant, unpleasant or neutral) is conditioned by sense impression and this feeling rises in relation to contacts at first through one then another sense door, ad infinitum. *Vedanā-paccayā taṇhā*—craving arises based on feeling. In terms of practice, this is the most important step of the *paṭiccasamuppāda* as it is at this point that we can learn to turn around the whole process and make it lead to the cessation of suffering.

The other (unnamed) factor which conditions craving along with feeling is ignorance (the same as the first factor)—the inability to see that in reality there is nothing worth craving for, nothing that can actually be held, and no ongoing being truly capable of having its desires satisfied. At this link volition can alter the old habitual sequences and the feeling part of the mind by means of training in the Noble Eightfold Path can be made to condition the arising of wisdom, and *paññā* will forestall the arising of *taṇhā* (and the whole mass of suffering that is conditioned by this craving). *Taṇhā-paccayā upādānaṃ*—craving gives rise to clinging, tenacious desire. Actually, for most of us, the application of wisdom and mindfulness is very rarely such that it can totally prevent the deep habits of *taṇhā* from surfacing after feeling, but what we can do is prevent either of the next two links—*upādāna* and *bhava*—from developing out of the initial spurt of desire. *Upādāna-paccayā bhavo*—conditioned by clinging, becoming arises. Due to the power of the accumulation of *saṅkhāras*, of *kamma* (*taṇhā, upādāna* and *bhava* being simply mental volitions of increasing strength), the very strong *kamma* which is responsible for the process of becoming arises and it is these *bhava-saṅkhāras* that generate the momentum for a new birth at the appropriate moment. *Bhava-paccayā jāti*—becoming conditions birth in a future life at the dissolution of this present five-aggregate phenomenon. If we seriously consider the matter, we can perceive that all desires are just particular manifestations of the will to exist or to continue; and all such craving and clinging are future directed energies whose function is the seeking of fulfillment. This force of *kammic* energy does not cease with death. Becoming is just the very strong form of desire and it contains sufficient momentum behind it that at the time of death it is the force that makes for a new birth. This energy manifests and a new *nāma-rūpa* begins. Thus once again the start of life is shown to be a completely impersonal, conditioned process working totally irrespective of anyone's wishes, hopes or desires, leading to a phenomenon with no essence or "I." This link repeats the second one in the series just in different words. *Jāti-paccayā jarāmaraṇaṃ*—once there is birth there automatically comes to be old age and death and all the other manifold forms of suffering encountered in life—the First Noble Truth. And thus the cycle beginning with our inherited ignorance leads inexorably towards more and more suffering in the future.

The inverse form of the cycle is stated alongside the form above. It is the inverse that demonstrates the Third Noble Truth, how with the cessation of the cause, the effect must cease; so *avijjā nirodha, saṅkhāra nirodho,* etc.—when ignorance ceases, no more *saṅkhāras* are generated and carried through all the intervening links, the way of ending all suffering is thus shown.

This is but a very rough sketch of the workings of the *paṭiccasamuppāda* that must be wisely considered and thoroughly elaborated on and then incorporated into the meditator's own thought processes for it to serve him as a means to liberation. Each link has to be investigated in terms of the Four Noble Truths—to understand the factor itself, its arising, its ceasing and the way leading to its cessation (always the Fourth Noble Truth—the Path). The Buddha has Sāriputta explain to him the way the meditator in training, who is still a learner, considers things. Sāriputta states: "'This has come to be,' Lord—thus by right insight he sees as it really is; and seeing it in this way he practices revulsion from it, and that it may fade away and cease. He sees by right insight continual becoming from a certain sustenance, and that it may fade away and cease. From the ceasing of a certain sustenance that which has come to be is liable to cease—so he sees by right insight as it really is. And seeing that in this way he practices revulsion from that which is liable to cease that it may fade away and cease." The revulsion to be practiced in relation to *all* conditioned phenomena, to all things that have arisen dependent on causes, is closely akin to detachment and dispassion. Unlike aversion, revulsion is based on wisdom and developed in relation to all pleasant, unpleasant or neutral experiences. The *arahant* makes the same observations about the unstable nature of conditioned phenomena, but for him the stage of practicing has passed, and when by right insight, the fully liberated one sees "This has come to be," then "because of revulsion at that which has come to be, because of its fading away and ceasing he becomes free, grasping at nothing..." (K.S., II, pp. 36–37). So the lesson to be learned from the doctrine of Dependent Origination—as from all the Dhamma—is that nothing that arises due to causes and conditions can possibly provide secure happiness due to its inherent changeability and instability; so there is absolutely nothing on any plane of existence worth developing the slightest interest in or attachment to as all such involvement can only lead to suffering. So detachment and revulsion are the result of a complete understanding of the workings of the causal law—and this is liberation.

In one place, the Buddha actually describes the series of causes leading to liberation itself, beginning with suffering, thus: "What is that which is the cause of liberation? Passionlessness is the answer... and repulsion is causally related to passionlessness... knowledge-and-vision of things as they really are is causally associated with repulsion... concentration is causally associated with knowledge-and-vision... happiness is causally associated with concentration... serenity is causally associated with happiness... rapture is causally associated with serenity... joy is causally associated with rapture... faith is causally associated with joy... And what is the cause of faith? Suffering is the answer. Suffering is causally related with faith" (K.S., II, pp. 25–26). The Buddha then continues with the origins of suffering back to ignorance following the usual *paṭiccasamuppāda* formulation backwards, thus showing the whole length of the route—the Path, the Fourth Noble Truth—out of the causal cycle. It is because of the experience of suffering that beings seek a way out and put their faith in the Buddha as a guide and in his teachings as the true method to attain freedom from all ill. Thus the causal cycle proceeds from *dukkha,* the end of the usual twelve-link Dependent Origination formula, through *saddhā* (faith) and all the steps here named to final and total emancipation.

Kamma is one of the basic causes in the cycle of Dependent Origination (in the past life it goes under the name of *saṅkhāra* and in the present life it encompasses *taṇhā, upādāna* and *bhava*) and a deep investigation of its significance and operation must be made, as, after all, it is through our own wholesome and unwholesome *kamma* that we are tied down to the infinite cycle of rebirths and it is by means of good *kamma* that we are able to transcend this universe of *kamma*, rebirth and *dukkha.*

It is important to remind ourselves and to discover how in our own minds, at every moment, we are creating new *kammas.* When we investigate the thinking process carefully in our meditation, we come to observe that all our thoughts are related to some *taṇhā,* some desire or aversion, some volition. And each moment the *kamma* we are creating is either beneficial or harmful to us both in the immediate and in the far distant future; there is not an instant when we are not molding our future fate. And no matter how good an act of body or speech may seem, it is only a gross manifestation of a mental volition, and if the thought behind it is impure, the *kammic* effects are in the long run bound to be painful. Hence it is vital to analyze our own minds and then cultivate the beneficial volitions that aid us on the Path to Liberation, otherwise the old habitual tendencies rooted in ignorance are bound to take us to the unhappy realms for rebirth, and once reborn there it is almost impossible to be reborn on the human plane for an extremely long period of time.

But we must also consider that in the ultimate analysis, even good volitions must be given up, as "That which we will, brethren, and that which we intend to do, that wherewithal we are occupied—this becomes an object for the persistence of consciousness," and so anything we think about will become nourishment for a new birth either in the lower or higher realms, depending on the purity of the willing, the intention or the occupation (K.S., II, p. 45). And ultimately in order to totally eradicate all suffering (even the very subtle *dukkha* that is inherent in the fact that the life span of even the most long-lived Brahma is limited, finite), rebirth must be eliminated—and this means rooting out its causes as explained in the cycle of Dependent Origination.

Particularly for the Western mind this infinite *saṃsāric* cycle of rebirth has to be thought about quite thoroughly before our understanding of it can influence our behavior, making us act on the basis of a very long-term view. "Incalculable is the beginning, brethren, of this faring on. The earliest point is not revealed of the running on, the faring on of beings cloaked in ignorance, tied to craving... For many a long day, brethren, have ye experienced death of mother, of son, of daughter, have ye experienced the ruin of kinfolk, the calamity of disease. Greater is the flood of tears shed by you crying and weeping of one and all these as ye fare on, run on this many a long day, united with the undesirable, sundered from the desirable, than are the waters in the four seas. (Because) incalculable is the beginning, brethren, of this faring on" (K.S., II, p. 120).

Ledi Sayādaw reminds us that, "Lack of wholesome *kamma* will lead to the lower worlds where one has to suffer grievously. Fearing such suffering, one has to perform wholesome *kamma* which can lead one to be reborn as man or deva in the existences to come" (*Manuals of Buddhism,* p. 227, *Maggaṅga Dīpanī*). One important aspect of Right View which has to be investigated relates to *kamma.* We have to know for ourselves that "Only the wholesome and unwholesome actions of beings are the origin of their wanderings in many a becoming or world cycle"; and that only these actions "are their real refuge wherever they may wander" (*Maggaṅga Dīpanī,* p. 221). There is nothing very strange in this idea of *kamma* being the one thing that endures (while always being influenced and altered by present mental volitions), carrying over from one life to the next. If we ponder over the matter, we see that just as a moral cause and effect works within this life to only some extent, the effects of many *kammas* can only show up in future lives; so over an infinite span of lives *kusala* (wholesome) *kammas* ultimately must bring good results and *akusala* (unwholesome) *kammas* bring unhappy states. As we study the cycle of Dependent Origination it clearly shows that there is no entity or ongoing being involved anywhere in all these births, deaths and rebirths, but only past *kamma* manifesting in a five-aggregate phenomenon which changes every moment and which in turn continues to generate new *kamma* leading to new births, in a process that evolves endlessly from moment to moment.

As seen above, it is of vital importance to investigate thoroughly the causal law and *kamma* in order for full insight into the nature of existence to develop, for some causes lie behind the arising of absolutely everything. "Whether any... mental or physical phenomena arise, the arising of any thing whatsoever is dependent on conditions, and without condition, nothing can ever arise or enter into existence."[7] It is only through giving systematic thought to the twelve factors and the connections between them in the *paṭiccasamuppāda* cycle that we can introduce the appropriate causes to make this law cease operating. And only thus can we bring to an end the process of rebirth and its attendant suffering, by substituting wisdom for ignorance when feeling arises—and so prevent the development of *taṇhā,* which would inexorably lead to rebirth. Most important of all to train the mind in wisdom is to understand clearly how completely impersonally and automatically moment to moment every link in the cycle operates; the sequence goes on strictly as a matter of cause and effect with no room for, no need for, any "I" to explain the continual rise and fall of *nāma-rūpa.*

> In this religion, brethren, a pondering brother ponders: "This diverse and manifold ill that arises in the world as old age and death—what is this ill based on, how comes it to pass?... What being there does old age-and-death come to be? What not being there does old age-and-death not come to be?" He pondering comes to know that this... is based on birth... He comes to know old age-and-death, he comes to know its arising, he comes to know its ceasing and he comes to know the way going to its ceasing.
>
> —K.S., II, pp. 56–57

He ponders similarly on all the other factors in the Dependent Origination and thus he is called a "brother who has wholly practiced for the complete destroying of ill." Full comprehension

7. *Buddhist Dictionary, Manual of Buddhist Terms and Doctrines,* Nyanatiloka, Buddhist Publication Society, Kandy, p. 135.

through very careful analysis of the *paṭiccasamuppāda* must make us detached, must make us see that there is nothing which really corresponds to the word "I," and must make us learn to cease creating *saṅkhāras* by willing actions. Once we cease to create any more *kamma* of any kind, the other links in the cycle must automatically fall away. And the Buddha ends this discourse emphatically referring to this process of breaking the causal chain saying, "Believe me, brethren, be convinced of this, be ye without doubt herein, without hesitation just this is the end of suffering!"

4. The Five Aggregates (*Khandha*)

Dhammavicaya, in addition to the definition used in the previous three sections of investigation of the Dhamma, may also be interpreted as meaning investigation of *dhammas*, of all things, all phenomena, mental or physical, real or imaginary, conditioned or unconditioned. In this connection the most important things to be examined are, perhaps, first the five *khandhas* or aggregates that make one life continuum, one *nāma-rūpa,* a "person"; and second the six sense doors—five physical ones and the mind, and their corresponding six categories of sense objects.

We have to examine one aggregate of body and four of the mind—perception, feeling, mental volitions and consciousness—that in combination make up this thing we have been calling "I", very thoroughly and deeply in order to see how ultimately there is nothing lasting, satisfying or which deserves to be considered "myself" in any of them; to know how all that we associate with "me" is just *anicca, dukkha* and *anattā,* and to understand how these aggregates arise to pass away. The *khandhas* are the basic components which make up what we perceive of as an individual. But each of these aggregates in itself has no essence; each is merely a process of continual minute momentary risings and fallings.

Viññāṇa is consciousness, just the process or faculty of knowing, or awareness, that arises immediately upon the coming together of any sense organ and its respective object. *Saññā* is perception or recognition of the object, defining it by associating it with past memories. *Vedanā* is the feeling that arises as an immediate result of contact when the internal and external sense bases get together and the appropriate consciousness comes into being. *Vedanā* can be pleasant, unpleasant or neutral feeling of body or of mind. *Saṅkhāra* is mental volitions or activities; the thinking process of the mind is the facet of *nāma* governed by this *khandha*. The past mind-moment with its consciousness, feeling, perception and volition is the condition for the arising of the next, but there is nothing of any of those four mental components (nor anything outside of them) that continues over from one instant to the next. The body aggregate, too, is utterly impermanent and insubstantial, just like any other form of matter, living or inorganic. All matter is made up of the infinitely small *kalāpas* (sub-atomic particles or vibrations) which come to be and vanish at only a slightly slower rate than the mind, but still so extremely quickly that we get the illusion of continuity, unity and substance where these do not actually exist.

The Buddha tells the monks the importance of such examination of the aggregates thus: "So soon, brethren, as beings thoroughly understand, as they really are, the satisfaction as such, the misery as such, the way of escape as such in these five factors of grasping (the aggregates) then, brethren, beings do remain aloof, detached... with barriers of the mind done away with" (K.S., III, p. 30). Once we intellectually realize that none of the *khandhas* can rightly be called "mine," then we are faced with the urgent task of rooting out, eliminating this aspect of personality-belief from our minds, of becoming truly aloof and detached. The Buddha described this work thus: "What is not of you, brethren, put it away. Putting it away will be for your profit and welfare. And what, brethren, is not of you? Body... feeling... perception... the activities, consciousness is not of you. Put it away" (K.S., III, pp. 231–2). Putting away or giving up or letting go of what we incorrectly think of as "mine" is a gradual and long-term process. In fact, not only is this process of investigating and giving systematic attention to the *anicca, dukkha, anattā* nature of the aggregates the work of the beginner, the same thing is done by beings at any stage along the way, even by the fully-liberated ones. "The grasping groups, friend Koṭṭhita," says the great disciple of the Buddha, Sāriputta, "are the conditions which should be pondered with method by a virtuous brother, as being impermanent, sick, as a boil, as a dart, as pain, as ill-health, as alien, as transitory, empty and soulless... It is possible for a virtuous brother so pondering with method... to realize the fruits of stream winning... of once returning... of never returning... of arahantship... For the *arahant*, friend, there is nothing further to be done... Nevertheless, these things, if practiced and enlarged conduce to a happy existence and self-possession even in this present life" for him (K.S., III, p. 143).

Very frequently the Buddha refers to the five aggregates or groups of existence as the *upādānakkhandha* or grasped-at groups, aggregates (as objects) of clinging, etc. It is worthwhile to contemplate why he considered these components of life so inseparable from *taṇhā* and *upādāna* that he actually called them clinging-aggregates. First of all, these aggregates only come into being because of *taṇhā;* through craving and clinging the past *saṅkhāras* gave rise to the present birth, the current *nāma-rūpa,* which is precisely the same as these five grasped-at groups. What has its cause in clinging must have clinging as its very core. Secondly, these aggregates are the means by which we are *conscious* of and *perceive* through the six sense doors; an impression is then *felt* and as a result of this process the input leads to mental *volitions* as well as to actions of *body* directed by some *taṇhā* to gain, grasp at, cling to something. Thirdly, and most important, it is just these five constituent groups that we tend to cling to most tenaciously, convinced that they are "I" and "mine." We have already looked into this misperception of reality and by means of a strong simile the Buddha illustrated the danger in such clinging to any of the aggregates or seeing in them any security:

Suppose... a mountain torrent... rising from afar, swift-flowing, and on both its banks are growing grasses overhanging the stream;... and a man is swept away by that stream and clutches at the grasses, but they might break away and owing to that he might come by his destruction.

Even so, brethren, the untaught manyfolk... regard the body as the self, or the self as having body, or the body as being in the self, or the self as being in the body. Then the body breaks away, and owing to that they come by their destruction.

And so with feeling, perception, the activities... consciousness.

—K.S., III, p. 116

We also subject ourselves to tremendous suffering because we "are possessed by this idea" that the body belongs to "me," for, when the body or any of the aggregates "alters and changes, owing to the unstable nature of the body, then sorrow and grief, woe, lamentation and despair arise" if these changes are not what we wanted (K.S., III, p. 3).

Only by completely investigating the ultimate reality of these five aggregates will we see that they are incapable of giving satisfaction and so not worth grasping at, that actually they are so unstable that holding on to them is impossible, and there is no one who can cling anyhow (as the "self" arises and vanishes every moment and so cannot possibly continue to possess anything for any period of time). So, in order to attain liberation, one must attain insight into these five aggregates so that the necessary dispassion arises, for "by not thoroughly knowing, by not understanding, by not being detached from, by not renouncing body (and the other *khandhas*) one is unfit for the destruction of suffering... But, brethren, by thoroughly knowing (them)... one is fit for the destruction of suffering" (K.S., III, p. 26).

5. The Sense Bases (*Āyatana*)

The investigative process also must be applied to the internal and external sense bases (*āyatana*), so that the pleasure and misery in them, their cause and cessation, and their *anicca, dukkha* and *anattā* nature are fully comprehended. Only with this insight are we able to let go of our attachments to, desire for and clinging to the eye and visible objects, the ear and sounds, the nose and smells, the tongue and tastes, the body and things tangible, the mind and mental objects. One must especially learn how the mind operates as just another sense organ, whose field is all the perceptions and thoughts that have occurred in the past, in order to dissociate the workings of the mind from the "I" notion. In his third sermon, the Buddha stated, "The all is on fire" and the nature of this conflagration must be seen and understood before it can be extinguished and freedom gained from it. "The eye, brethren, is on fire, objects are on fire, eye-consciousness... eye contact... that weal or woe or neutral state experienced, which arises owing to eye-contact (*vedanā,* feeling);... that also is on fire... On fire with the blaze of lust, the blaze of ill-will, the blaze of infatuation, the blaze of birth, decay and death, sorrow..." (K.S., IV, p. 10) and so are tongue and mind-related phenomena—and by extrapolation those coming from the other senses as well.

The six internal sense organs (*saḷāyatana*) and their corresponding objects have a crucial role in the present lifetime phase of the *paṭiccasamuppāda*. Consciousness, *viññāṇa*, is not permanent or abiding; instead it arises and ceases every moment, and it is the coming together of one of the sense organs and its respective object that causes the arising of a moment of consciousness. Thus every consciousness is eye-consciousness, or ear-consciousness, or nose- or tongue- or body- or mind-consciousness, depending on which sense organ at that instant has met its object. The cycle of causality continues on from there: "Owing to eye and objects arises eye-consciousness. The coming together of the three is contact. Dependent on contact is feeling. Dependent on feeling is craving... grasping... becoming. Dependent on becoming is rebirth, decay and death, sorrow and grief... This is the arising of the world" (K.S., IV, p. 33). From thus analyzing the genesis of existence (the "world") and of *dukkha* (as it is more often formulated) we can understand the absolutely impersonal nature of the arising of consciousness, as well as the germinal role in creating *saṅkhāras* played by the internal and external sense bases.

Consciousness, or mind, is analogous to the proverbial monkey constantly on the move high up in the trees in the jungle, always grasping at something or the other. Similarly with the mind, at each and every mind-moment when awake, consciousness must be connected with one or another of the sense doors; there is no underlying substratum of consciousness that endures through time, but only momentary clutching after sights, grabbing for sounds, clinging to smells, holding on to tastes, attachment to tangibles or (and often most predominantly) hanging on to mind objects. It is because the sense organs and their objects inherently contain the danger of tempting us to create craving (*taṇhā*) and an urge to renewed existence (*bhava-saṅkhāra*) that the Buddha frequently warned the monks about keeping the sense doors well guarded, since the external objects cannot be eliminated. By means of ongoing mindfulness, rooted in insight into the true nature of all the phenomena that appear at the sense doors, it is necessary to observe how craving starts to rear its head (as it inevitably will, due to the old completely automatic mental conditioning) once contact and feeling have taken place, and not allow the desire to take over the mind and become a strong rebirth producing force.

If we do not keep watch over our senses and reactions attentively, we are like the fish attracted by the well-baited hook on the line held by the fisherman. "Just as a fisherman, brethren, casts a baited hook in some deep pool of water, and some fish greedy for the bait gulps it down and thus... comes to destruction—even so, brethren, there are these six hooks in the world, to the sorrow of beings... objects cognizable by the eye inciting to lust... If a brother delights therein, persists in clinging to them, such a one is called 'hook-swallower'... is come to destruction" (K.S., IV, p. 99). And of course the other hooks to be wary of in the world are alluring sounds, smells, tastes, tangibles and mental objects. If we give careful, systematic attention to these external sense objects as we meet them, we cannot help but realize that the pain of swallowing the hooks by clinging to the sense objects far outweighs the possible momentary pleasure of tasting the bait.

The basic aim of investigating the sense organs is the same as for the aggregates—to see how thoroughly they are *anicca* and *dukkha* and so to cease to cling to them as "I" and "mine." "A brother beholds no trace of the self nor what pertains to the self in the six-fold sense sphere. So beholding, he is attached to nothing in the world. Unattached he is not troubled. Untroubled he is of himself utterly set free" (K.S., IV, p. 104).

The specific subjects in the Dhamma that must be investigated for insight have in this section been given initial exploration. The task is to turn these thoughts and ideas into real wisdom, so that the whole course of the life becomes oriented to and aimed at liberation. We must learn to keep before us at all times the ultimate nature of all *dhammas*—all phenomena of any conceivable kind that can enter consciousness—so that the gross perceptual illusion or hallucination of the apparent truth loses its strength and the ignorance it fosters vanishes and with it all craving. We have to analyze completely this body-and-mind and all the external phenomena that appear from time to time at the six sense doors until the pleasure and misery in them are understood, until the causes of their arising and ceasing are comprehended, until their ultimately impermanent, unsatisfactory, conditioned and essenceless nature is clearly known. This is done by means of careful investigation in meditation on these *dhammas* along the lines of the Four Noble Truths, the Three Signata of Existence and the Doctrine of Dependent Origination. With this insight fully developed there can be no clinging or craving, no ill-will or aversion, and ultimately one becomes "independent, unattached to anything in the world," and so with all its causes uprooted, liberation from all suffering is achieved.

Investigation in Meditation

There are a number of other aspects of Dhamma investigation that have to be examined now that the contents of such exploration have been discussed. The very basic and essential relationship between investigative thinking and insight meditation, how the two are required to support each other and send the meditator's mind to its goal of ending all possibility of *dukkha*, is the appropriate one to deal with first.

For investigation of Dhamma to lead to liberating insight it must be combined with and done in the course of insight meditation. It is just through investigation and wise consideration of phenomena that insight into their ultimate nature develops. At the time of the Buddha there were people who became fully Enlightened in just a few moments of time, but even for them some sort of thought process had to go on. But these individuals had accumulated such a vast store of *pāramīs*—accumulated good acts and mental dispositions of the past—that the liberating wisdom came with nearly instantaneous impact. While just a Bodhisatta, the Buddha went back to the first *jhāna*, a deep absorption (after having mastered seven still deeper, more profound concentrative states)—which includes thinking—when he sat under the Bodhi Tree with the final and total determination to become fully liberated. "Before my Enlightenment, while I was still only an unenlightened Bodhisatta, I thought: This world has fallen into a slough for it is born, ages and dies, it passes away and reappears, and yet knows no escape from this suffering. When will an escape from this suffering be described? I thought: What is there when aging and death come to be? What is their necessary condition? Then with ordered attention I came to understand... birth is a necessary condition for them." And so as he exerted the utmost effort to become a Buddha, a fully self-liberated being, he proceeded carefully thinking through all the links of the cycle of Dependent Origination in both directions. "I thought: This is the path to Enlightenment that I have now reached... that is how there is a cessation to this whole aggregate mass of suffering. 'The cessation, the cessation' such was the insight, the knowledge, the understanding, the vision, the light, that arose in me about ideas not heard of before."[8]

Also to gain the full understanding of the *khandhas* at this crucial juncture of this life, the Bodhisatta used careful intellectual consideration. "I thought: In the case of material form, of feeling, of perception, of formations, of consciousness what is the gratification, what is the danger, what the escape? Then I thought: In the case of each the bodily pleasure and mental joy that arise in dependence on these things (the five categories) are the gratification; the fact that these things are all impermanent, painful and subject to change is the danger; the disciplining and abandoning of desire and lust for them is the escape."[9]

These quotations show how vital wise investigative thinking was to the Buddha himself in his meditations while moving towards his Enlightenment and so must we, too, carefully combine the thought process and meditation to liberate ourselves from suffering.

The long quotation given in the section on investigating the *khandhas* shows how it is the process of pondering deeply on things that brings us dispassion towards them all, and so to the stages of Enlightenment. So insight, clarity of vision into the ultimate nature of reality, *bhāvanā-māya-paññā* (wisdom born of meditation) the personal direct knowledge that bears concrete fruit in our behavior in life, is really based on careful thinking so that the apparent truths are seen through and no longer allowed to delude us by coloring and covering up the real nature of our minds and bodies and of the external world.

This liberating insight can, however, only develop if the investigating is done by a person who meditates regularly. Meditation provides us with the relatively concrete evidence of personal experience to guarantee the validity of our more

---

8. *The Life of the Buddha*, Bhikkhu Ñāṇamoli, Buddhist Publication Society, pp. 25, 27, quoting from *Saṃyutta Nikāya*, XII, 65.

9. *Ibid.*, p. 28.

abstract thinking. There are times when meditation consists of just observing, in a very one-pointed manner, the rise and fall of the sensations (*vedanā*) caused by the subtle biochemical changes going on in the body. But there are other occasions either when thinking is going on quite strongly or when there is a tendency to sloth and torpor, and at these times it is very beneficial to do Dhamma investigation. When the mind is busy thinking, it is always involved in ignorance, always full of clinging or aversion, always dwelling in the past or future because this is the nature of the conditioning that it has gotten from the past. By this kind of thinking we are creating "heaps and heaps" of unwholesome mental volitions, *saṅkhāras, akusala kamma,* which are bound to bear fruit in some sort of *dukkha* in the future. If instead we apply the mind in a systematic way to thinking about Dhamma, trying to eliminate craving, trying to see through to the ultimate realities of phenomena, we are creating very powerful good *kamma* for ourselves which has to lead us towards liberation. At the same time, this kind of consideration clarifies in our minds the fundamental truths of Buddha Dhamma that we have read or heard previously so that they become fully comprehensible and meaningful. Thus carefully directed thought, while sitting in *vipassanā* meditation, is a vital tool for the rooting out of all our ignorance and for contrasting the path to emancipation.

Also investigation is important to practice strenuously when there is a tendency to a daydreaming, lazy kind of meditation, when the hindrances of sloth and torpor are attacking. The Buddha told the monks, "... at such time, monks, as the mind is sluggish, then is the season for cultivating the limb of wisdom that is Norm-investigation, the season for cultivating the limb of wisdom that is energy, the season for cultivating the limb of wisdom that is zest. Why so? Because, monks, the sluggish mind is easily raised up by such conditions" (K.S., V, p. 96). By energetically applying the mind to trying to understand more thoroughly than before the Four Noble Truths or another important aspect of Dhamma, the mind will be directed and stimulated. When this happens, the tendency of the mind to drift must disappear and zest for meditation and the clarity of mind which is crucial to real understanding return.

Thus to use investigation in meditation is to apply Right Thought, one of the factors of the Noble Eightfold Path. Obviously, analytical thinking takes places in relation to Dhamma outside of meditation as well—when listening to discourses or when doing Dhamma reading, for example. But for the information gained from outside to become truly meaningful to us, for it to become our own "wisdom-born-of-meditation" (*bhāvanā-mayā-paññā*), for this information to influence how we live our lives, it must be thoroughly thought through while we are actually sitting in meditation. At such times the mind is much more concentrated and subtle than usual and as the hindrances to concentration and insight (i.e., doubt, excitement and restlessness, sloth and torpor, greed, and ill-will) are at a fairly low level, the mind is much more pliable and fit to assimilate pure Dhamma thoughts. As we increase our understanding and wisdom through meditative investigation, we decrease our ignorance, and as ignorance diminishes we are loosening the bondage of our suffering and becoming more and more free of craving (*taṇhā*).

Systematic Attention and Control of the Hindrances

Another important role played by investigation is in preventing the arising of all the hindrances that tend to block our progress now and again. It is by means of analytical thought, systematic attention, *yoniso-manasikāra,* that we can keep the hindrances under control. In this process the two Enlightenment Factors of investigation and mindfulness are employed, as it takes careful thought in combination with continuous awareness to keep control of the mind. "And what, monks, is no food for the arising of sensual lust not yet arisen?" The Buddha answers his own question saying that sensual lust is kept from growing by "systematic attention" to "the repulsive feature of things." To counter the hindrance of ill-will, systematic attention must be given to *mettā,* the quality of unbounded loving kindness. To deal with sloth and torpor, systematic attention must be applied to "the element of putting forth effort, the element of exertion, the element of striving." Against excitement, one must apply systematic attention to tranquillity of mind. To still doubt, one must give systematic attention to Dhamma, or in the Buddha's words, to "things good and things bad, things blameworthy and things not blameworthy, things mean and things exalted, things that are constituent parts of darkness and light" (K.S., V, p. 88).

These five great hindrances to concentration, to meditation, to living the Dhamma life are all quite familiar habits to us. But we can develop the tools to prevent their arising and to control them when they do come up. And chief amongst these is the application of systematic attention to the external situations that stimulate the sensual lust, the ill-will, the sloth and torpor, the excitement and the doubt that lie latent in our minds, and to the internal negative tendencies themselves. Thus when it is seen that with wisdom these hindrances are ultimately nothing but irrelevant and inappropriate deep-rooted, habitual mental reactions to impermanent, unsatisfactory and essenceless phenomena, the hindrances must lose strength and gradually disappear, leaving behind a pure mind.

Investigation Conduces to Insight

Investigation of Dhamma is one of the four factors which the Buddha frequently describes as conducing "to growth in wisdom, to acquiring insight, to growth of insight, the increase of insight." The four elements involved are: "Association with good men (following after the good), hearing *Saddhamma* (the Good Norm), thorough work of mind (systematic attention to Dhamma) and behavior in accordance with Dhamma (living in accordance with the precepts of the Norm)." When the Buddha spoke, of course, the good man to associate oneself with was specifically the Tathāgata himself and his *arahant* disciples, all fully liberated beings. Today we do not have this opportunity, but we certainly can choose our associates from amongst those who are on the Path and who are striving to gain wisdom. If we associate with the foolish, we are wasting our time and tempting ourselves unnecessarily, making our task of self-purification all the more difficult. But if we spend time with other strivers, we will reinforce our own motivation and also perhaps get some direct help or encouragement in times of need. As for the second factor, only rarely do we get the opportunity to actually "hear" the Dhamma and then of course not directly from the Fully Enlightened One. But when we take a meditation course, this purpose is served by the teacher's discourses, which are designed to inform us of and elucidate to us the fundamentals of the Dhamma. Naturally this opportunity, too, is limited, and to supplement live Dhamma teachings regularly, we have to do some reading both of the direct words of the Buddha as preserved in the translated Pāli texts, and also of what later meditators have written about him and his teachings. Without this beneficial material for our minds to thoroughly think about, to consider wisely, to give systematic attention to, we are apt to find our meditation getting into ruts which become so habitual as to lose their impact on our minds—and on how we live our lives as well. On the other hand, reading Dhamma as an intellectual pastime, without combining it with meditation and trying to make what we read our own wisdom which can influence our life patterns is a complete waste of time. But if we are associating with a Sangha (the community of those walking on the Noble Eightfold Path), if we are learning the basics of Dhamma and carefully and persistently applying our minds to it, then our behavior cannot help but reflect the wisdom we are so gaining. Thus these four factors must "if cultivated and made much of, conduce to realizing the fruits of stream-winning... of once-returning, of non-returning and of arahantship" (K.S., V, p. 351).

The Seven Factors of Enlightenment

Investigation of Dhamma, *dhammavicaya,* usually the second in the list of the seven Factors of Enlightenment, has a unique place amongst these limbs of wisdom whose function is to purify and train the mind and to "conduce to downright revulsion, to dispassion, to cessation, to calm, to full comprehension, to wisdom, to Nibbāna" (K.S., V, p. 69). Thinking over the Buddha's teachings is the very basis for the development of these seven factors, as described in the following quotation:

> When a monk ... remembers and turns over in his mind that teaching of the Norm, it is then that the limb of wisdom which is mindfulness is established in that monk;... Thus, he, dwelling mindful, with full recognition investigates and applies insight to that teaching of the Norm and comes to close scrutiny of it.

> Now, monks, at such a time as a monk, dwelling thus mindful, with full recognition investigates and applies insight to that teaching of the Norm, then it is that limb of wisdom which is Norm-investigation that, as he comes to close scrutiny of it, by his culture of it, it comes to perfection.
>
> —K.S., V, p. 6

Clearly, from the Buddha's description of the cultivation of the two limbs of wisdom of mindfulness and investigation, they are closely tied up with each other; certainly neither can be perfected without the help of the other. But thinking about the Norm is the most basic feature involved in the development of these seven *Bojjhaṅgas* because it is the original motivator behind their development. That is why the Buddha placed it at the very beginning of his description of the seven as well as in its regular spot as the second factor, *dhammavicaya.*

Mindfulness is a vital skill to develop, for without mindfully observing one's mind and body to see the defilements as they tend to creep in, it is impossible to purify oneself. But without some degree of understanding of the ultimate facts of existence (*anicca, dukkha* and *anattā* and the relationship between *taṇhā* and *dukkha* particularly), the practice of "bare attention" (*sati*) would probably be futile. Just watching what is going on at the gross level of bodily action is unlikely in and of itself to take us to that deep insight that automatically begins to rid our minds of greed, hatred and delusion, the roots of *taṇhā* and hence of *dukkha.* Only if our minds are also carefully at work to try and delve into the ultimate realities is mindfulness, constant watchfulness, guaranteed to bear fruit. The Buddha describes this when he defines "the cultivation of a station of mindfulness. Herein a monk dwells contemplating the rise of things in body. He so dwells contemplating the fall of things in body... and also in feeling, mind and mind-states" (K.S., V, p. 160). In other words, it is by the consideration of the *anicca* (and by extrapolation, the *dukkha* and *anattā* nature as well) of the body, the feelings, the mind and the mind-states that mindfulness is actually developed.

On the other hand, investigation alone also tends to be sterile, a merely intellectual knowledge. Only by continuing meditative mindfulness and observation of whatever comes into the mind via any of the six sense doors can we put into practice our understanding of Dhamma. The Pāli phrase "*yoniso-manasikāra*" combines the two factors of mindfulness and investigation in itself, although the stress seems to be on the latter. *Yoniso-manasikāra* is translated as systematic attention or wise consideration. Systematically, mindfully, with full awareness, one considers the Dhamma; one thinks about the matter at hand until its apparent nature has been penetrated and the ultimate truth is clear. Once the wisdom is gained and the mindfulness of the ultimate reality of the body, feelings, mind and mental states (the Four Stations of Mindfulness) is constant, then it is only a matter of effort, of energy (the third Enlightenment Factor), of just patiently and persistently doing the work—the results of these conditions (detachment leading to liberation) must come about automatically.

This energy is the Enlightenment Factor which follows *dhammavicaya.* "As with full recognition he investigates and applies insight to that Norm-teaching, then unshaken energy is established in him" (K.S., V, p. 56). On the basis of understanding the utter suffering of existence we become so convinced of the need to escape from the perpetual rounds of *saṃsāra* that we are completely willing to put out all the effort needed to do so. Knowing that we are doing what has to be done brings us *pīti,* the next limb of wisdom. *Pīti* is pure joy or pleasurable interest or zest—it is the positive feeling that arises from knowing we have the technique for eliminating our suffering, which sustains us further, encouraging us to continue to apply that method wholeheartedly. Tranquillity of mind and body, the next limb, develops, with *pīti*; with the elimination of doubt a deep sense of peace of mind based on wisdom comes about. When one has thought about life very carefully and knows that there is nothing in the world worth getting the least bit involved with or attached to, then the mind runs after objects less and less and tends to settle down and get well concentrated (the sixth factor), as no possible phenomenon at any of the six sense doors appears worthwhile for it to try and grasp onto. This pure concentration as it is rooted in insight and allows insight to grow more and more makes the mind balanced and calm, and so equanimity (the final limb of wisdom) grows. This is not bored, mundane callousness, but an equanimity that is rooted in clear thought and deep understanding which has made it apparent that there can be absolutely nothing, mental or physical, anywhere on any plane of existence, past, present or future, worth reacting to or getting involved with.

Thus it is that the Buddha declared, "As a matter concerning one's own self, monks, I see no other single factor so potent for the arising of the seven limbs of wisdom as systematic attention. Of a monk who is possessed of systematic attention we may expect that he will cultivate, that he will make much of the seven limbs of wisdom," and developing these seven Enlightenment Factors is precisely developing liberation from suffering (K.S., V, pp. 34–35). Hence, careful investigation, persistently pursued is the root cause of, as well as the route to, wisdom in all its facets.

The Noble Eightfold Path

The Buddha states that it is this same factor of systematic attention (*yoniso-manasikāra*) that brings one onto the Noble Eightfold Path, the Fourth Noble Truth, which leads to the cessation of all suffering.

> Just as the dawn, monks, is the forerunner, the harbinger of the sun, even so possession of systematic thought, monks, is the forerunner, the harbinger, of the arising of the Ariyan Eightfold Way.
>
> Of a monk who is possessed of systematic thought, it may be expected that he will cultivate, that he will make much of the Ariyan Eightfold Way. And how, monks, does a monk so possessed make much of the Ariyan Eightfold Way?
>
> Herein a monk cultivates right view, that is based on seclusion, that is based on dispassion, on cessation, that ends in self-surrender, and he makes much of it... He cultivates right aim (thought), right speech, right action, right living (livelihood), right effort, right mindfulness, he cultivates and makes much of right concentration that is based on seclusion, on dispassion, on cessation, that ends in self-surrender.
>
> —K.S., V, p. 27

The Noble Eightfold Path is divided into three sections: the first is *paññā* (wisdom) and includes the first two factors of *sammā-diṭṭhi* (Right View or Understanding) and *sammā-saṅkappa* (Right

Thought); second is *sīla* (morality), which includes *sammā-vācā* (Right Speech), *sammā-kammanta* (Right Action) and *sammā-ājīva* (Right Livelihood); the third division is *samādhi* (concentration) including the final three elements of the Path—*sammā-vāyāma* (Right Effort), *sammā-sati* (Right Mindfulness) and *sammā-samādhi* (Right Concentration). Investigation is important to each group. Although it is virtually identical with the *paññā* section of the Path, the faculty of reasoned contemplation has a significant role to play in the development of both *sīla* and *samādhi*, and *samādhi* and *sīla* in turn both support investigation.

Careful investigation of the apparent truth must enable us to break through the barriers of our conditioned, colored and unclear perception of things until we thoroughly penetrate and clearly comprehend their ultimate truth. This is *vipassanā*—insight; this is *paññā*—Right Understanding and Right Thought, wisdom. As the Buddha shows us in a simile, all perception is as unsubstantial and essenceless as a mirage. "Just as if, brethren, in the last month of the dry season at high noontide there should be a mirage and a keen-sighted man should observe it and look close into the nature of it, so observing it he would find it to be without essence" (K.S., III, p. 119). If we accept the information we get about the world both internal and external from our sense organs automatically without carefully examining it, we are bound to act on the basis of the mirage of ignorance as all the past thinking that influences the perception—and so the feeling and reaction which come along with it—was based on the inaccurate assumptions of permanence, beauty, happiness and self. But once we begin to develop Right View, we come to see gradually how in actual fact nothing lasts, nothing can really be called beautiful (since everything is always changing, undergoing corruption and decay), nothing can really bring us satisfaction and there is no essence in any of the apparently solid objects, beings or mental phenomena of the universe. And we come to understand that there can only be the conditioned processes of becoming that arise and cease strictly and solely in accordance with the appropriate conditions. Right Thought is a vital means to the attainment of this Right Understanding or View; and investigation of truth is one and the same with Right Thought.

"Whatsoever there is of thinking, considering, reasoning, thought, ratiocination, application... the mind being holy, being turned away from the world, and conjoined with the path, the holy path being pursued" is called Right Thought (Majjhima Nikāya, 117). Right Thought is also specifically, and on the more mundane level, thinking that is free from ill-will or cruelty and thinking relating to renunciation of greed and lust. Right Understanding grows deeper and deeper the more thoroughly we investigate the essentials of Buddha Dhamma. As we apply our minds to them, the Three Salient Characteristics of Existence, the nature of wholesome and unwholesome *kamma*, the doctrine of Dependent Origination and the Four Noble Truths all become more meaningful to us and we comprehend more clearly how they explain the phenomena of existence and the way out of all suffering. "He understands what is worthy of consideration... He considers the worthy... What suffering is he wisely considers; what the origin of suffering is, he wisely considers, what the extinction of suffering is he wisely considers, what the path that leads to the extinction of suffering is, he wisely considers" (Majjhima Nikāya, 2). And thus wisely considering, we come to act on the basis of such thought; with such purified deeds of body, speech and mind we are bringing ourselves nearer and nearer to the cessation of all suffering.

Sīla is morality; in the context of the Noble Eightfold Path it refers specifically to Right Speech, Action and Mode of Livelihood. However, there are many broader kinds of *sīla*—from the Five Precepts every lay disciple tries to live by to the 227 rules for monks. The culmination of *sīla* is the culmination of the Path—perfect purity of bodily and verbal action rooted in similarly cleansed mental volition; when the mind can no longer develop *taṇhā* for any object whatsoever, then it is completely pure and totally free from all suffering. We may keep the *sīla* precepts rather mechanically, by tradition, or automatically reciting the Five Precepts at the start of a meditation course and this may for a time seem to serve our purpose. But if such morality is not based on Right Understanding, it will be very weak when put under duress by adverse conditions. Unless we have thought through and understood the drastic *kammic* results, in future lives as well as in this one, that we must expect from breaking *sīla,* we may well be tempted to lie for our own gain, to earn our livelihood by some means involving subterfuge or dishonesty, or to take something that actually belongs to someone else. An understanding of the fact that "Only the wholesome and unwholesome volitional actions (*kamma*) done by beings are their own properties that always accompany them, wherever they may wander in many a becoming" (*Subha-sutta* quoted in Ledi Sayādaw, *Manuals of Buddhism*, p. 75, *Sammā-diṭṭhi Dīpanī*) will greatly strengthen one's resolve to abstain from doing unwholesome deeds of body, speech and most importantly mind. Clearly understanding the Path and how *sīla* relates to the other sections is also a great support for keeping the moral code. *Sīla* makes up the preliminary steps in self-purification. If we indulge in intoxicants or sexual misconduct (e.g., adultery) or break the other three precepts, we cannot hope to gain concentration or wisdom. This is because it is the nature of such behavior that it keeps the mind distracted, either over-excited or very dull. But if we keep our morality pure on this gross level of bodily and verbal actions, then we are able to undertake the task of mental concentration and purification which is the work of *samādhi* and *paññā*. *Samādhi*, by concentrating the mind, suppresses, and *paññā*, Right View or Right Understanding, roots out the causes of all our unwholesome mental volitions. With ignorance thus eliminated, free from *taṇhā* related thoughts, we automatically keep perfect *sīla* of body and speech. Working on these principles of Dhamma in our minds so that we really comprehend both the results of our immoral actions and the importance of keeping *sīla* as the basis for progress on the Path will make our *sīla* much stronger and less likely to break no matter what provocative situation may crop up.

The three final elements of the Path make up the concentration group. They are effort, mindfulness and concentration. Strenuous, tireless effort is required if we are to be able to apply our minds sufficiently to penetrate through the apparent truths of life and really understand the ultimate realities. Without some understanding and careful thinking we will not be able to clearly distinguish those unwholesome states of mind that effort must be put forth in order to eliminate from the wholesome ones which must be cultivated with similarly great energy. Unless these distinctions are known, the effort cannot be Right Effort which is the Path factor.

> A monk puts forth desire, makes an effort, begins to strive, applies his mind, lays hold of his mind to prevent the arising of ill unprofitable states not yet arisen. As to all unprofitable states that have arisen, he puts forth desire to destroy them. As to profitable states that have not yet arisen, he puts forth desire for their arising.
>
> As to the profitable states that have already arisen, he puts forth desire, makes an effort, begins to strive, applies his mind, lays hold of his mind for their continuance, for the non-confusion, for their more-becoming, increase, culture and fulfillment. That, monks, is called 'right effort'.
>
> —K.S., V, p. 8

Hence effort strengthens and supports thorough, deep investigation, and conversely, investigation leads to the understanding of how effort is to be correctly applied.

As has already been discussed at some length, there is a very close link between mindfulness and investigation; they are totally interdependent and it is often impossible in practice to distinguish them from each other at any given moment. The four stations of mindfulness—of body, of feelings, of mind and of mental objects—are to be cultivated by means of contemplating on, thinking through their *anicca* (and also *dukkha* and *anattā*) nature.

> A monk dwells contemplating the rise of things in body. He dwells contemplating the fall of things in body; he dwells contemplating both the rise and fall of things in body; and in feelings, in mind, in mind-objects, ardent, composed and mindful by having restrained coveting and dejection with regard to the world... This, monks, is called 'the cultivation of a station of mindfulness'.
>
> —K.S., V, p. 160

Mindfulness of the body must include a well thought out understanding of its transient nature, of the inevitability of its decay and death—*anicca*; of its unsatisfactoriness as, ultimately, we cannot control its fate as it brings with it the myriad forms of physical suffering—*dukkha*; and of the fact that it cannot rightly be considered "I" or "mine" since we cannot control its changes or make it remain as we wish to—*anattā*. The specific exercises in mindfulness of the body (such as on the breath or the thirty-two parts of the body) if practiced for insight not just for concentration, must include such contemplation on the essential nature of the body.

The same kind of thought is required for the proper cultivation of contemplation of feelings (*vedanānupassanā*), contemplation of mind (*cittānupassanā*), and contemplation of mind-objects (*dhammānupassanā*). The Buddha told a group of elder monks to instruct the novices in this fashion: "In feelings do ye abide contemplating feelings (as transient) ardent, composed, one-pointed, of tranquil mind, calmed down, of concentrated mind, for insight into feelings as they really are. In mind... for insight into mind as it really is. In mind-states... for insight into mind-states as they really are" (K.S., V, p. 123). This means that feelings, mind and mind objects are to be observed and considered most carefully, concentratedly and objectively in order to gain true insight into their ultimately unstable nature. In *vedanānupassanā* (the particular technique taught by S. N. Goenka, et al.), it is the combination of the meditative experience of *feeling*, the subtle changing sensations, produced in the body by its biochemical processes which reflect the changing *mind-states*, with Right Thought about the ultimate nature of all the five aggregates that can free us of all our ignorance and so of our *taṇhā* and *dukkha*. The experience of free flow—feeling the sensations throughout the body in one sweep or all at one time (the sensations which are continually being produced by the changing *kalāpas*, the subatomic particles of which the whole mass of the body is composed)—alone, without understanding the far-reaching significance of these sensations, can be just like any other experience, a thing of passing interest that has no substantive effect on our lives. Similarly infertile will be mere intellectualizing about ultimate realities without any direct way of knowing them within our own five aggregate phenomena through mindful meditation. Careful analysis and rational thinking must also be applied mindfully, in an ongoing way, to the activity of the *mind* and to the objects of thought. Thus in order to carry the four stations of mindfulness to their goal, the transiency, unsatisfactoriness and essencelessness of these phenomena must be comprehended.

On the other hand, without one-pointed concentration investigation will be shallow and unable to penetrate through the conventions of the apparent truths we perceive because the mind will not be able to remain on one subject long enough. Concentration cannot be powerful if the mind is constantly intrigued by and grasps at the thoughts that come and go; and only when we understand how useless and *dukkha*-ridden is everything in the mind will it become detached and disinterested and so naturally tend to stay put on the chosen salutary object.

Thus we see how investigative Dhamma thinking is an integral part of the development of Right Thought and Right Understanding, how careful contemplation strengthens morality, how *sīla* allows *dhammavicaya* to deepen, how careful consideration shows where effort is to be applied, the ultimate significance of the objects of mindfulness, which enables concentration to grow, and conversely how the development of these three elements of the *samādhi* section of the Path contributes to the deepening and widening scope of Dhamma investigation. So, once we begin to develop systematic attention, we are starting to walk on the Path, the Fourth Noble Truth set out by the Buddha, the Way which enables us to develop a mind which is totally detached and at peace, free from ignorance, from craving, and so from suffering. *Dhammavicaya*—Right Thought—supports us at all stages and all aspects of the Path and development of the other Path factors similarly contributes to the growth of investigation of Dhamma.

Conclusion

Dhammavicaya—investigation of reality—is one of the most important tools to be used by the meditator seeking liberating insight and freedom from *dukkha,* suffering, as has here been shown. By means of careful investigation in meditation we are able to penetrate the apparent truths and come to full realization of the ultimate nature of the phenomena of existence. So by keen thinking in the course of *vipassanā* meditation we come to understand thoroughly how our own five aggregates and all the external mental and material universe (*nāma-rūpa*) perceived by the senses are utterly transient, arising and passing away at every moment as the causes that produced them do likewise. Because every *dhamma* is so unstable, the five aggregates can never bring true happiness but only *dukkha,* as such changing and unsatisfactory phenomena are utterly essenceless and not worth clinging to, not to be taken as "I" or "mine." As we seriously consider all this and also investigate the cause-and-effect nature of all life processes and contemplate the Noble Truths of Dukkha, its Cause, its Cessation and the Way leading to its Cessation, while persevering in our meditation, craving (*taṇhā*) must weaken and detachment, liberation must develop. And as the other Enlightenment and Path Factors are also brought to perfection with the support of *dhammavicaya*—complete freedom from all future birth and so of future suffering is attained.

Our good tendencies from the past have put us in the exceedingly fortunate position of being born as human beings during the time of a Buddha's dispensation, and they have brought us into contact with this incomparable jewel, the Dhamma. So now is the time to exert and strengthen our present mental volition towards liberation. To free ourselves from *dukkha,* we must strive to experience and investigate, to realize and understand, the ultimate truths of existence. With this insight, this wisdom, the mind becomes utterly detached, and since it is completely independent of all the world's changing, unsatisfactory and essenceless phenomena, there is absolute Peace and Freedom.

May all beings be Happy!
May all beings be Peaceful!
May all beings be Liberated!

Contemplation of Feelings

The Related Discourses on Feelings
(Vedanā-Saṃyutta)
from the Saṃyutta Nikāya

Translated from the Pāli and Introduced by
Nyanaponika Thera

WHEEL PUBLICATION NO. 303/304

Introduction

Contemplation of Feelings

"To feel is everything!"—so exclaimed a German poet, and exuberant though these words may be, they do point to the key role that feeling plays in human life. Whether deliberately or not, most people pass their days and nights in an avid endeavour to increase pleasant feelings and to avoid unpleasant ones. All human ambitions and strivings are geared to that purpose. From the simple amusements of the common man to the power urge of the mighty and the creative activity of the great artist, what is basically wanted is to enjoy pleasure, to gain satisfaction and to obtain happiness. Pleasant feelings come in many forms, and the longing to experience them in all their variety and intensity gives rise to courses of action and ways of life as equally numerous and diverse. To satisfy "the pleasure principle" many heroic deeds have been performed, and many more that were unheroic. The modern world, particularly, has seen the craving for physical comfort, emotional gratification and sensual enjoyment expand at a geometric rate. In every major country thousands of industries and services have sprung up, employing millions of workers, harnessing all the magic of technology first to excite, and then to satisfy, the desire for pleasure and convenience. By providing questionable escape routes, these same purveyors of emotional and sensual titillation also try to allay the worry, boredom, frustration and discontent so rampant in this present "age of anxiety."

From this brief survey one may now appreciate the significance of the Buddha's terse saying that "all things converge on feelings." The central position of feeling in human life also makes it clear why the Buddha included feelings as a separate category among the five constituent aggregates of personality (*pañcakkhandhā*) and as a separate mode of contemplation in the four foundations of mindfulness (*satipaṭṭhāna*).

In the precise pinpointing of mental states undertaken in Buddhist psychology, feeling (*vedanā*) is understood as the bare sensation experienced as pleasant, unpleasant (painful) or neutral (indifferent). It is distinguished from *emotion,* a more complex phenomenon which arises from the basic feeling, but adds to it various overlays of an evaluative, volitional and cognitive character. Feeling, in the Buddhist sense, is the second of the five aggregates constituting what is conventionally called "a person." The specific factors operative in *emotion* belong to the aggregate of mental formations (*saṅkhāra-kkhandha*), the fourth aggregate. All four mental aggregates arise inseparably in all states of consciousness: feeling, perception, mental formations and consciousness. Because feeling is associated with emotional factors, the two tend to be confused, but on close analysis they are seen to be distinct.

Feeling arises whenever there is the meeting of three factors—sense-organ, object and consciousness. The meeting of these three is called in Buddhist psychology sense-impression, contact or impact (*phassa*). Sense-impression is a mental, not a physical, event. It is sixfold, as being conditioned either by one of the five physical senses or by the mind. This sixfold sense-impression is the chief condition for the corresponding six kinds of feeling born of contact through the five physical senses and of mind-contact. In the formula of dependent origination (*paṭicca-samuppāda*), this relationship is expressed by the link: "Sense-impression conditions feeling" (*phassa-paccayā vedanā*). When emotions follow, they do so in accordance with the next link of dependent origination: "Feeling conditions craving" (*vedanā-paccayā taṇhā*).

The feeling that arises from contact with visual forms, sounds, odours and tastes is always a neutral feeling. Pleasant or unpleasant feelings do not always follow in relation to these four sense perceptions; but when they *do* follow, they then mark an additional stage of the perceptual process, subsequent to the neutral feeling which is the first response. But bodily impressions such as touch or pressure can cause either pleasant or unpleasant feelings. Mental impressions can cause gladness, sadness or neutral indifferent feeling.

Feeling is one of those mental factors (*cetasika*) common to all types of consciousness. In other words, every conscious experience has a feeling-tone, pleasant, painful or neutral, the latter being also a distinct quality in its own right. The subsequent emotional, practical, moral or spiritual values attached to any particular feeling are determined by the associated mental factors belonging to the aggregate of mental formations. It is the quality of those other mental functions that makes the co-nascent feeling either good or bad, noble or low, *kammic* or non-*kammic*, mundane or supramundane.

Since feeling, in its primary state, simply registers the impact of the object, in itself it is quite devoid of any emotional bias. Only when volitional evaluations are admitted will there appear emotions such as desire and love, aversion and hate, anxiety and fear, as well as distorting views. But these admixtures need not arise, as the emotions are not inseparable parts of the respective feelings. In fact, many of the weaker impressions we receive during the day stop at the mere registering of a very faint and brief feeling, without any further emotional reaction. This shows that it is psychologically possible to stop at the bare feeling and that this can be done intentionally with the help of mindfulness and self-restraint, even in cases when the stimulus to convert feelings into emotions is strong. Through actual experience it can thus be confirmed that the ever-revolving round of dependent origination can be stopped at the stage of feeling, and that there is no inherent necessity for feeling to be followed by craving. Here we encounter feeling as a key factor on the path of liberation and can see why, in the Buddhist tradition, the *contemplation of feeling* has always been highly regarded as an effective aid on the path.

The contemplation of feeling is one of the four foundations of mindfulness (*satipaṭṭhāna*). As such it may be undertaken in the framework of that meditative practice aiming at the growth of insight (*vipassanā*). It is, however, essential that this contemplation should also be remembered and applied in daily life whenever feelings are prone to turn into unwholesome emotions. Of course, one should not intentionally try to *produce* in oneself certain feelings just for the sake of practice; they should rather be taken up for mindful observation only when they naturally occur. There will be many such occasions, provided the mind is alert and calm enough to notice the feelings clearly at their primary stage.

In the contemplation of feelings, there should first be a mindful awareness of the feelings when they arise. One should clearly distinguish them as pleasant, unpleasant (painful) or neutral. There is no such thing as "mixed feelings."

Mindfulness should be maintained throughout the short duration of a specific feeling, down to its cessation. If the vanishing point of feelings is repeatedly seen with increasing clarity, it will become much easier to forestall the emotions, thoughts and volitions which normally follow them so rapidly and so often become habitually associated with them. Pleasant feeling is habitually linked with enjoyment and desire; unpleasant feeling with aversion; neutral feeling with boredom and confusion, and also serving as a background for wrong views. But when bare attention is directed towards the arising and vanishing of feelings, these polluting additives will be held at bay. If they do arise, they will be immediately recognized as soon as they appear, and that recognition may often be sufficient to stop them from growing stronger by unopposed continuance.

If feelings are seen blowing up and bursting like bubbles, their linkage with craving and aversion will be weakened more and more until it is finally broken. As attachments to likes and dislikes are reduced by this practice, an inner space will open up for the growth of the finer emotions and virtues: for loving kindness and compassion, for contentment, patience and forbearance.

In this contemplation it is of particular importance to dissociate the feelings from even the faintest thoughts of "I" and "mine." There should be no ego-reference to oneself as subject: "I feel (and, therefore, I am)." Nor should there be any thought of being the owner of the feelings: "I have pleasant feelings. How happy I am!" With the thought, "I want to have more of them," craving arises. Or when thinking, "I have pains. How unhappy I am!" and wishing to get rid of the pains, aversion arises.

Avoiding these wrong and unrealistic views, one should be aware of the feelings as a conditioned and transient process. Mindfulness should be kept alert, focused on the bare fact that there is just the mental function of such and such a feeling; and this awareness should serve no other purpose than that of knowledge and mindfulness, as stated in the Satipaṭṭhāna Sutta. As long as one habitually relates the feelings to a person who "has" them, and does so even during meditation, there cannot be any progress in contemplation.

To be aware of the feelings without any ego-reference will also help to distinguish them clearly from the physical stimuli arousing them, as well as from the subsequent mental reactions to them. Thereby the meditator will be able to keep his attention focused on the feelings alone, without straying into other areas. This is the purport of the phrase "he contemplates feelings in feelings" as stated in the Satipaṭṭhāna Sutta. At this stage of the practice, the meditator will become more familiar with the "insight-knowledge of discerning mentality and materiality" (*nāma-rūpa-paricchеda*).

Further progress, however, will require persistency in the mindful observation of the arising and passing away of every instant of feeling whenever it occurs. This will lead to a deepening experience of impermanence (*anicca*), one of the main gates to final liberation. When, in insight meditation, the vanishing moment of feelings becomes more strongly marked, the impermanent nature of the feelings will impress itself deeply on the meditator's mind. This experience, gained also from other mental and bodily processes, will gradually mature into the "insight-knowledge of dissolution" (*bhaṅga-ñāṇa*). On reaching this stage, the meditator will find himself well on the road to further progress.

It is within the practice of insight meditation that the contemplation of feelings can unfold its full strength as an efficient tool for breaking the chain of suffering at its weakest link. But considerable benefits can also be derived from this contemplation by those who, in their daily life, can only devote a little quiet reflection to their feelings and emotions. Even if they do this retrospectively, they will soon find that feelings and emotions are "separable." This reflective and retrospective contemplation will help them to a fuller awareness of feelings and emotions when they actually occur, and this again can save them from being carried away by the emotional cross-currents of elation and dejection. The mind will then gradually reach a higher level of firmness and equipoise, just by that simple procedure of examining and reviewing one's feelings and emotions.

This, however, should not, and need not, be made a constant practice. It should be taken up on suitable occasions for a limited period of time until one has become familiar with the mechanism of feelings followed by emotions. Such an understanding of the process will result in an increasing control over one's emotional reactions, a control gained in a natural, spontaneous way. One need not fear that focusing the mind on feelings and emotions in the manner described will lead to a cold aloofness or an emotional withdrawal. On the contrary, mind and heart will become more open to all those finer emotions like friendship, human sympathy and forbearance. It will not exclude warm human relationships, nor the enjoyment of beauty in art and nature. But it will remove from them the fever of clinging, so that these experiences will give a deeper satisfaction than is possible when the mind is overrun by tempestuous emotions.

A life lived in this way may well mature in the wish to use the contemplation of feelings for its highest purpose: mind's final liberation from suffering.

The Related Discourses on Feelings (Vedanā-Saṃyutta)

1. Concentration

There are, O monks, these three feelings: pleasant feelings, painful feelings, and neither-painful-nor-pleasant feelings.

A disciple of the Buddha, mindful,
clearly comprehending, with his mind collected,
he knows the feelings[1] and their origin,[2]
knows whereby they cease[3] and knows the path
that to the ending of feelings lead.[4]
And when the end of feelings he has reached,
such a monk, his thirsting quenched, attains Nibbāna.[5]

2. Happiness

There are, O monks, these three feelings: pleasant feelings, painful feelings, and neither-painful-nor-pleasant feelings.

Be it a pleasant feeling, be it painful, be it neutral,
one's own or others', feelings of all kinds[6]—
he knows them all as ill, deceitful, evanescent.
Seeing how they impinge again, again, and disappear,[7]
he wins detachment from the feelings, passion-free.

---

1. Comy: He knows the feelings by way of the Truth of Suffering.
2. Comy: He knows them by way of the Truth of the Origin of Suffering.
3. Comy: He knows, by way of the Truth of Cessation, that feelings cease in Nibbāna.
4. Comy: He knows the feelings by way of the Truth of the Path leading to the Cessation of Suffering.
5. *Parinibbuto,* "fully extinguished"; Comy: through the full extinction of the defilements (*kilesa-parinibbānāya*).
6. On "feelings of all kinds," see Text 22.
7. *Phussa phussa vayaṃ disvā.* The Comy explains differently, paraphrasing these words by *ñāṇena phusitvā phusitvā,* "repeatedly experiencing (them) by way of the knowledge (of rise and fall)." These verses occur also in Suttanipāta, verse 739, with one additional line.

3. Giving Up

In the case of pleasant feelings, O monks, the underlying tendency[8] to lust should be given up; in the case of painful feelings, the underlying tendency to resistance (aversion) should be given up; in the case of neither-painful-nor-pleasant feelings, the underlying tendency to ignorance should be given up.

If a monk has given up the tendency to lust in regard to pleasant feeling, the tendency to resistance in regard to painful feelings, and the tendency to ignorance in regard to neither-painful-nor-pleasant feelings, then he is called one who is free of (unwholesome) tendencies, one who has the right outlook. He has cut off craving, severed the fetters (to future existence), and through the full penetration of conceit,[9] he has made an end of suffering.

If one feels joy, but knows not feeling's nature,
bent towards greed, he will not find deliverance.
If one feels pain, but knows not feeling's nature,
bent toward hate, he will not find deliverance.

And even neutral feeling which as peaceful
the Lord of Wisdom has proclaimed,
if, in attachment, he should cling to it,
he will not be free from the round of ill.

But if a monk is ardent and does not neglect
to practise mindfulness and comprehension clear,
the nature of all feelings will he penetrate.

And having done so, in this very life
will be free from cankers, free from taints.
Mature in knowledge, firm in Dhamma's ways,
when once his life-span ends, his body breaks,
all measure and concept he has transcended.

---

8. *Anusaya.*

9. "Conceit" refers in particular to self-conceit (*asmi-māna*), i.e., personality belief, on both the intellectual and the emotional levels.

4. The Bottomless Pit

When, O monks, an untaught worldling says that in the great ocean there is a (bottomless) pit,[10] he speaks about something unreal and not factual.[11] The (bottomless) pit, O monks, is rather a name for painful bodily feelings. When an untaught worldling is afflicted by painful bodily feelings, he worries and grieves, he laments, beats his breast, weeps and is distraught. He is then said to be an untaught worldling who cannot withstand the bottomless pit and cannot gain a foothold in it. But when a well-taught noble disciple[12] is afflicted by painful bodily feelings, he will not worry nor grieve and lament, he will not beat his breast and weep, nor will he be distraught. He is then said to be a noble disciple who can withstand the bottomless pit and has gained a foothold in it.

> Who cannot bear the painful body-feelings that arise
> endangering his life, he trembles when afflicted.
> He wails and cries aloud, a weak and feeble man.
> He cannot stand against the pit,
> nor can a foothold he secure.
>
> But one who bears the painful body-feelings that arise,
> not trembling when his very life is threatened,
> he truly can withstand that pit
> and gain a foothold in its depth.

---

10. *Pātāla.*

11. Comy (paraphrased): According to popular belief, there is in the ocean a very deep abyss hollowed out by the force of the water, which is the abode of aquatic animals as well as dragon deities (*naga*), etc. Hence, for these beings, this abyss provides a basis for their existence, a comfortable abode. Therefore, to call it a bottomless pit is unrealistic and not factual, because it gives an inadequate and non-evident meaning to the word. It is rather bodily pain, inseparable from bodily existence, which deserves to be called a "bottomless pit" of suffering, being a part of unfathomable *saṃsāra*.

12. Comy: In this Discourse, by the words "noble disciple," it is, in the first place, a Stream-winner (*sotāpanna*) that is meant. But also a meditator with strong insight and keen intellect is capable of withstanding feelings that arise without being carried away by them. He, too, ought to be included here (because he penetrates the feelings to some extent; Sub-comy).

5. To Be Known

There are, O monks, these three feelings: pleasant, painful and neither-painful-nor-pleasant. Pleasant feelings should be known as painful, painful feelings should be known as a thorn, and neither-painful-nor-pleasant feelings should be known as impermanent. If a monk has known the feelings in such a way, it is said of him that he has the right outlook. He has cut off craving, severed the fetters (to existence) and, through the full penetration of conceit, he has made an end of suffering.

> Who sees the pain in happiness and views the painful feeling as a thorn,
> perceives the transience in neutral feeling which is peaceful—
> right outlook, truly, has such a monk who fully understands these feelings;
> And having penetrated them, he will be taint-free in this very life.
> Mature in knowledge, firm in Dhamma's ways,
> when once his life-span ends, his body breaks,
> all measure and concept he has transcended.

6. The Dart

An untaught worldling, O monks, experiences pleasant feelings, he experiences painful feelings and he experiences neutral feelings. A well-taught noble disciple likewise experiences pleasant, painful and neutral feelings. Now what is the distinction, the diversity, the difference that exists herein between a well-taught noble disciple and an untaught worldling?

When an untaught worldling is touched by a painful (bodily) feeling, he worries and grieves, he laments, beats his breast, weeps and is distraught. He thus experiences two kinds of feelings, a bodily and a mental feeling. It is as if a man were pierced by a dart and, following the first piercing, he is hit by a second dart. So that person will experience feelings caused by two darts. It is similar with an untaught worldling: when touched by a painful (bodily) feeling, he worries and grieves, he laments, beats his breast, weeps and is distraught. So he experiences two kinds of feeling: a bodily and a mental feeling.

Having been touched by that painful feeling, he resists (and resents) it. Then in him who so resists (and resents) that painful feeling, an underlying tendency of resistance against that painful feeling comes to underlie (his mind). Under the impact of that painful feeling he then proceeds to enjoy sensual happiness. And why does he do so? An untaught worldling, O monks, does not know of any other escape from painful feelings except the enjoyment of sensual happiness. Then in him who enjoys sensual happiness, an underlying tendency to lust for pleasant feelings comes to underlie (his mind). He does not know, according to facts, the arising and ending of these feelings, nor the gratification, the danger and the escape, connected with these feelings. In him who lacks that knowledge, an underlying tendency to ignorance as to neutral feelings comes to underlie (his mind). When he experiences a pleasant feeling, a painful feeling or a neutral feeling, he feels it as one fettered by it. Such a one, O monks, is called an untaught worldling who is fettered by birth, by old age, by death, by sorrow, lamentation, pain, grief and despair. He is fettered to suffering, this I declare.

But in the case of a well-taught noble disciple, O monks, when he is touched by a painful feeling, he will not worry nor grieve and lament, he will not beat his breast and weep, nor will he be distraught. It is one kind of feeling he experiences, a bodily one, but not a mental feeling. It is as if a man were pierced by a dart, but was not hit by a second dart following the first one. So this person experiences feelings caused by a single dart only. It is similar with a well-taught noble disciple: when touched by a painful feeling, he will not worry nor grieve and lament, he will not beat his breast and weep, nor will he be distraught. He experiences one single feeling, a bodily one.

Having been touched by that painful feeling, he does not resist (and resent) it. Hence, in him no underlying tendency of resistance against that painful feeling comes to underlie (his mind). Under the impact of that painful feeling he does not proceed to enjoy sensual happiness. And why not? As a well-taught noble disciple he knows of an escape from painful feelings other than by enjoying sensual happiness. Then in him who does not proceed to enjoy sensual happiness, no underlying tendency to lust for pleasant feelings comes to underlie (his mind). He knows, according to facts, the arising and ending of those feelings, and the gratification, the danger and the escape connected with these feelings. In him who knows thus, no underlying tendency to ignorance as to neutral feelings comes to underlie (his mind). When he experiences a pleasant feeling, a painful feeling or a neutral feeling, he feels it as one who is not fettered by it. Such a one, O monks, is called a well-taught noble disciple who is not fettered by birth, by old age, by death, by sorrow, lamentation, pain, grief and despair. He is not fettered to suffering, this I declare.

This, O monks, is the distinction, the diversity, the difference that exists between a well-taught noble disciple and an untaught worldling.

7. At the Sick Room—I

Once the Blessed One dwelt at Vesālī, in the Great Forest, at the Gabled House. In the evening, after the Blessed One had risen from his seclusion, he went to the sick room and sat down on a prepared seat. Being seated he addressed the monks as follows:

O monks, mindfully and clearly comprehending should a monk spend his time! This is my injunction to you!

And how, O monks, is a monk mindful? He dwells practising body-contemplation on the body, ardent, clearly comprehending and mindful, having overcome covetousness and grief concerning the world. He dwells practising feeling-contemplation on feelings, ardent, clearly comprehending and mindful, having overcome covetousness and grief concerning the world. He dwells practising mind-contemplation on the mind, ardent, clearly comprehending and mindful, having overcome covetousness and grief concerning the world. He dwells practising mind-object-contemplation on mind-objects, having overcome covetousness and grief concerning the world. So, monks, is a monk mindful.

And how, O monks, is a monk clearly comprehending? He applies clear comprehension in going forward and going back; in looking straight on and in looking elsewhere; in bending and in stretching (his limbs); in wearing the robes and carrying the almsbowl; in eating, drinking, chewing and savouring; in obeying the calls of nature; in walking, standing, sitting, falling asleep, waking, speaking and being silent—in all that he applies clear comprehension. So, monks, is a monk clearly comprehending.

If a monk is thus mindful and clearly comprehending, ardent, earnest and resolute, and a pleasant feeling arises in him, he knows: "Now a pleasant feeling has arisen in me. It is conditioned, not unconditioned. Conditioned by what? Even by this body it is conditioned.[13] And this body, indeed, is impermanent, compounded, dependently arisen. But if this pleasant feeling that has arisen is conditioned by the body which is impermanent, compounded and dependently arisen, how could such a pleasant feeling be permanent?"

In regard to both the body and the pleasant feeling he dwells contemplating impermanence, dwells contemplating evanescence, dwells contemplating detachment, dwells contemplating cessation, dwells contemplating relinquishment. And in him who thus dwells, the underlying tendency to lust in regard to body and pleasant feeling vanishes.

If a painful feeling arises in him, he knows: "Now a painful feeling has arisen in me. It is conditioned, not unconditioned. Conditioned by what? Even by this body it is conditioned. And this body, indeed, is impermanent, compounded, dependently arisen. But if this painful feeling that has arisen is conditioned by the body, which is impermanent, compounded and dependently arisen, how could such a painful feeling be permanent?"

In regard to both the body and the painful feeling he dwells contemplating impermanence, dwells contemplating evanescence, dwells contemplating detachment, dwells contemplating cessation, dwells contemplating relinquishment. And in him who thus dwells, the underlying tendency to resistance in regard to body and painful feeling vanishes.

If a neutral feeling arises in him, he knows: "Now a neutral feeling has arisen in me. It is conditioned, not unconditioned. Conditioned by what? Even by this body it is conditioned. And this body, indeed, is impermanent, compounded, dependently arisen. But if this neutral feeling that has arisen is conditioned by the body which is impermanent, compounded and dependently arisen, how could such a neutral feeling be permanent?"

---

13. The term *body* may be taken here as referring to the first five of the six bases of sense-impression (*phassāyatana*).

In regard to both the body and the neutral feeling he dwells contemplating impermanence, dwells contemplating evanescence, dwells contemplating detachment, dwells contemplating cessation, dwells contemplating relinquishment. And in him who thus dwells, the underlying tendency to ignorance in regard to body and neutral feeling vanishes.

If he experiences a pleasant feeling, he knows it as impermanent; he knows, it is not clung to; he knows, it is not relished. If he experiences a painful feeling... a neutral feeling, he knows it as impermanent; he knows, it is not clung to; he knows, it is not relished.

If he experiences a pleasant feeling, he feels it as one unfettered by it. If he experiences a painful feeling, he feels it as one unfettered by it. If he experiences a neutral feeling, he feels it as one unfettered by it.

When having painful feelings endangering the body, he knows: "I have a painful feeling endangering the body." When having painful feelings endangering life, he knows: "I have painful feelings endangering life." And he knows: "After the dissolution of the body, when life ends, all these feelings, which are unrelished, will come to (final) rest, even here."

It is like a lamp that burns by strength of oil and wick, and if oil and wick come to an end, the flame is extinguished through lack of nourishment. Similarly this monk knows: "After the dissolution of the body, when life ends, all these feelings which are unrelished will come to (final) rest, even here."

8. At the Sick Room—II[14]

Once the Blessed One dwelt at Vesālī, in the Great Forest, at the Gabled House. In the evening, after the Blessed One had arisen from his seclusion, he went to the sick room and sat down on a prepared seat. Being seated, he addressed the monks as follows:

O monks, mindfully and clearly comprehending should a monk spend his time! This is my injunction to you!

---

14. This *sutta* is identical to the preceding one except that here the feeling of pleasure, etc. (in paragraphs 5–10), is said to be dependent on *sense-impression* (contact: *phassa*) rather than on the *body*.

And how, O monks, is a monk mindful? He dwells practising body-contemplation on the body, ardent, clearly comprehending and mindful, having overcome covetousness and grief concerning the world. He dwells practising feeling-contemplation on feelings, ardent, clearly comprehending and mindful, having overcome covetousness and grief concerning the world. He dwells practising mind-contemplation on the mind, ardent, clearly comprehending and mindful, having overcome covetousness and grief concerning the world. He dwells practising mind-object-contemplation on mind-objects, having overcome covetousness and grief concerning the world. So, monks, is a monk mindful.

And how, O monks, is a monk clearly comprehending? He applies clear comprehension in going forward and going back; in looking straight on and in looking elsewhere; in bending and in stretching (his limbs); in wearing the robes and carrying the almsbowl; in eating, drinking, chewing and savouring; in obeying the calls of nature; in walking, standing, sitting, falling asleep, waking, speaking and being silent—in all that he applies clear comprehension. So, monks, is a monk clearly comprehending.

If a monk is thus mindful and clearly comprehending, ardent, earnest and resolute, and a pleasant feeling arises in him, he knows: "Now a pleasant feeling has arisen in me. It is conditioned, not unconditioned. Conditioned by what? Even by this *sense-impression*[15] it is conditioned. And this *sense-impression*, indeed, is impermanent, compounded, dependently arisen. But if this pleasant feeling that has arisen is conditioned by a *sense-impression* which is impermanent, compounded, and dependently arisen, how could such a pleasant feeling be permanent?"

In regard to both *sense-impression* and the pleasant feeling, he dwells contemplating impermanence, dwells contemplating evanescence, dwells contemplating detachment, dwells contemplating cessation, dwells contemplating relinquishment. And in him who thus dwells, the underlying tendency to lust in regard to *sense-impressions* and pleasant feeling vanishes.

If a painful feeling arises in him, he knows: "Now a painful feeling has arisen in me. It is conditioned, not unconditioned.

15. *Sense-impression*, or contact (*phassa*), is a mental factor and does not signify physical impingement.

Conditioned by what? Even by this *sense-impression* it is conditioned. And this *sense-impression*, indeed, is impermanent, compounded, dependently arisen. But if this painful feeling that has arisen is conditioned by a *sense-impression* which is impermanent, compounded and dependently arisen, how could such a painful feeling be permanent?"

In regard to both *sense-impression* and painful feeling, he dwells contemplating impermanence, dwells contemplating evanescence, dwells contemplating detachment, dwells contemplating cessation, dwells contemplating relinquishment. And in him who thus dwells, the underlying tendency to resistance in regard to *sense-impression* and painful feeling vanishes.

If a neutral feeling arises in him, he knows: "Now a neutral feeling has arisen in me. It is conditioned, not unconditioned. Conditioned by what? Even by this *sense-impression* it is conditioned. And this *sense-impression*, indeed, is impermanent, compounded, dependently arisen. But if this neutral feeling that has arisen is conditioned by a *sense-impression*, which is impermanent, compounded and dependently arisen, how could such a neutral feeling be permanent?"

In regard to both *sense-impression* and neutral feeling, he dwells contemplating impermanence, dwells contemplating evanescence, dwells contemplating detachment, dwells contemplating cessation, dwells contemplating relinquishment. And in him who thus dwells, the underlying tendency to ignorance in regard to *sense-impression* and neutral feeling vanishes."

If he experiences a pleasant feeling, he knows it as impermanent; he knows it is not clung to; he knows it is not relished. If he experiences a painful feeling... a neutral feeling, he knows it as impermanent; he knows it is not clung to; he knows it is not relished.

If he experiences a pleasant feeling, he feels it as one unfettered by it. If he experiences a painful feeling, he feels it as one unfettered by it. If he experiences a neutral feeling, he feels it as one unfettered by it.

When having painful feelings endangering the body, he knows: "I have a painful feeling endangering the body." When having painful feelings endangering life, he knows: "I have painful feelings endangering life." And he knows: "After the dissolution of the body, when life ends, all these feelings which are unrelished will come to (final) rest, even here."

It is like a lamp that burns by strength of oil and wick, and if oil and wick come to an end, the flame is extinguished through lack of nourishment. Similarly this monk knows: "After the dissolution of the body, when life ends, all these feelings which are unrelished will come to (final) rest, even here."

9. Impermanent

The three kinds of feelings, O monks, are impermanent, compounded, dependently arisen, liable to destruction, to evanescence, to fading away, to cessation—namely, pleasant feelings, painful feelings and neutral feelings.

10. Rooted in Sense-Impression

There are, O monks, these three feelings, rooted in sense-impression, caused by sense-impression, conditioned by sense-impression: pleasant, painful and neutral feelings.

Dependent on a sense-impression that is liable to be felt as pleasurable, there arises a pleasant feeling. When that very sense-impression liable to be felt as pleasurable has ceased, then the sensation born from it[16]—namely the pleasant feeling that arose dependent on that sense-impression—also ceases and is stilled.

Dependent on a sense-impression that is liable to be felt as painful (neutral), there arises a painful (neutral) feeling. When that very sense-impression liable to be felt as painful (neutral) has ceased, then the sensation born from it—namely the painful (neutral) feeling that arose dependent on that sense-impression—also ceases and is stilled.

Just as from the coming together and rubbing of two sticks of wood heat results and fire is produced, and by the separation and disconnection of the sticks, the heat produced by them ceases and disappears, so it is also with these three feelings which are born of sense-impression, rooted in sense-impression, caused by sense-impression, dependent on sense-impression: dependent on a sense-impression of a certain kind there arises a

16. *Tajjaṃ vedayitaṃ.*

corresponding feeling; by the cessation of that sense-impression the corresponding feeling ceases.

11. Secluded

Once a certain monk came to see the Blessed One and, after saluting him respectfully, sat down at one side. Seated thus, he spoke to the Blessed One as follows:

"When I went into seclusion, while I was in solitude, this thought occurred to me: 'Three feelings have been taught by the Blessed One: pleasant, painful and neutral feelings. But the Blessed One has also said that whatever is felt is within suffering.' Now, with reference to what was it stated by the Blessed One that whatever is felt is within suffering?"

"Well spoken, monk, well spoken. While three feelings have been taught by me, the pleasant, the painful and the neutral, yet I have also said that whatever is felt is within suffering. This, however, was stated by me with reference to the impermanence of (all) conditioned phenomena (*saṅkhāra*). I have said it because conditioned phenomena are liable to destruction, to evanescence, to fading away, to cessation and to change. It is with reference to this that I have stated: 'Whatever is felt is within suffering.'

"I have further taught, monk, the gradual cessation of conditioned phenomena. In him who has attained the first meditative absorption (*jhāna*), speech has ceased. Having attained the second absorption, thought-conception and discursive thinking have ceased. Having attained the third absorption, joy has ceased. Having attained the fourth absorption, inhalation and exhalation have ceased. Having attained the sphere of the infinity of space, perception of form (matter) has ceased. Having attained the sphere of the infinity of consciousness, the perception of the sphere of the infinity of space has ceased. Having attained the sphere of no-thingness, the perception of the sphere of infinity of consciousness has ceased. Having attained the sphere of neither-perception-nor-non-perception, the perception of the sphere of no-thingness has ceased. Having attained the cessation of perception and feeling, perception and feeling have ceased. In a taint-free monk greed has ceased, hatred has ceased, delusion has ceased.

"I have further taught, monk, the gradual stilling of conditioned phenomena (*saṅkhāra*). In him who has attained the first meditative absorption, speech has been stilled. Having attained the second absorption, thought-conception and discursive thinking have been stilled... (*continued as above, up to*:) Having attained the cessation of perception and feeling, perception and feeling have been stilled. In a taint-free monk greed has been stilled, hatred has been stilled, delusion has been stilled.

"There are, monk, these six quietenings. In him who has attained the first absorption, speech is quietened. Having attained the second absorption, thought-conception and discursive thinking are quietened. Having attained the third absorption, rapture is quietened. Having attained the fourth absorption, inhalation and exhalation are quietened.[17] Having attained the cessation of perception and feeling, perception and feeling are quietened. In a taint-free monk greed is quietened, hatred is quietened, delusion is quietened."

12. In the Sky—I

In the sky, O monks, various kinds of winds are blowing: winds from the east, west, north and south, winds carrying dust and winds without dust, winds hot and cold, gentle and fierce. Similarly, monks, there arise in this body various kinds of feelings: pleasant feelings arise, painful feelings arise and neutral feelings arise.

> Just as in the sky above winds of various kinds are blowing:
> Coming from the east or west, blowing from the north or south,
> some carry dust and others not, cold are some and others hot,
> some are fierce and others mild—their blowing is so different.
> So also in this body here, feelings of different kinds arise:
> The pleasant feelings and the painful and the neutral ones.
>
> But if a monk is ardent and does not neglect
> to practise mindfulness and comprehension clear,

17. In the section on "being quietened" (*paṭippassaddha*), the four immaterial absorptions (*arūpajjhāna*) are not mentioned. According to Comy they are implied in the "cessation of perception and feelings" (for the attainment of which they are a condition).

the nature of all feelings will he understand,
and having penetrated them,
he will be taint-free in this very life.
Mature in knowledge, firm in Dhamma's ways,
when once his life-span ends, his body breaks,
all measure and concept he has transcended.

13. In the Sky—II

(This text repeats the prose section of No. 12, without the verses.)

14. The Guest House

In a guest house, O monks, people from the east may take lodgings, or people from the west, north or south. People from the warrior caste may come and take lodgings there, and also Brahmins, middle-class people and menials.

Similarly, O monks, there arise in this body various kinds of feelings; there arise pleasant feelings, painful feelings and neutral feelings; worldly feelings that are pleasant, painful or neutral, and unworldly (spiritual) feelings that are pleasant, painful or neutral.

15. Ānanda—I

Once the Venerable Ānanda went to see the Blessed One. Having saluted him respectfully, he sat down at one side. Thus seated, he said:

"What are the feelings, O Lord? What is the origin of feelings, what is their cessation and the way leading to their cessation? What is the gratification in feelings? What is the danger in feelings? And what is the escape from them?"

"There are, Ānanda, three kinds of feelings: pleasant, painful and neutral. Through the origin of sense-impression there is origin of feelings; through the cessation of sense-impression there is cessation of feelings. It is the noble eightfold path that is the way leading to the cessation of feelings, namely: right understanding, right thought, right speech, right action, right livelihood, right effort, right mindfulness and right concentration.

"It is the happiness and gladness arising dependent on feelings that is the gratification in feelings. Feelings are impermanent, (liable to bring) pain and are subject to change; this is the danger in feelings. The removal and the giving up of the desire and lust for feelings is the escape from feelings.

"I have further taught, Ānanda, the gradual cessation of conditioned phenomena (*saṅkhāra*). In him who has attained the first meditative absorption, speech has been stilled. Having attained the second absorption, thought-conception and discursive thinking have ceased. Having attained the third absorption, joy has ceased. Having attained the fourth absorption, inhalation and exhalation have ceased. Having attained the sphere of the infinity of space, perception of form (matter) has ceased. Having attained the sphere of the infinity of consciousness, the perception of the sphere of the infinity of space has ceased. Having attained the sphere of no-thingness, the perception of the sphere of infinity of consciousness has ceased. Having attained the sphere of neither-perception-nor-non-perception, the perception of the sphere of no-thingness has ceased. Having attained the cessation of perception and feeling, perception and feeling have ceased. In a taint-free monk greed, hatred, and delusion are quietened."

16. Ānanda—II

(In this discourse, the Buddha himself puts to Ānanda the same questions as in Text 15, and being requested by Ānanda to give the explanation himself, the Buddha answers in the same way as in Text 15.)

17–18. Many Monks

(Here, again, the same questions and answers are repeated, in the case of "many monks." The introductory parts correspond to those in Texts 15 and 16.)

19. Carpenter Fivetools (Pañcakaṅga)[18]

Once Carpenter Fivetools went to see the Venerable Udāyi. Having saluted him respectfully, he sat down at one side. Thus seated, he asked the Venerable Udāyi:

"How many kinds of feelings, Reverend Udāyi were taught by the Blessed One?"

18. This text is identical with MN 59 (Bahuvedanīya Sutta).

"Three kinds of feelings, Carpenter, were taught by the Blessed One: pleasant, painful and neutral feelings. These are the three feelings taught by the Blessed One."

After these words, Carpenter Fivetools said: "Not three kinds of feelings, Reverend Udāyi were taught by the Blessed One. It is two kinds of feelings that were stated by the Blessed One: pleasant and painful feelings. The neutral feeling was said by the Blessed One to belong to peaceful and sublime happiness."

But the Venerable Udāyi replied: "It is not two feelings that were taught by the Blessed One, but three: pleasant, painful and neutral feelings."

(This exchange of views was repeated for a second and a third time), but neither was Carpenter Fivetools able to convince the Venerable Udāyi nor could the Venerable Udāyi convince Carpenter Fivetools. It so happened that Venerable Ānanda had listened to that conversation and went to see the Blessed One about it. Having saluted the Blessed One respectfully, he sat down at one side. Thus seated, he repeated the entire conversation that had taken place between the Venerable Udāyi and Carpenter Fivetools.

The Blessed One said: "Ānanda, Udāyi's way of presentation, with which Carpenter Fivetools disagreed, was correct, indeed. But also Carpenter Fivetool's way of presentation, with which Udāyi disagreed, was correct. In one way of presentation I have spoken of two kinds of feelings, and in other ways of presentation I have spoken of three, of six, of eighteen, of thirty-six, and of one hundred and eight kinds of feelings.[19] So the Dhamma has been shown by me in different ways of presentation.

"Regarding the Dhamma thus shown by me in different ways, if there are those who do not agree with, do not consent to and do not accept what is rightly said and rightly spoken, it may be expected of them that they will quarrel, and get into arguments and disputes, hurting each other with sharp words.

"Regarding the Dhamma thus shown by me in different ways, if there are those who agree with, consent to and accept what is rightly said and rightly spoken, it may be expected of them that they will live in concord and amity, without dispute, like milk (that easily mixes) with water, looking at each other with friendly eyes.

19. See Text 22.

"There are five strands of sense desire. What are these five? Forms cognizable by the eye that are wished for, desirable, agreeable and endearing, bound up with sensual desire and tempting to lust. Sounds cognizable by the ear... odours cognizable by the nose... flavours cognizable by the tongue... tangibles cognizable by the body, that are wished for, desirable, agreeable and endearing, bound up with sense desire and tempting to lust. These are the five strands of sense desire. The pleasure and joy arising dependent on these five strands of sense desire, that is called sensual pleasure.

"Now, if someone were to say: 'This is the highest pleasure and joy that can be experienced,' I would not concede that. And why not? Because there is another kind of pleasure which surpasses that pleasure and is more sublime. And what is this pleasure? Here, quite secluded from sensual desires, secluded from unwholesome states of mind, a monk enters upon and abides in the first meditative absorption (*jhāna*), which is accompanied by thought conception and discursive thinking and has in it joy and pleasure born of seclusion. This is the other kind of pleasure which surpasses that (sense) pleasure and is more sublime.

"If someone were to say: 'This is the highest pleasure that can be experienced,' I would not concede that. And why not? Because there is another kind of pleasure which surpasses that pleasure and is more sublime. And what is this pleasure? Here, with the stilling of thought conception and discursive thinking... a monk enters upon and abides in the second meditative absorption... the third... the fourth meditative absorption... in the sphere of the infinity of space... of the infinity of consciousness... of no-thingness... of neither-perception-nor-non-perception.

"If someone were to say: 'This is the highest pleasure that can be experienced,' I would not concede that. And why not? Because there is another kind of pleasure which surpasses that pleasure and is more sublime. And what is this pleasure? Here, by completely surmounting the sphere of neither-perception-nor-non-perception, a monk enters upon and abides in the cessation of perception and feeling. This is the other kind of pleasure which surpasses that pleasure and is more sublime.[20]

---

20. Comy: "From the fourth *jhāna* onwards, it is the neither-painful-nor-pleasant feeling (that is present in these meditative states). But this neutral

"It may happen, Ānanda, that Wanderers of other sects will be saying this: 'The recluse Gotama speaks of the Cessation of Perception and Feeling and describes it as pleasure. What is this (pleasure) and how is this (a pleasure)?'

"Those who say so, should be told: 'The Blessed One describes as pleasure not only the feeling of pleasure. But a Tathāgata describes as pleasure whenever and whereinsoever it is obtained.'"

20. Bhikkhus

(This discourse, addressed to Bhikkhus, repeats the main part of Text 19, without its introductory section.)

21. Sīvaka

Once the Blessed One dwelled at Rājagaha in the Bamboo-Grove Monastery, at the Squirrels' Feeding Place. There a wandering ascetic, Moḷiya Sīvaka by name, called on the Blessed One and, after an exchange of courteous and friendly words, sat down at one side. Thus seated, he said:

"There are, revered Gotama, some ascetics and brahmins who have this doctrine and view: 'Whatever a person experiences, be it pleasure, pain or neither-pain-nor-pleasure, all that is caused by previous action.' Now, what does the revered Gotama say about this?"

---

feeling, too, is called 'pleasure' (*sukha*), on account of its being peaceful and sublime. What arises by way of the five cords of sensual desire and by way of the eight meditative attainments is called 'pleasure as being felt' (*vedayita-sukha*). The state of Cessation of Perception and Feeling is a 'pleasure, not being felt' (*avedayita-sukha*). Hence, whether it be pleasure felt or not felt, both are assuredly 'pleasure,' in the sense of their being pain-free states (*niddukkhabhāva-saṅkhātena sukhena*)."

In AN 9:34, the Venerable Sāriputta exclaims: "Nibbāna is happiness, friend; Nibbāna is happiness, indeed!" The monk Udāyi then asked: "How can there be happiness when there is no feeling?" The Venerable Sāriputta replied: "Just this is happiness, friend, that therein there is no feeling." The continuation of that Sutta may also be compared with our text. On Nibbāna as happiness, see also AN 6:100.

"Produced by (disorders of the) bile, there arise, Sīvaka, certain kinds of feelings. That this happens, can be known by oneself; also in the world it is accepted as true. Produced by (disorders of) phlegm... of wind... of (the three) combined... by change of climate... by adverse behaviour... by injuries... by the results of Kamma—(through all that), Sīvaka, there arise certain kinds of feelings. That this happens can be known by oneself; also in the world it is accepted as true.

"Now when these ascetics and brahmins have such a doctrine and view that 'whatever a person experiences, be it pleasure, pain or neither-pain-nor-pleasure, all that is caused by previous action,' then they go beyond what they know by themselves and what is accepted as true in the world. Therefore, I say that this is wrong on the part of these ascetics and brahmins."

When this was spoken, Moḷiya Sīvaka, the wandering ascetic, said: "It is excellent, revered Gotama, it is excellent indeed!... May the revered Gotama regard me as a lay follower who, from today, has taken refuge in him as long as life lasts."

22. Hundred and Eight Feelings

I shall show you, O monks, a way of Dhamma presentation by which there are one hundred and eight (feelings). Hence listen to me.

In one way, O monks, I have spoken of two kinds of feelings, and in other ways of three, five, six, eighteen, thirty-six and one hundred and eight feelings.

What are the two feelings? Bodily and mental feelings.

What are the three feelings? Pleasant, painful and neither-painful-nor-pleasant feelings.

What are the five feelings? The faculties of pleasure, pain, gladness, sadness and equanimity.

What are the six feelings? The feelings born of sense-impression through eye, ear, nose, tongue, body and mind.

What are the eighteen feelings? There are the (above) six feelings by which there is an approach (to the objects) in gladness; and there are six approaches in sadness and there are six in equanimity.

What are the thirty-six feelings? There are six feelings of gladness based on the household life and six based on renunciation;

six feelings of sadness based on the household life and six based on renunciation; six feelings of equanimity based on household life and six based on renunciation.

What are the hundred and eight feelings? There are the (above) thirty-six feelings of the past; there are thirty-six of the future and there are thirty-six of the present.

These, O monks, are called the hundred and eight feelings; and this is the way of the Dhamma presentation by which there are one hundred and eight feelings.

Texts 23–29

(Repeat paragraphs 3 and 4 of Text 15; only the interlocutors differ.)

Text 30

(Contains only an enumeration of the three kinds of feeling.)

31. Cessation

There is, O monks, worldly joy (*pīti*), there is unworldly joy and there is a still greater unworldly joy. There is worldly happiness (*sukha*), there is unworldly happiness and there is a still greater unworldly happiness. There is worldly equanimity, there is unworldly equanimity and there is a still greater unworldly equanimity. There is worldly freedom, there is unworldly freedom and there is a still greater unworldly freedom.

Now, O monks, what is worldly joy? There are these five cords of sense desire: forms cognizable by the eye that are wished for and desired, agreeable and endearing, associated with sense-desire and tempting to lust. Sounds cognizable by the ear... odours cognizable by the nose... flavours cognizable by the tongue... tangibles cognizable by the body, wished for and desired, agreeable and endearing, associated with sense-desire and tempting to lust. It is the joy that arises dependent on these five cords of sense-desire which is called "worldly joy."

Now, what is unworldly joy? Quite secluded from sense-desires, secluded from unwholesome states of mind, a monk enters upon and abides in the *first meditative absorption* (*jhāna*), which is accompanied by thought-conception and discursive thinking, and has joy and happiness born of seclusion. With the stilling of thought-conception and discursive thinking, he enters upon and abides in the *second meditative absorption,* which has internal confidence and singleness of mind without thought-conception and discursive thinking, and has joy and happiness born of concentration. This is called "unworldly joy."

And what is the still greater unworldly joy? When a taint-free monk looks upon his mind that is freed of greed, freed of hatred, freed of delusion, then there arises joy. This is called a "still greater unworldly joy."

Now, O monks, what is worldly happiness? There are these five cords of sense-desire: forms cognizable by the eye... sounds cognizable by the ear... odours cognizable by the nose... flavours cognizable by the tongue... tangibles cognizable by the body that are wished for and desired, agreeable and endearing, associated with sense-desire and alluring. It is the happiness and gladness that arises dependent on these five cords of sense-desire which are called "worldly happiness."

Now, what is unworldly happiness? Quite secluded from sense desires, secluded from unwholesome states of mind, a monk enters upon and abides in the *first meditative absorption*... With the stilling of thought-conception and discursive thinking, he enters upon and abides in the *second meditative absorption*... With the fading away of joy as well, he dwells in equanimity, mindfully and fully aware he feels happiness within, and enters upon and abides in the *third meditative absorption* of which the Noble Ones announce: "He dwells in happiness who has equanimity and is mindful." This is called "unworldly happiness."

And what is the still greater unworldly happiness? When a taint-free monk looks upon his mind that is freed of greed, freed of hatred, freed of delusion, then there arises happiness. This is called a "still greater unworldly happiness."

Now, O monks, what is worldly equanimity? There are these five cords of sensual desire: forms cognizable by the eye... tangibles cognizable by the body that are wished for and desired, agreeable and endearing, associated with sense-desire and alluring. It is the equanimity that arises with regard to these five cords of sense-desire which is called "worldly equanimity."

Now, what is unworldly equanimity? With the abandoning of pleasure and pain, and with the previous disappearance of gladness and sadness, a monk enters upon and abides in the *fourth meditative absorption,* which has neither pain-nor-pleasure and has purity of mindfulness due to equanimity. This is called "unworldly equanimity."

And what is the still greater unworldly equanimity? When a taint-free monk looks upon his mind that is freed of greed, freed of hatred and freed of delusion, then there arises equanimity. This is called a "still greater unworldly equanimity."

Now, O monks, what is worldly freedom? The freedom connected with the material. What is unworldly freedom? The freedom connected with the immaterial. And what is the still greater unworldly freedom? When a taint-free monk looks upon his mind that is freed of greed, freed of hatred and freed of delusion, then there arises freedom.

Miscellaneous Texts

For Use in the Contemplation of Feelings

Feelings are like bubbles.

SN 22:95

All things converge on feelings.

AN 9:14

All feeling—whether it is of the past, the future or the present, whether in oneself or in others, whether coarse or sublime, inferior or superior, far or near—should be seen with right understanding as it actually is: "This is not mine, this I am not, this is not a self of mine."

SN 22:59

Pleasant feeling is pleasant when present; it is painful when changing.

Painful feeling is painful when present; it is pleasant when changing.

Neither-painful-nor-pleasant feeling is pleasant if one understands it; it is painful if there is no understanding.

MN 44

A well-taught noble disciple... does not consider feeling as the self nor the self as the owner of the feeling, nor feeling as included within the self, nor the self as included within the feeling.

Of such a well-taught noble disciple it can be said that he is unfettered by the bondage of feeling, unfettered by bondages inner or outer. He has seen the coast, he has seen the Other Shore, and he is fully freed from suffering—this I say.

SN 22:117

> It was said that one should know the feelings, their conditioned origin, their diversity, their outcome, their cessation and the way to their cessation. Why was this said?

What are the feelings? These three: pleasant, painful and neither-painful-nor-pleasant.

What is the conditioned origin of these feelings? Sense-impression is the conditioned origin of the feelings.

What is the diversity in feelings? There are pleasant feelings, worldly and unworldly; there are painful feelings, worldly and unworldly; and there are neutral feelings, worldly and unworldly.

What is the outcome of feelings? It is the personalized existence (*attabhāva*) born of this or that (feeling), be it of a meritorious or demeritorious character, which one who feels causes to arise.

What is the cessation of feelings? It is the cessation of sense-impression that is the cessation of feelings.

And it is the Noble Eightfold Path that is the way leading to the cessation of feelings, namely: right understanding, right thought, right speech, right action, right livelihood, right effort, right mindfulness and right concentration.

If a noble disciple knows in such way the feelings, their conditioned origin, their diversity, their outcome, their cessation and the way to their cessation, he will be one who knows this penetrative Holy Life, namely the cessation of feelings.

AN 6:63

> The Four Noble Truths are the Dhamma taught by me, which is unrefuted, untarnished, irreproachable and uncensored by intelligent ascetics and Brahmins. What is that Dhamma?

Based on the six elements[21] there is descent into the womb. When such descent into the womb takes place, there will be mind-and-body (*nāma-rūpa*). Mind-and-body conditions the sixfold sense-base. The sixfold sense-base conditions sense-impression. Sense-impression conditions feeling. Now, it is for one who feels[22]

---

21. These are the elements of earth, water, fire, wind, space and consciousness. See MN 140.

22. The commentary applies this to one who *understands* feeling and quotes

that I make known, "This is suffering," "This is the origin of suffering," "This is the cessation of suffering," "This is the way leading to the cessation of suffering."

AN 3:61

> "Sisters, suppose there is a lamp burning: its oil, its wick, its flame, its radiance, all are impermanent and liable to change. Now, would anyone speak correctly when saying: 'When this lamp is burning, its oil, wick and flame are impermanent and liable to change, but its radiance is permanent, everlasting, eternal, and not liable to change?'"—"Certainly not, venerable sir."—"Why not?"—"Because, venerable sir, when that lamp burns, its oil is impermanent and liable to change, and so are the wick, the flame and the radiance."

"In the same way, sisters, would anyone speak correctly when saying: 'These six (organ) bases in oneself are impermanent, but what, dependent on them, I feel as pleasant or painful or neither-painful-nor-pleasant, that is permanent, everlasting, eternal and not liable to change?'"—"Certainly not, venerable sir."—"Why not?"—"Because, venerable sir, each kind of feeling arises dependent on its appropriate condition, and with the cessation of the appropriate condition the corresponding feeling ceases."

"Well said, sisters, well said! When a noble disciple perceives this, he sees it with right understanding, as it actually is."

MN 146

> Pleasant feeling is impermanent, conditioned, dependently arisen, having the nature of wasting, vanishing, fading and ceasing. The painful feeling and the neutral feeling, too, are impermanent, conditioned, dependently arisen, having the nature of wasting, vanishing, fading and ceasing.

When a well-taught disciple perceives this, he becomes dispassionate towards pleasant feelings, dispassionate towards painful feelings and dispassionate towards neutral feelings. Being

---

the beginning of the Contemplation of Feeling from the Satipaṭṭhāna Sutta. Alternatively, "One who feels" may also refer to all beings who feel suffering and seek a release from it.

dispassionate, his lust fades away, and with the fading away of lust, he is liberated. When liberated, there comes to him the knowledge that he is liberated. He now knows: "Birth is exhausted, the Holy Life has been lived, done is what was to be done, there is no more of this to come."

A monk whose mind is thus liberated, concurs with none and disputes with none; he employs the speech commonly used in the world, but without misapprehending it.

MN 74

* * *

Aphorisms from the Exegetical Literature

To know, as it actually is, the origin (cessation, and the way to cessation) of feeling, etc., leads to liberation without clinging, because it partakes of the path.

The lack of full penetration of the origin, etc., of feeling leads to imprisonment in the jail house of *saṃsāra*, because (such ignorance) is a condition for the *kamma*-formations (*saṅkhāra*).

Delusion, which hides the true nature of feelings, leads to enjoyment of feelings.

But an understanding of feeling as it actually is leads to the penetration of feeling and to dispassion regarding it.

By not understanding the danger and misery (*ādīnava*) in feelings, the craving for feelings will grow; and this happens because one only considers what is enjoyable in feelings (*assāda*).

When there is lust for what is felt, one will be wriggling in the grip of the notions of self and self's property, and in the grip of the notions of eternalism, and so on. This is due to the proximity of the cause for it, since clinging (to ego-belief and views) is conditioned by craving.

For those who proclaim doctrines of eternalism, etc., or feel emotions corresponding (to them), sense-impression is the cause (*hetu*). This applies because (having such ideas or emotions) cannot occur without the meeting of sense-organ, object, and consciousness (which constitute sense-impression).

Sub-Commentary to Brahmajāla Sutta
DN 1

The Paccekabuddha: A Buddhist Ascetic

A Study of the Concept of the Paccekabuddha in Pāli Canonical and Commentarial Literature

by

Ria Kloppenborg

WHEEL PUBLICATION NO. 305/306/307

Preface

The Paccekabuddha is an important figure in the Buddhist tradition who exemplifies the ascetic and introspective tendencies of the Buddhist and pre-Buddhist Indian heritage. Most of the textual references—canonical as well as commentarial—concerned with the Paccekabuddha relate the popular stories which describe the individual Paccekabodhisatta's search for enlightenment, rather than elaborate on the doctrinal aspects of the phenomenon of the solitary enlightened one.

Therefore a systematic study of the place of the Paccekabuddha in Buddhist thought is stimulated less by the texts than by an attempt to uncover and convey the special reality of the individual's choice for his own way towards liberation.

For me, this study has again emphasized the importance of the ancient ascetic, individualistic and world-rejecting tradition.

I wish to express my deep gratitude to the Venerable Nyanaponika Mahāthera for his critical remarks and his friendly, unobtrusive guidance. I am indebted to Mrs. Helen Wilder's efforts to select the passages from my original book as published by E. J. Brill, Leiden, in 1974, for this version in the *Wheel Series*, and to the publishers for their kind permission to revise and reprint the original work.

Ria Kloppenborg
Utrecht, June 1982

Introduction

The Paccekabuddha has received little detailed attention in the study of Buddhism. The most elaborate contributions are to be found in dictionaries and encyclopaedias. There an attempt has been made to establish his position among other enlightened individuals, as can be found in the systematic approaches of the *Abhidhamma* and commentarial texts, and to enumerate his basic characteristics. In this respect a short reference may be made to the articles in the Pali Text Society's *Pāli-English Dictionary* where he is described as "one enlightened by himself, i.e. one who has attained to the supreme and perfect insight, but dies without proclaiming the truth to the world." In Childers[1] he is thus described: "one who has attained, like a Buddha, by his unaided powers the knowledge necessary to Nirvāna, but does not preach it to men ... is not omniscient ... in all respects inferior to a Sammāsambuddho"; and Edgerton: "a Buddha for himself alone, who has won enlightenment but lives in solitude and does not reveal his knowledge to the world" (*Buddhist Hybrid Sanskrit Dictionary*).

To find an adequate English equivalent for the term *Paccekabuddha* (Sanskrit: *Pratyekabuddha*) is almost impossible, for, as is the case with many technical terms used in Buddhist texts, the word has various connotations and bears different shades of meaning. It has the meaning of: "one who is enlightened by himself, or for himself," and also as "an enlightened one who is on his own."

The term encompasses the basic characteristics of the type of person set forth in the explanations given in the canonical and commentarial literature, such as the fact of his solitary way towards enlightenment and his solitary way of life. One may be justified in saying that the rendering "an enlightened one who is on his own" accentuates the most typical characteristic. This fact is stressed over and over again in the literature, in narrative as well as in more systematic passages, especially when he is compared with a *Sammāsambuddha* and an *arahant*. For "one

1. R. C. Childers, *A Dictionary of the Pāli Language*, London, 1876.

who is enlightened by himself" can refer to a Paccekabuddha as well as to a *Sammāsambuddha*.

The Paccekabuddha is rarely dealt with in the secondary literature. Most studies mention him as a possible type of enlightened personality recognised in the Canon, but go no further into the matter. The reason for this seems to lie in his lack of a sense of mission. As Eliot observes in his *Hinduism and Buddhism*[2]: "Their knowledge is confined to what is necessary for their own salvation and perfection. They are mentioned in the *Nikāyas* as worthy of all respect, but are not prominent in either the earlier or later works, which is only natural, seeing that by their very definition they are self-centred and of little importance for mankind. The idea of a (Paccekabuddha) ... is interesting, inasmuch as it implies that even when the four truths are not preached they still exist and can be discovered by anyone who makes the necessary mental and moral effort."

The present work aims at filling in this gap with a detailed study of the concept of the Paccekabuddha. This study has been limited to the *Theravāda* tradition and is mainly based upon the works incorporated in the Pāli Canon and the main commentaries.

The *Vinayapiṭaka* gives no direct information on the subject, as its function is to provide rules of conduct for the monastic community. But since it also illuminates aspects of the organization of the ascetic's life and of ascetic communities, it can also shed some light on the way of life of the Paccekabuddha as this has been described in other scriptures.

The *Suttapiṭaka*, especially the *Khuddakanikāya* with its varied collection of works, contains many references to the concept of the Paccekabuddha. Among these, the forty-one verses of the *Khaggavisāṇasutta* of the *Suttanipāta* are of major importance, as they are regarded as belonging to the most ancient ascetic tradition and the later development of a systematic classification of the different enlightened persons. The term Paccekabuddha itself is not used in the verses, perhaps because at the time the verses were composed the concept of the Paccekabuddha in its technical sense had not yet been developed within the Buddhist

2. Sir C. Eliot, *Hinduism and Buddhism,* 3 Volumes, London, 1922, I 344–45.

system of thought. But the idea of a solitary ascetic seems clearly to be implied. The same observation can be made about other texts regarded as part of the older layer of Buddhist literature. In the works of the *Abhidhamma-piṭaka* the Paccekabuddha is only mentioned in the systematic lists of persons who attain enlightenment, and no detailed information can be found.

Commencing in the 3rd century B.C.E. commentarial literature was written in Sri Lanka in Sinhalese. The commentaries continued to increase until at least the second century C.E., drawing new material from the Sinhalese Buddhist social and religious life. Buddhaghosa based his own systematised commentarial work on these older texts. Most of the information about the Paccekabuddha has been handed down to us by this scholar, who drew upon the living tradition of the previous centuries.

The concept of the Paccekabuddha underwent further developments in the *Mahāyāna* schools of Buddhism, but these lie beyond the scope of the present work.

The adaptation of the concept of the Paccekabuddha in Buddhism seems to have been inspired by the Indian tradition of asceticism and individualism, and the popular reverence and esteem for ascetics, wandering religious men, *munis* and sages.

Since the earliest times, ascetics who leave society to evade the hindrances of worldly ties and to search for insight into reality and salvation have been mentioned as one of the most typical characteristics of Indian religions. The *Rg-Veda* mentions a class of holy men distinct from the brahmins, the *munis* who are said to possess supernatural powers, especially the ability to fly through the air and to read other people's thoughts. This asceticism seems to have developed among different groups or individuals along a similar line, and shows similar characteristics of practice and circumstances: a solitary life outside the community, residence in forests or on the outskirts of towns and villages, dressing in clothes of bark or of rags, living on begged food or plants, shaving the hair, etc. Some of these ascetics lived in isolation, others in groups; still others wandered in groups or alone, begging for alms, preaching their doctrines to those who wished to listen. The fact that there are only a few references to these ascetics in Vedic literature does not imply that they were rare. They formed a religious group distinct from the orthodox sacrificial priests and developed their own culture and style of living. Many of the impulses for new developments in thought came from these groups.

The motives for abandoning society in the search for final release were based on the belief that life formed an endless chain of existence from which deliverance was necessary. The sense of freedom from worldly cares and ties has been one of the main themes in the religious literature of India, Hindu and Buddhist.

The acquisition of supernatural powers is often mentioned as another motive for asceticism. Throughout the entire literature it is stated that one of the main aims of the Indian ascetic is the acquisition of powers to control the course of nature. These powers, gained through ascetic practices, offered the opportunity to rise above the brahmanical sacrificial priest, not only on the level of spiritual development, but also on the material plane. Consequently, the ascetics were honoured, respected and even feared by the people. The ascetics who achieved their goals were more powerful than any other persons in the universe; even the gods were subordinate to them.

The tradition of asceticism, and the idea that release could only be attained by the individual, seems to have reached its culmination in the time of the Buddha. During that period numerous groups of ascetics appeared, living alone or following a leader, dwelling in forests or wandering as mendicants. The idea prevailed that escape from rebirth and salvation could only be obtained by renunciation of the ordinary societal ties in favour of a special way of life. In this period the ancient tradition of *munis* and *śramaṇas* found new continuity and a suitable soil for new developments in Buddhism and Jainism, which were both ascetic in making renunciation of life in the world essential for release and in continuing the tradition of the individual attainment of enlightenment.

Although the Buddha rejected austere asceticism and the practice of ritual in the way these were followed by the *śramaṇas* (ascetics; Pāli: *samaṇas*) of his time, and favoured a less rigid separation from society for his monks, his teaching exemplified the main traits of the Indian ascetic contemplative tradition: a stress on renunciation, entrance upon religious life and solitary meditation as important aids to the attainment of insight. Most of the monks chose to live within the communal structure of the

Order, and to combine their meditative practice with such tasks as preaching, teaching, study discussion, and social activities. But there were some monks who preferred to follow the older ideal of the solitary recluse, remaining bound to the community only by means of the fortnightly *uposatha*-celebration,[3] at which the rules of the Order were recited. In the early Buddhist community the thera Mahākassapa was especially esteemed for this type of austerity. Those who followed the Buddha's Path in this personal way continued the ancient tradition of asceticism and were respected and honoured by the people on the same level as were the *munis*, *śramaṇas* and other ascetics. Later, in Sri Lanka, the monks who lived in the forests became a separate group, the *Vanavāsi-nikāya*.

The concept of the Paccekabuddha presented the opportunity to include pre-Buddhist recluses and seers in Buddhism and in doing so it continued these pre-Buddhist traditions. In this respect it becomes clear why Paccekabuddhas are referred to in the scriptures with all other terms that could be used to denote ascetics: *muni*, *isi*, *samaṇa*, *tāpasa*, *jaṭila*, terms which emphasize different aspects of asceticism.

In order to find a legitimate place within Buddhist teaching, these ascetics had to fit in with the system of thought. They were given their place as a way of recognising that the *Dhamma*, the eternal and highest truth, is always accessible and can be attained by those of great virtue and spiritual maturity even when the formulated *Dhamma* of a Buddha is not available. For the *Dhamma*, as the formulated teaching, is subject to the law of origination,

3. The bimonthly *uposatha* days (on the first and the fifteenth day of the lunar month) are used to preach the *Dhamma* and for the recitation of the *Pātimokkha*, the rules of the order, and the confession ceremony preceding the recitation. When one speaks of Paccekabuddhas celebrating this day, one should keep in mind that the ceremony as described in the Vinaya is, of course, not meant for Paccekabuddhas who do not possess any knowledge of the *Pātimokkha* laid down only during periods in which the *Dhamma* is preached. One should rather connect the "celebration of *uposatha* by Paccekabuddhas" with the general custom of ascetics and religious communities in India, who, from Vedic times onwards, used to hold some sort of *uposatha*-celebration.

growth and decay. It appears in history, revealed by a Buddha, and for a period is studied, practised, and taught by human beings. But these periods during which the *Dhamma* is known alternates with other periods during which it has disappeared, remaining only on the level of absolute truth. This does not mean, however, that the truth cannot be attained during this time. It only means that the truth must be personally discovered without the guidance of an articulated doctrine and map of the path, an achievement calling for a very highly developed faculty of wisdom.

Those who discover the *Dhamma* by themselves are of two types: the *Sammāsambuddha*, who, after realising the *Dhamma*, teaches it in its fullness and re-establishes the dispensation in the world; and the Paccekabuddha, who does not reveal it or preach it to the great mass of people. To proclaim the *Dhamma* anew requires special qualities—omniscience and supreme compassion—and even then the decision to reveal the abstruse, ultimate truth is difficult to make. The figure of the Paccekabuddha provided the means to accommodate the notion of one who discovers the truth for himself without possessing all the powers of a supreme Buddha, and thus chooses not to try to teach the truth at large. This same figure also serves to confirm the validity of the achievements of ascetics and sages of pre-Buddhist times.

With the emergence of ideas which finally took shape in the *Mahāyāna* schools, the ideals of the *Pratyekabuddha* and of the *arahant* came to stand for what was called "the *Hīnayāna*." In contrast to the individualistic outlook of the earlier schools, the Mahāyānists, challenged by what seemed to them self-centredness, felt that it was impossible for any enlightened being not to teach to others the truth he had discovered. The change of view caused a different attitude towards the *arahant* and the *Pratyekabuddha*. They were now considered egoists, and contrasted unfavourably with the *Bodhisattva*, whose dedication was praised. Another change which took place concerned the conception of time. The phenomenal world was no longer regarded as proceeding in time, but as operating idealistically. Therefore Buddhas were no longer conceived as following one another in time, as historical persons, but as manifesting themselves in this world spontaneously. The concept of Buddhahood was no longer directly connected with an historical figure, but considered as the ultimate goal for all, the germ of Buddhahood being present in every person. This outlook made the concept of *Pratyekabuddha* a mere possibility of the older schools and deprived it of its historical reality within the tradition of Indian religiosity.

However as it was impossible to negate the concept, attempts were made to make it fit in with the new ideas. A discussion started as to whether there was any difference between the goals of the *śrāvaka* and the *Pratyekabuddha* on the one hand, and of the *Bodhisattva* on the other. Their Ways were different, but did this also result in different goals, in a different Enlightenment and *Nirvāna*?

This question resulted in the diverse opinions of the Mahāyānist philosophers regarding the three vehicles and the one vehicle, their distinctions and similarities.

Although it is not the intention of this paper to treat the concept of the *Pratyekabuddha* as it occurs in the *Mahāyāna* schools, a few fundamental differences between the *Mahāyāna* and *Theravāda* conceptions should be mentioned.

The idea that the three *yānas* lead to their own specific *Bodhi* and *Nirvāna*, as is found in the *Saṃdhinirmocanasūtra* and the *Mahāyānasūtrālamkāra*, and the idea that *śrāvaka* and *Pratyekabuddha* (*dviyāna*) on the one hand and *Bodhisattva* (*ekayāna*) on the other attain distinctive goals, as it can be found in the *Laṅkāvatārasūtra* and most of the *Mādhyamika* and *Yogācāra* works, were both refuted by other Mahāyānists. They postulated that there can be only one vehicle (*ekayāna*) since there is only one insight. This view has been expressed in the *Saddharmapuṇḍarīka* thus: "The venerable Mahākāsyapa asked: 'If, O Lord, there are no three vehicles, for what reason has one at the present period formed the conception of disciples, Pratyekabuddhas and Buddhas?' Being thus addressed, the Lord said to the venerable Mahākāsyapa: 'A potter makes many vessels out of the same clay. Some of them hold sugar, others ghee, others curd and milk, and others again impure waste matter. There is no difference in the clay, but only in the substances which are put in the resulting pots. Just so, O Kāsyapa, there is just this one single Buddha-vehicle, and a second or third vehicle does not exist.' Being thus addressed the venerable Mahākāsyapa said to the Lord: 'But if, O Lord, those beings who have found their way out of the threefold world, have different dispositions, will their Nirvāna be one, two or three?' The Lord said: 'Nirvāna results from understanding the sameness of all *dharmas*. Hence there is but one Nirvāna, not two or three"' (132 f.).

In this connection no separate existence is allotted to the *śrāvaka*—and *Pratyekabuddha*—vehicles. To attain *Bodhi* and *Nirvāna* one has to follow the *ekayāna*, the only way of the *Bodhisattva*. However, in many *Mahāyāna* works distinctions are made between the *śrāvaka*, *Pratyekabuddha* and the *Bodhisattva*. The most important of these is the fact that *śrāvaka*s and Pratyekabuddhas are said to be capable of purifying only the hindrance of the defilements (*klesāvaraṇa*) and not the hindrance of the knowable, the intellectual faults (*jñeyāvaraṇa*), while Bodhisattvas are said to purify both hindrances. The wisdom and knowledge of a *Pratyekabuddha* are very small compared to the wisdom of a Buddha: "If the ten points of space were filled with Pratyekabuddhas, free from faults, gifted with acute faculties and standing, in the last stage of their existences, as numerous as reeds and bamboos in the woods; and if combined for an endless number of myriads of *koṭis* of aeons, they were to investigate a part only of my superior laws, they would never find out its real meaning" (*Saddharmapuṇḍarika* 32, vs. II, 12–13).

Some *Mahāyāna* works differentiate between the *śrāvaka* and the *Pratyekabuddha* by asserting that the former attains insight through meditation on the four noble truths, the latter through meditation on dependent origination (*pratityasamutpāda*). This idea gave rise to the use of the term Pratyayabuddha, "one who has become enlightened by (understanding) the causes," for "by a thorough insight into causes and conditions (*hetupratyaya*) they hope to win final Nirvāna for themselves" (*Saddharmapuṇḍarika* III 80, 9). In Chinese and Tibetan translations this aspect has been given much attention, because in Tibetan the *Pratyekabuddha* is often referred to as "one who meditates on *pratitya*" (*rten-'brel-bsgom*), "who understands only the causes" (*rkyen-gcig-rtogs*). Reverence paid to Pratyekabuddhas remained, also in *Mahāyāna* surroundings, a means of acquiring merit; it has even been recommended by rulers in their edicts.

I. The Paccekabuddha

The *Apadāna* of the *Khuddakanikāya* belongs to the later works of the Pāli *Tipiṭaka* and consists of a collection of stories in verse in which the instructive life-histories (*apadāna*) of saints and arahants have been related. The second section deals with the Paccekabuddha *apadāna.* In it the *Khaggavisāṇasutta* of the *Suttanipāta* has been inserted. Here the beginning and the concluding verses are given in translation.

1. The *muni* Vedeha, bowing his body, asked the *Tathāgata*, who was staying in the Jetavana: "Paccekabuddhas are said to exist, by what reasons do they become wise?"

2. Then the best of the omniscient, the great wise one, said to Ānandabhadda ("Ānanda, the virtuous") in a sweet voice: "Those who have fulfilled their duties under all (former) Buddhas, without attaining liberation during the period in which the teaching of the *Jinas* is known.

3. "Who are wise because of their repulsion,[4] whose wisdom is very sharp, who attain insight by themselves even by means of a small object of meditation without the instruction of Buddhas.

4. "And what is more, in this whole world, there is no one except me equal to the Paccekabuddhas. I shall clearly express the following, only an abridged description of the distinction of the great *munis.*

5. "Listen, all of you who wish for the highest medicine, your thoughts very calm, to the good words which are sweet like honey, of those great wise men, who are fully enlightened by themselves.

6. "To these expositions of Paccekabuddhas, who assembled (on Mount Gandhamādana), pronounced one after the other about the wretchedness and the cause of the absence of passion, and how they attained insight.

7. "Their consciousness without passion with regard to the objects of passion, their minds dispassionate in an impassionate world, having abandoned the world of conceptualisation (*papañca*). The agitations conquered (by them), thus they attained insight.

4. I.e., a feeling of repulsion and emotion caused by the contemplation of the miseries of the world.

8. "Putting aside violence to all beings, not hurting any of them, good and compassionate, with a mind filled with friendliness, one should live alone, like the horn of a rhinoceros (Here follow the forty-one verses of the *Khaggavisāṇasutta* of the *Suttanipāta*.)

50. "Their morality pure, their wisdom purified, concentrated, practising watchfulness, contemplating, seeing the characteristics of the dhamma, they understand, having gone through the Path factors of the way[5] and the elements of enlightenment.[6]

51. "Having practised the aspiration regarding the attainment of merit, which is thus characterised, they do not attain the state of a disciple during the Jina's teaching, (but) they become *Paccekajinas*, self-existent and wise.

52. "Their dhamma is great, their many bodies are according to the dhamma, they are masters of their Minds, they have overcome the flood of all sufferings, their minds exalted, they have seen the highest truth, like lions are they, like the horn of a rhinoceros.

53. "With serene senses, calm, concentrated, practising mindfulness with regard to the people of border districts, illuminating like lamps in the other world and in this world, thus are these Paccekabuddhas, always good.

54. "Having destroyed all hindrances, kings of men, illuminators of the world, shining like solid gold, undoubtedly worthy of gifts in the world, are these Paccekabuddhas, always good.

55. "These are in this world together with the world of the gods, the good words of Paccekabuddhas. Those fools who, having heard them, do not act accordingly, whirl round in sufferings again and again.

56. "Those who, having heard the good words of the Paccekabuddhas, which are like a sweet stream of honey, act accordingly, become seers of the truth, possessing wisdom.

57. "These excellent verses have been spoken by the Paccekabuddhas, the conquerors, after they had gone forth, and they have been made known by the Lion of the Sakyas, the highest of men, for the sake of the understanding of the *Dhamma*."

---

5. Right view, right resolve, right speech, right behaviour, right living, right effort, right mindfulness and right concentration.

6. Mindfulness, investigation of the dhamma, energy, joy, calmness, concentration and equanimity.

58. Out of compassion for the world these miraculous deeds of these Paccekabuddhas have been made known by the Lion of the self-existent ones, in order to increase (the number of) those who are victorious in battle because of their repulsion (Ap I 7–14).

I.1. The Paccekabuddha: his position, compared with the Sammāsambuddha and the *sāvaka*

The Commentary on the *Khuddakapāṭha* gives an exposition of the classes of living beings and classifies them from the lower to the higher stages of existence.

Human beings are divided into women and men. The men are further classified into those who are householders and those who have left their houses, the *anagārika*. The *anāgārika* are divided into ordinary people (*puthujjana*) and noble ones (*ariya*). The *ariya* are again classified into those who need further instruction (*sekha*) and those who do not need further instruction (*asekha, i.e.,* the arahants). These are divided into those who, in their prior practice went the way of pure insight (*sukkhavipassaka*) and those who had started with the practice of quietude (*samathayānika*). The *samathayānika* are divided into those who have not attained the perfections of a disciple (*sāvaka*) and those who have. Then follow the Paccekabuddhas, who are called higher than the disciples because of the greatness of their virtue. "Even several hundreds of disciples who are like Sāriputta and Moggallāna do not attain a hundredth part of the virtues of one Paccekabuddha."

Higher than the Paccekabuddhas are the Sammāsambuddhas because of the greatness of their virtue: "For even (*a group of*) Paccekabuddhas seated on the whole of the (*continent of*) Jambudīpa so close together that sitting cross-legged (*their knees*) would touch each other, do not attain a portion, or a sixteenth part or a small fraction (*of that*) of the virtues of one perfectly enlightened one" (I 177–178).

A hierarchy is clearly evident from this passage: The Paccekabuddhas are higher than the perfected disciples, and the perfect Buddhas are ranked above the Paccekabuddhas. These three groups are often mentioned together, e.g., in connection with their common attainments and way of life. In this section we shall mainly emphasize their differences.

The *Puggalapaññatti* enumerates nine individuals, first the *Sammāsambuddha*, secondly the Paccekabuddha, thirdly the *sāvaka*, etc. The first two are distinguished as follows: "What individual is the *Sammāsambuddha*? In this world a certain individual awakes by himself to the truths among teachings that are not heard of before and then attains omniscience (*sabbaññutā*) and mastery of the powers (*bala*); this individual is called a *Sammāsambuddha*.

"What individual is the Paccekabuddha? To this world a certain individual awakes by himself to the truths among teachings that are not heard of before and then he does not attain omniscience or mastery of the powers; this individual is called a Paccekabuddha" (Pug 10).

So the Paccekabuddha attains enlightenment, but not the omniscience or the powers which are the special attainments of the *Sammāsambuddha*.

There are more points of difference. In the *Milindapañhā* ("The Questions of Milinda") the thoughts of various classes of beings are classified. The sevenfold classification consists of the ordinary person, the person who has entered the stream (*sotāpanna*), who is to be born once more (*sakadāgāmin*), who will not be reborn in the world of the senses (*anāgāmin*), the *arahant*, the Paccekabuddha and the *Sammāsambuddha*. The text says:

"The arahants, O great king, whose evil influences (*āsava*) have been annihilated, whose stains have been washed away, whose defilements have been left behind, who have reached perfection, who have attained the highest good, who have destroyed the bonds of existence, who have attained mastership in analysis (*paṭisambhidā*), are pure on the stages of the *sāvaka*. In the province of the *sāvaka* their thoughts arise lightly and move lightly, (but) on the stages of the Paccekabuddha they arise with difficulty and move sluggishly. And why? Because they have been fully purified in the province of the *sāvaka* and because they have not been fully purified in the province of the Paccekabuddha" (Mil 101).

And about the thoughts of the Paccekabuddha:

"Those Paccekabuddhas, O great king, are self-existent (*sayambhū*), without a teacher, living solitarily (*ekacāri*), resembling the horn of a rhinoceros, in their own province possessing thoughts which are pure and stainless; in their own province their thoughts arise lightly and move lightly, (but) on the stages of the omniscient Buddha they arise with difficulty and move sluggishly. And why? Because they have been fully purified in their own province and because of the greatness of the province of the omniscient Buddha.

"It is, O great king, like a man who on his own land might cross a small river by night or by day, whenever he wants, without fear, but who might be afraid, might tarry and might not dare to cross the great ocean, having seen that it is deep, wide and unfathomable, and with no other shore in sight, and why? Because of the familiarity with his own land and of the greatness of the great ocean" (Mil 105).

The distinctions regarding the families in which they are born are described in the *Suttanipāta* Commentary, where it is said: "Having fulfilled the perfections, when (future) Buddhas are reborn in the world, they are born in a family of *khattiyas*, *brāhmaṇas* or householders; and chief disciples, like Buddhas, are also born in families of *khattiyas* or *brāhmaṇas*" (Sn-a 51).

It is noteworthy that in this passage future Buddhas and chief disciples are described as being born in the same kinds of families, and that future Paccekabuddhas are also born in families of householders, i.e. apparently socially lower classes than those of the *khattiyas* and *brāhmaṇas*.

The text continues: "perfect Buddhas do not arise in the world period of devolution, but they arise in the world period of evolution, Paccekabuddhas arise without having come to know Buddhas and not at the times of the birth of a Buddha."

Here the important fact of the Paccekabuddha's period of appearance is mentioned. Only in times in which there are no Buddhas is it possible to attain Paccekabuddhahood.

And further: "Buddhas are enlightened by themselves and enlighten others: Paccekabuddhas are enlightened by themselves (but) do not enlighten others: they comprehend only the essence of meaning (*attharasa*), not the essence of the idea (*dhammarasa*). Because they are not able to put the supramundane *Dhamma* into concepts and teach it, their realization of the *Dhamma* is like a dream seen by a dumb man and like the taste of a curry from the city to one who lives in the forest; they reach the whole that consists of supernatural power (*iddhi*), attainments (*samāpatti*) and analysis (*paṭisambhidā*).

As to the eminence of their virtues, they are lower than Buddhas and higher than disciples; making others enter upon the religious life they teach the practice of lesser ethics (*abhisamācārika*)[7] with this instruction: "Austerity regarding the mind should be practised, perfection should not fall into stagnation."

All the principal points of difference between Buddhas and Paccekabuddhas are mentioned here: Paccekabuddhas usually do not bring others to enlightenment; they do not understand the full range of the *Dhamma*; they are not able to formulate it by way of concepts. They possess supernatural powers, reach high levels of meditation, and can influence others indirectly to take up a religious life.

The commentary continues: "They announce *uposatha* saying: 'Today is *uposatha,'* or with a similar saying. And having announced *uposatha* they celebrate (it) after having gathered on (Mount) Gandhamādana at the root of the Mañjūsaka tree in the Jewel-Yard."

A distinction between the knowledge (*ñāṇa*) of disciple, Paccekabuddha and Buddha is made in the *Sāratthappakāsinī*, where the Buddha is shown admonishing Ānanda thus: "Why did you not penetrate the knowledge of the perfections of a disciple like Sāriputta and Moggallāna, who fulfilled the perfections in the course of one hundred thousand *kalpas* plus one incalculable period, and (why) did you not penetrate the knowledge of self-enlightenment like the Paccekabuddhas who fulfilled the perfections in the course of one hundred thousand *kalpas* plus two incalculable periods?" (S-a II 93).

Buddhaghosa's commentary on the *Dīghanikāya* describes three different categories of knowledge as follows: "The knowledge of the perfections of a disciple is deep, (but) therein is no determination (*vavatthāna*). And further the knowledge of a Paccekabuddha is deeper than that, (but) also in that there is no determination. And the knowledge of omniscience is deeper than that. And there is no other that is deeper ..." (D-a I 100).

---

7. I.e., what is called the "minor precepts," as they are expounded in the Khandhaka section of the Vinaya. *Visuddhimagga* II equates this practice with the third, fourth and fifth stages of the Noble Eightfold Way, right speech, right behaviour and right living.

And in the *Sāratthappakāsinī*: "Disciples ... attain the knowledge of the perfections of a disciple, Paccekabuddhas the knowledge of self-enlightenment, (and) Buddhas the knowledge of omniscience" (S-a III 208). The *Majjhimanikāya* enumerates fourteen offerings graded according to the state of the individual to whom they are presented: the first is the offering presented to a *Sammāsambuddha*; the second the offering presented to a Paccekabuddha, the third to an *arahant*-disciple of a Buddha (M III 254).

In addition to the classification of Buddha, Paccekabuddha and disciple, another classification occurring in the commentarial literature speaks of four kinds of Buddhas: the omniscient Buddha, the Paccekabuddha, the four-truths Buddha and the learned Buddha (S-a I 25). These are explained as follows: "Here (the person) who, having fulfilled all the thirty perfections,[8] attains perfect enlightenment, is called an omniscient Buddha. (He), who, having fulfilled the perfections in the course of one hundred thousand *kalpas* plus two incalculable periods, attains the state of a self-existent one, is called a Paccekabuddha. The remaining ones who have destroyed the evil influences are called four-truths-Buddhas. And those who are very learned (are called) learned Buddhas" (S-a I 25). In this classification the third member of the threefold series, the disciple, has been divided into the liberated disciple or *arahant* and the disciple who is learned in the teaching but not yet liberated.

Besides the differences between Buddhas, Paccekabuddhas and disciples, according to the technical use of the terms, certain shared similarities can also be found in the texts. Thus Buddhas, Paccekabuddhas and disciples are equally called noble (*ariya*), and their lineage is the lineage of the noble (*ariyavaṃsa*).

Four persons are called worthy of a stupa, namely a *Sammāsambuddha*, a Paccekabuddha, a disciple and a king who is a world-ruler. The function of a stupa of a Paccekabuddha is that "having made their hearts confident, thinking: 'This is the stupa of a

8. Thirty *pāramī*: usually a group of ten perfections is mentioned, viz. regarding generosity, morality, renunciation, wisdom, energy, patience, truthfulness, resolution, friendliness, equanimity. When they are subdivided into the ordinary (*pāramitā*), the intermediate (*upapāramitā*) and the supreme (*paramatthapāramitā*) grades, the number thirty is reached.

Lord Paccekabuddha,' (people) attain a good form of existence, a heavenly world, on the dissolution of their bodies at death."

The *Kathāvatthu* states that Paccekabuddhas, Sammā-sambuddhas and disciples cannot arise in the world of the gods, because among the gods there is no one who follows a religious life. They can only arise in the human world where a religious life, i.e., a life of renunciation and meditation, is possible (Kv I 95 and 97). Although Buddhas, Paccekabuddhas and disciples live in the world of sensual desire, they do not remain subject to the five strands of sensual pleasures.

Māra is mentioned in references to Buddhas as well as to Paccekabuddhas. Both are said to have conquered the evil one and his army. Towards both Māra sometimes plays the role of the offended king of evil, who, by means of sly tricks, tries to embitter the life of his conqueror. One example is the following well-known story, which is told about the Buddha as well as a Paccekabuddha: "In a time in which no Buddha existed ... one Paccekabuddha entered the city for alms. Because Māra had beguiled all the citizens, he did not receive any offering of alms and went away with an empty bowl. Then Māra, having gone to the city gate, stood there in disguise, and asked the Paccekabuddha when he arrived: 'Reverend Sir, did you not receive anything?'—'Are you not the cause I did not receive anything?'—'Then turn back and enter (the city) again; now I shall cause (you to receive alms)'—'I shall not turn back again.' For, if he had turned back, (Māra) would have again entered into the bodies of all the citizens, hit (him) with his band, and ridiculed him" (Dhp-a I 2, 196).

An interesting relationship occurs between a (future) Buddha and a Paccekabuddha when they are disciple and teacher in a former existence. A future Paccekabuddha is often mentioned as a disciple of a Buddha during one of his former existences. Not being able to reach arahantship at that time, he eventually attains *Paccekabodhi*. Examples of the reverse relationship are also found in the *Jātakas*, where it is told that the future Buddha Sakyamuni received advice and help from Paccekabuddhas on his way to enlightenment. In the following fragment from the *Pañcuposathajātaka*, a Paccekabuddha assists the Bodhisatta (then an ascetic) to overcome the pride which prevents him from attaining *jhāna*:

"Then one Paccekabuddha, perceiving that he (the future Buddha) was possessed with pride, (thought): This is no common being, he is destined to be a Buddha; even in this world-period he will attain omniscience. Having made him subdue his pride I shall cause him to develop attainments (*samāpatti*). Then he left the northern Himalayas. While the ascetic was seated in his hut, the Paccekabuddha sat down on his slab of stone. Coming out of his hut the ascetic saw him seated on his own seat and because of his pride could no longer control himself. He went towards the Paccekabuddha and snapped his fingers, saying: 'Fall dead, you vile, black-eared, bald-headed little ascetic; why are you sitting on my stone seat?' And the Paccekabuddha said to him: 'Good man, why are you possessed with pride? I am one who has penetrated the knowledge of *Paccekabodhi*, (and) even in this world period you will become an omniscient Buddha; you are destined to be a Buddha. When you have fulfilled the perfections, and when another world period like this has come, you will be a Buddha. In this state of Buddhahood you will be named Siddhattha.' He depicted everything to him, name, family, clan, chief disciples, etc., saying: 'Why are you so rough, out of pride? Such a thing is unworthy of you!' and he gave him advice. Even being addressed by him in this way the ascetic did not honour him nor ask: 'When shall I be a Buddha?' and other things. Then the Paccekabuddha said to him: 'Know the difference between your greatness based upon your birth and mine based upon my virtues: if you can, move in the air like me!' He then rose up into the air and, shaking off the dust of his feet on (the ascetic's) tuft of hair, he went to the northern Himalayas. After this admonition the ascetic was overcome with grief and having fulfilled several observances, reached the brahmaloka" (J-a IV, 328).

I.2. The Paccekabuddha: his outward appearance

There are several references in the texts to the outward appearance of the Paccekabuddha. Generally he is depicted as an ascetic or wandering monk. In some places his appearance is described with more details, as in *Jātaka* IV 114:

"(With) their hair two fingerbreadths (*aṅgula*) long, wearing yellow robes, they live in the northern Himalayas on the Nandamūlaka slope ... A red double cloth was wrapped (around him), a girdle which looked like a flash of lightning was tied (around him), an upper robe and mantle with the colour of pink lac was hanging over one shoulder, a ragged robe with the colour of a storm-cloud was draped over the (other) shoulder and an earthen bowl of bee-brown colour dangled at his left side."

From this description we learn that the Paccekabuddha was thought of as having the same clothes and attributes as the Buddhist monk or the wandering ascetic: the short-cut or shaven hair, the three robes made of rags and dyed in red-brown colours, the bowl, etc.

The Aṅguttara Commentary says: "Paccekabuddhas ... have (their) hair and beards two fingerbreadths long and have the eight requisites fastened round their bodies" (A-a I 354).

And the Sutta-Nipāta Commentary relates in similar words: "And he touched his head with his right hand: at once the characteristics of a householder disappeared, and the appearance of one who has undertaken a religious life became manifest; his hair and beard were two fingerbreadths long; he was provided with the eight requisites and looked like a senior monk a hundred years old" (Sn-a 63).

As was customary in the case of monks and ascetics, Paccekabuddhas were also presented with the requisites of an ascetic (*samaṇaparibhoga*), namely the three robes, bowl, razor, needle, girdle and water-strainer.

The fact that the Paccekabuddha is described as having the outward appearance of a monk—the only difference being the usually short-cut hair and beard of the Paccekabuddha, in contrast to the shaven hair and beard of the monk—sheds some light on the problem of why images or representations of Paccekabuddhas are so strikingly rare in Buddhist art. Most probably representations of Paccekabuddhas were made, but they cannot be distinguished from those of monks unless an inscription shows them to be indeed images of Paccekabuddhas.

I.3. The Paccekabuddha: names and individuals

The Majjhima Nikāya (M III 69–71) enumerates 119 names of a group of five hundred Paccekabuddhas who are said to reside on Mount Isigili. Of these names only a few are mentioned in Pāli texts elsewhere: the most important ones are Tagarasikhin,

Uparittha, Mātaṅga and Mahāpaduma. The Paccekabuddha Uparittha occurs in a story in the *Manorathapurāṇī*, where he plays a role in one of the previous existences of the Buddha's cousin Anuruddha, who, as the poor Annabhāra, presents him with alms. "Then one day on Mount Gandhamādana, the Paccekabuddha named Uparittha, having entered the attainment of suppression (*nirodhasamāpatti*), came out of this (meditation) and reflected: 'To whom ought compassion be shown today?' For Paccekabuddhas are compassionate towards those who have entered a bad form of existence." Having chosen Annabhāra as a suitable object for his compassion, he went to him to receive alms. Then Annabhāra filled the Paccekabuddha's bowl with his own meal and presented him with it, expressing the wish to be released from his miserable existence, and he then made the Paccekabuddha sit down upon his own cloak to eat (A-a I 185).

The same text mentions the Paccekabuddha Mahāpaduma, the first of the five hundred Paccekabuddhas who are the sons of Padumavatī. He is the only one who is said to have been born from her womb, the others having been born from moisture. He is the first of the group to enter *Nibbāna*.

Tagarasikhin is the most frequently mentioned Paccekabuddha. He is the third son of Padumavatī and lives on Mount Gandhamādana "in the happiness resulting from the attainment of the fruit." Tagarasikhin is mentioned in the *Udāna*, where he is insulted by the son of the wealthy merchant, named Suppabuddha, who called him a leper. As a result of this offence Suppabuddha was reborn in hell and remained there for many hundreds of thousands of years, after which he obtained a human existence as a leper. In one of the *Jātakas* Tagarasikhin figures in a story in which he receives a gift from an unbeliever, who regrets his generosity afterwards.

Padumavatī, the mother of the five hundred Paccekabuddhas, is regarded as a previous incarnation of the nun Uppalavaṇṇā. How she acquired the merit which enabled her to attain this state is explained in the following fragment from the *Manoratha-pūraṇī* (A-a I 346): "At that time one Paccekabuddha, having come out of the attainment of suppression on Mount Gandhamādana went to a place not far from where she was and stood (there). Having seen the Paccekabuddha, she took fried grain and a lotus-flower, came down from her car, and threw the fried grain into the Paccekabuddha's bowl. Having covered the bowl with the lotus-flower, she gave (it to him). Shortly after the Paccekabuddha had left she thought: 'Those who have entered upon religious life have no need of a flower; I shall adorn myself with the flower.' She went (to him) and took the flower (back) from the Paccekabuddha's hand, but then she thought: 'If the Lord should not have needed the flower, he would not have allowed (it) to lie on top of the bowl. Surely he has need of it!' And again going to him, she laid it on top of the bowl, apologized to him and expressed this wish: 'Reverend Sir, as a result of (the presenting of) these grains may I have as many sons as the number of the grains; may a lotus-flower arise from each (of my) footprints every place where I shall be reborn as a result of (the presenting of) the lotus-flower.' (Then) before her very eyes the Paccekabuddha went through the air to Gandhamādana. Having made a foot-wiper flower for the (other) Paccekabuddhas, he placed himself near the stairs of approaching. As a result of her deed, the woman came to rebirth in the world of the gods. From the time (of this) existence onwards a big lotus-flower grew out of each of her footprints."

In the *Apadāna* she commemorates her good deed in two verses: "Having seen the Paccekabuddha and having presented him with five hundred fried grains covered with lotuses, I wished for five hundred sons. Having given honey in these lonely places to the self-existent one, I passed from (that existence) and was born in a forest in the interior of a lotus" (Ap II 555, verses 56–57).

The Paccekabuddha Sunetta is mentioned in the Petavatthu Commentary, where it is related how he was murdered while meditating on the bank of the Ganges. Another Paccekabuddha, whose death had been violent, is mentioned in the *Jātaka*, where it is related that he was shot with an arrow as a result of being mistaken for a deer in the forest.

The Paccekabuddha Mātaṅga, the last of the Paccekabuddhas who lived before the *Bodhisattva* entered his last existence, received the announcement of this and entered final *Nibbāna.*

I.4. The Paccekabuddha: his predicates

The *Majjhimanikāya* (III 69–71) provides a list of names and predicates of Paccekabuddhas. These predicates, also used in descriptions of the *Sammāsambuddha* and the disciple, include: undisturbed (*anigha*), without longing (*nirāsa*), incomparable, enlightened, truthful, stainless, wise, of superior energy (*anomanikkhama*), beautiful, essence of being, silent one (*muni*), one who defeats Māra's army, one who cut away pride, one who bears his last body, one who cuts away the bonds of existence, one whose passion is gone and one whose mind is released.

Many other predicates besides these are used in the descriptions of Paccekabuddhas. The most prevalent will be briefly enumerated; they occur again in the translations that follow.

Very often Paccekabuddhas are defined as ascetics (*samaṇa*) and as seers (*isi*) who have the Himalayas and the places Isigili and Isipatana as their favourite residences. Another interesting designation is that of *muni*, "silent one." The *Mahāniddesa* enumerates six *munis* "who possess the three *muni* qualities" (i.e. "silence" of body, speech and thought): the *muni* who remains in the house, the *muni* who has left the house, the *muni* who needs further instruction, the *muni* who does not need further instruction (i.e., the *arahant*), the *Paccekamuni* (i.e., the Paccekabuddha) and the *muni-muni* (i.e., the *Sammāsambuddha*) (Nidd I 58).

The *Cullaniddesa* explains the three moral perfections of a *muni*, called the *muni* qualities (*moneyya*) of body, speech and thought (*manomoneyya*):

"What is the *muni* quality of the body? It is the annihilation of the threefold wrong activity of the body,[9] the threefold good activity of the body is the *muni* quality of the body; knowledge of the condition of the body, full understanding of the body, the way (of action) which is connected with this understanding; annihilation of the desire for excitement by means of the body,

9. The three wrong activities of the body are: taking life, taking what is not given and (for the *muni* and the monk) unchastity; the fourfold wrong activity of speech is telling lies, slander, harsh speech and frivolous talk; the threefold wrong activity of the mind is covetousness, malevolence and heretic views. The good activities are the reverse or absence of these ten wrong activities.

cessation of the conditioning of the body,[10] the attainment of the fourth stage of *jhāna.*

"What is the *muni* quality of speech? The annihilation of the fourfold wrong activity of speech is the *muni* quality of speech; knowledge of the condition of speech, full understanding of speech, the way (of action) which is connected with full understanding, annihilation of the desire for excitement by means of speech, is the *muni* quality of speech, cessation of the conditionings of speech,[11] the attainment of the second stage of jhāna. This is the *muni* quality of speech.

"What is the *muni* quality of thought? The annihilation of the threefold wrong activity of the mind is the *muni* quality of thought; it is the knowledge of the condition of the mind, full understanding of the mind, the way which is connected with this understanding, annihilation of the desire for excitement by means of the mind, cessation of the conditionings of the mind, the attainment of the suppression of consciousness and sensation" (Nidd II 228–229).

One of the most important characteristics of the Paccekabuddha is his solitary way of life. Because of this he is described by the predicate *eka,* meaning solitary, alone or unique. More will be said about this below. Like most ascetics, the Paccekabuddha lives on offerings of alms. As a recipient of alms he is called "a field for merit," and "worthy of the best gifts." Thus the *Upāsakajanālaṅkāra* says: "From the moment (they attain the) sublime fruit, they become men called Paccekabuddhas and they are worthy of the best gifts in this world together with its gods" (Upās 344). Again, like all those who follow the religious way of life, the Paccekabuddha is called "learned" and "wise." Apparently, the preferred predicate in describing him in this connection is *bahussuta,* "one who has heard much," i.e., learned, erudite. Having attained enlightenment, he is also called "without worry," "not afraid," especially regarding the end of his life.

---

10. *Kāya-saṅkhārā*; here the inhalations and exhalations are meant, which subside temporarily in the fourth jhāna.

11. Thought-conception and discursive thinking (*vitakka-vicāra*), which may be called "interior speech," subside temporarily in the second jhāna.

II. The Way towards Paccekabodhi

The *Upāsakajanālaṅkāra* summarizes the way to *Paccekabodhi* as follows:

"After making the resolve (*abhinīhāra*), in the course of one hundred thousand world periods plus two incalculable periods, the lay-disciples accumulate the conditions necessary to obtain enlightenment (*bodhisambhāra*). Gradually, having accumulated the conditions necessary for *Paccekabodhi*, at the time of (their) last existence, they reach an object of thought and a steady inner stirring because of the ripening of their knowledge. Seeing the complete wretchedness of existence, etc., they define the cause of all that happens by means of the knowledge of the self-existent, thoroughly realising: 'This is suffering,' and the other (truths). Devoting themselves to the object of meditation, which consists of the four truths, they crush the conditionings, conforming to their own resolve. In due course they practise insight, successively attain the sublime way, and become enlightened with *Paccekabodhi*. From the moment (they attain) the sublime fruit, they come to be called *Paccekasambuddha*" (Upās 344).

II.1. The Way towards Paccekabodhi: the period in which no Buddha exists

Paccekabuddhas are said to exist only in periods when there are no Buddhas. "A person realizes *Paccekabodhi* only when reborn at a time when there is no Buddha" (S-a III 189 and 208). Other expressions to denote this period are: "the time which lies between (the appearances of) a Lord" (A-a I 194); "a period in which no Teacher has appeared" (Pv-a III 144); and "the period between the Buddha (-periods)" (A-a II 192). One of the main characteristics of the Paccekabuddha's career is that he attains insight during such a period. But this does not mean that his whole aspiration to enlightenment is restricted to this time; it is invariably a matter of many existences of hard work, during which he practises the perfections and accumulates the conditions for enlightenment.

Sometimes a person does not attain arahantship during a Buddha-period and so is driven onwards to strive for enlightenment by himself: "When one has attained the condition (for arahantship), (*upanissaya*), one attains arahantship (if possible) during the first part of one's life, then during the middle part, and if one does not attain it during the middle part, then at the moment of death; if one does not attain it at the moment of death, then one attains if after having become a demi-god (*devaputta*); but if one does not attain it after having become a demi-god, then one enters final *Nibbāna* having become a Paccekabuddha. And if one has not become a Paccekabuddha and does not enter final *Nibbāna*, then one becomes a person of quick intuition like the thera Bāhiya, or a person of great wisdom like the thera Sāriputta" (Sn-a 58). Even the wicked Devadatta could, as a result of taking refuge in the Triple Gem at the moment of death, be assured of future *Paccekabodhi* under the name of Aṭṭhissara after being released from hell.

II.2. The Way towards Paccekabodhi: conditions and resolve

From the moment he makes his resolve (*abhinīhāra*) for *Paccekabodhi*, the future Paccekabuddha is called a *Paccekabodhisatta*. He retains this description through the many existences during which he strives for enlightenment, until his self-enlightenment has been effected. The period during which he practises the perfections is always said to consist of one hundred thousand world periods plus two calculable periods. During this time he could have contact with the Buddhas who arise in the world.

The conditions needed to make the resolve to go the way leading to *Paccekabodhi* are enumerated in several works. The commentary to the *Suttanipāta* gives the following list: being human, possessing the male sex, seeing those who are free of evil influences, meritorious act and desire.

These conditions are explained as follows:

"Being human" means: "birth as a human being. If the one who lives in other than human births, in all births, even birth as a god, the aspiration (*paṇidhi*) is not successful."

"Possessing the male sex" means: "existence as a man; of those who live in a human birth, but as a woman, as someone without sex or as a hermaphrodite, etc., the aspiration is not successful."

"Seeing those who are free of evil influences" means: "seeing Buddhas, Paccekabuddhas and disciples."

"Meritorious act" means: "doing the superior thing, the meaning of which is renunciation; for having renounced life, etc., there is success for the one who has the aspiration."

"Desire" means: "willingness to do something. One who possesses this strong (desire) will be successful" (Sn-a 48–31).

Here also, the Paccekabuddha's conditions differ from those of the *Sammāsambuddha* and the disciple. Instead of five conditions, the *Sammāsambuddha*'s list comprises eight, namely: being human, possessing the male sex, the cause (*hetu,* i.e. the condition for arahantship), seeing a teacher, entering upon religious life (*pabbajjā*), possessing virtue, meritorious act and desire. The conditions for the disciple are: meritorious act and desire.

II.3. The Way towards Paccekabodhi: instruction

The fact that future Paccekabuddhas do not receive instruction and that Paccekabuddhas do not teach is often mentioned as one of their main characteristics. This is correct as there is no account of his systematic teaching. But it is said that he teaches the *Dhamma*. This section deals with the instruction received by the Paccekabodhisatta and not with instruction given by a Paccekabuddha. However, since Paccekabuddhas sometimes instruct aspirants for *Paccekabodhi*, it is difficult to separate the two. There are several methods by which the future Paccekabuddha can be induced to enter the way leading to self-enlightenment. Most of the methods help him to concentrate on that object of meditation which is his specific starting-point on the way. These ways of instruction mainly consist of subtle influences, instigations and pushes into the right direction, rather than of thorough instruction regarding the nature of the way and the reality of enlightenment. The Paccekabodhisatta receives help in the first stage of his development, but from that point onward he has to fulfil the way by himself. In this respect one is justified saying that he does not receive instruction. Others only provide him with an opportunity to start upon the way by helping him to find and concentrate upon his object of meditation, which is his personal key to insight.

Sometimes the influence is exercised on purpose, sometimes it seems accidental. An example of the first possibility can be found in the *Suttanipāta* commentary, where it is related how a

Paccekabuddha tricks a Paccekabodhisatta into coming to his hut in order to provide him with an opportunity to meditate. The commentary to the verses of the *Suttanipāta* relates many examples of "accidental" influence. The Paccekabodhisatta's maturity enables him to recognize these events as not being accidental, but as extremely meaningful in his own spiritual development.

Another way of "instruction" often found in connection with the Paccekabodhisatta is that of example. This can be the exemplary behaviour and way of life of the Paccekabuddha which impresses the Paccekabodhisatta: a Paccekabuddha is supposed to teach by means of the body (*kāyika*). It can also be the example of some natural event, as for instance in the verse and its commentary in which the freedom of deer gives rise to a meditation on freedom and bondage. A comparison used by an instructing Paccekabuddha can also provide the Paccekabodhisatta with an object of meditation. In addition to these ways of influence, a more systematic method of instruction may be used. This can take place during the past existences of the Paccekabodhisatta before he made his resolve to enter the way to *Paccekabodhi*, and it may have been given by past Buddhas. But after the resolve to strive for *Paccekabodhi* has been made, whatever instruction he receives comes from Paccekabuddhas, and is said to be confined to the giving of the entrance to religious life (*pabbajjā*) and the transmission of the basic rules of conduct of ascetics (*abhisamācārika*).

The instruction, if it occurs, is very limited, and provides the person striving for enlightenment with only vague indications regarding the stages he will have to pass and the difficulties attached to these.

An element of the greatest importance for the Paccekabodhisatta's way towards enlightenment is his attainment of an object of meditation. This object provides him with a means to attain *jhāna* and insight. It is always obtained and developed by the Paccekabodhisatta himself, although sometimes with the help of persons or circumstances. The attainment of an object of meditation conducive to insight is the first step on the last and decisive part of the way. It provides the Paccekabodhisatta with the means to develop wisdom and consequently to attain enlightenment. The primary objects of meditation will be discussed below (see II. 5.).

II.4. The Way towards Paccekabodhi: the entrance upon religious life (*pabbajjā*)

Pabbajjā is not considered essential for the attainment of *Paccekabodhi*, as is clear from its omission from the list of conditions for the resolve. The *Jātakas* also describe a few cases in which *Paccekabodhi* has been attained without formal entrance upon religious life. For example, in one story, one of two friends steals his friend's drinking-water, but then repents and attains enlightenment shortly after reflecting: "If it increases, this thirst of mine will throw me into lower states of existence."

The same *Jātaka* passage provides us with four more examples of quick and sudden attainment of *Paccekabodhi*:

"A man who could not divert his attention from the beautiful wife of another man thought: 'If it increases, this greed of mine will throw me into lower states of existence'; then, with agitated mind, he cultivated insight and produced the knowledge of *Paccekabodhi*. Standing in the air he taught the *Dhamma* and then went to the Nandamūlaka slope.

"A father and son, waylaid by robbers while travelling, agreed to conceal the nature of their relationship from the robbers so that the latter would not think of taking one of them hostage for a ransom. The son afterwards regretted his lie: 'If it increases, this sin will throw me into lower states of existence; I shall subdue this fault.' He then cultivated insight and produced the knowledge of *Paccekabodhi*. Standing in the air, he taught the *Dhamma* to his father and then went to the Nandamūlaka slope.

"A village headman, who had forbidden the slaughter of animals, had to consent to such slaughter as an offering to the *yakkhas* during their annual festival. But people slaughtered more animals after having received his consent. Thinking: 'These people who are killing those living beings kill because of the consent (given by) me alone,' he felt remorse. While still standing by the window, he cultivated insight and produced the knowledge of *Paccekabodhi*. Thereupon he taught the *Dhamma*, standing in the air, and then went to the Nandamūlaka slope.

"Another village headman, who had forbidden the sale of spirituous liquors, consented to its consumption during the drinking festival with the result that fights arose, people were wounded and killed and many penalties were inflicted. Thinking: 'If this had not been permitted by me, they would not have known this suffering,' he felt remorse. He then cultivated insight and produced knowledge of *Paccekabodhi*. Thereupon he taught the *Dhamma*, standing in the air, saying: 'Be vigilant,' and then went to the Nandamūlaka slope" (J-a IV, 114–116).

In these cases *Paccekabodhi* was attained in the lay state. But it should be mentioned that after attaining *Paccekabodhi* as laymen and going to the Nandamūlaka slope, these newly enlightened Paccekabuddhas formally entered upon religious life.

However, in nearly all the accounts of the Paccekabodhisatta's typical career, mention is made of *pabbajjā* as an important phase of the way preceding and leading to enlightenment. The term *pabbajjā* used with regard to the Paccekabodhisatta's entrance upon religious life denotes his abandoning the world and adopting the way of life of an ascetic as a means to attain insight and enlightenment. The event is also called *samaṇaka pabbajjā*, "entrance upon the life of an ascetic." It is not identical with the ceremony of *pabbajjā* described in the *Vinaya* texts, as this ceremony marking formal admission into the *Saṅgha* is quite distinct from the Paccekabodhisatta's act of leaving the world to devote himself to solitary asceticism.

The events which stir the Paccekabodhisatta to his renunciation are of several characteristic types: disgust after one has recognized greed as a negative, obstructive factor; the behaviour of wicked friends; the realization that the way of life of an ascetic is to be preferred; the wish not to be bound to this world and its obligations. The result of reflection along these lines is in most cases a feeling of dissatisfaction or even disgust with the present situation and the decision to enter upon religious life, which means donning the yellow robe and leading the life of an ascetic.

With the *pabbajjā*, the Paccekabodhisatta takes a final step to dedicate the rest of his life to the attainment of enlightenment. He enters upon religious life alone, both in the sense of being self-motivated and of being physically isolated: in this he is said to be solitary. However, there are some references to a kind of *pabbajjā*-ceremony performed by Paccekabuddhas for someone striving for *Paccekabodhi* who wishes to live in their community. The candidate expresses a wish to enter upon religious life, and the Paccekabuddhas acknowledge this by stating that they accept him.

This simple ceremony seems to have the function of protecting from profanation the instruction to be given to the candidate. Only he who enters upon religious life can receive instruction.

Taking up a life of asceticism means accepting a life with various hardships. The *Suttanipāta*-commentary says: "Hard is the entrance upon religious life, like walking up and down upon the edge of a razor." And the various difficulties of the ascetic's way of life are described, such as lying down on a mat of grass or a bed of ropes, exposure to cold, wind, biting insects, hunger and thirst, walking for a long time to collect alms, eating dirty food, etc. But the Paccekabodhisatta who is able to endure this hard life, by means of either the power of his will to attain enlightenment or the power of consideration, attains to *Paccekabodhi*. Concerning the willpower needed to persevere in the midst of privation: "Those who have entered upon religious life are not subject to (external) conditions. They exercise power over a thought (to find better conditions), they are not in the power of such a thought."

Sometimes the problems and hardships may be too much for a young Paccekabodhisatta. He then may leave the religious life and enter it again after having regained the necessary energy. *Pabbajjā* is said to be only "practised by noble people, having many advantages, being extremely pleasant, (and) although it is this, (it is) not coveted and not wished for by low people who are overwhelmed by greed."

If there are no good teachers during the period in which he lives, a Paccekabodhisatta who intends to enter upon religious life can be confronted with the problem of his ignorance regarding the way of life of an ascetic. In such a case the instruction he needs can be given by a Paccekabuddha who descends from Gandhamādana to teach the proper ways of conduct for a Paccekabodhisatta. When a Paccekabuddha tries to explain the way of life of those whose goal is *Paccekabodhi*, he shows the young Paccekabodhisatta, by means of supernatural power, a place in the Himalayas where Paccekabuddhas live: "And there he saw Paccekabuddhas leaning on a balustrade, standing and walking to and fro and doing things like dyeing and needle-work (and the Paccekabuddha explained): 'from the time of *pabbajjā* onwards, ascetics are indeed allowed for the sake of effecting their own salvation to go to (any) place they wish and desire, this is right'" (Sn-a 98–105).

II.5. The Way towards Paccekabodhi: the meditations

Having entered upon religious life, the Paccekabodhisatta lives the life of an ascetic and dedicates himself to meditation practices. Except for the instances of sudden and spontaneous enlightenment, the aspirant for *Paccekabodhi* has to strive to reach his goal through the hard practice of meditation.

Several forms of meditation are mentioned in the texts with reference to the Paccekabodhisatta's practice. He can choose whichever method he wishes, according to personal preference, to prepare his mind for the attainment of enlightenment.

One type of practice is *kasiṇa*-meditation, meditating on a specially prepared object capable of leading to *jhāna.* The *kasiṇas* are ten: the earth, water, fire, air, blue, yellow, red, white, space and consciousness *kasiṇas.*

Another type of practice, developed by those who abide in thoughtfulness, is the four applications of mindfulness (*satipaṭṭhānā*), namely, mindfulness directed towards the body, feelings, thoughts and mind-objects. These meditations lead to wisdom.

Still another group of meditations often mentioned in connection with the Paccekabodhisatta's way towards enlightenment is the set of four called the immeasurable states (*appamaññā*) or divine abodes (*brahmavihāras*). The four are friendliness (*mettā*), compassion (*karuṇā*), sympathy (*muditā*) and equanimity (*upekkhā*). Of these four, friendliness is described most frequently as applied by Paccekabodhisattas.

The consequence of this stress on friendliness is the great protective power ascribed to the Paccekabuddha. The *Apadāna* mentions his mindfulness regarding the inhabitants of border districts, and there are indications that images of Paccekabuddhas were used for the purpose of protection. This could well be the outcome of their reputation for extended practice of *mettā*, popularly believed to be a protective power which counteracts inimical influences. Two stories provide evidence for this. The commentary on the *Udāna* mentions the story of a robber who shot a Paccekabuddha to get his bowl and robe, probably to use as a disguise as well as a good-luck charm (*iddhimaya-patta-cīvara*), (Ud-a 95). And in the *Jātakas* (J-a II 197) a hunter is said to use the guise of a Paccekabuddha while hunting elephants for the same purposes, namely, as an appearance that inspires confidence and as a protection from wild beasts. The *Isigili Sutta*, in which the names of Paccekabuddhas are listed, is recited during the Sinhalese *Paritta*-ceremony; this tradition points in the same direction.

Sometimes insight into the truths or into certain doctrinal points is not the direct result of systematic practice, but arises spontaneously under the influence of circumstances. The first flash of insight occurs thus and then the Paccekabodhisatta can systematically contemplate it. This rather sudden insight, as described in the relevant texts, occurs either through understanding the doctrine of impermanence, suffering and non-self, or through understanding the origination by dependence (*paṭiccasamuppāda*). In some cases it arises through insight into the true nature of the round of existence, i.e., *saṃsāra*, and the end of the round, i.e., *Nibbāna*.

The attainments (*samāpatti*) are often mentioned in connection with the Paccekabodhisatta. They include the four stages of the world of form, i.e., the four *jhānas*, and the four stages of the world without form, i.e. the four immaterial attainments (*āruppa*). The attainment of suppression (*nirodhasamāpatti*) is most frequently mentioned in connection with the Paccekabuddha. He is supposed to abide in this state of meditation while living on Mount Gandhamādana and comes out of it only to go seeking for alms. The attainment of suppression belongs to the so-called liberations (*vimokkha*), among which it is ranked as the last, the eighth, the attainment of the suppression of consciousness and sensation (*saññāvedayita-nirodha-samāpatti*). It also comes as the ninth of the nine gradually ascending stages (*anupubbavihārā*), preceded by the four *jhānas* and the four immaterial attainments. The immaterial attainments were probably known and practised by yogis and ascetics before the time of the Buddha, for it is mentioned that they had been taught to him by his teachers, Ālāra Kālāma and Uddaka Rāmaputta.

The Paccekabuddha who has entered a state of deep meditation is described as being invulnerable. The Commentary on the Dhammapada relates the story of a Paccekabuddha who could not be injured while being in the midst of a fire: "Even after having brought a thousand cartloads of wood and having kindled (that), they could not even make a show of heat; therefore, having risen (from his meditation) on the seventh day, he went as he wished" (Dhp-a I 2, 225.5 ff.).

The Paccekabuddha's concentration (*samādhi*) is not in need of further training (*asekha*) (Nidd II 64) and is equated with the four *jhānas* (Sn-a 64):

The different stages of *jhāna* are described in several places. The Paccekabuddha's way to attain and develop these is the same as a Buddha's or disciple's way. The fourth *jhāna* is said to be characterized by equanimity and quietude, both qualities preferably attributed to the Paccekabuddha. Based on this *jhāna*, Buddhas, as well as Paccekabuddhas, attain enlightenment during one meditation.

Another important characteristic of the fourth jhāna is its function as the basis for higher knowledge (*abhiññā-pādaka*). This is of special interest to the Paccekabuddha because, based on this higher knowledge, he is able to fly through the air, according to the texts his usual way of transportation from his residence to the places where he intends to go and beg for alms. In addition to using these *abhiññās* as a means for his own transportation, he can also use them "to increase the faith" of those who are watching his miraculous powers, sometimes combining this with a teaching of the *Dhamma*.

II.6. The Way towards Paccekabodhi: insight and enlightenment

The devoted practice of meditation leads towards quietude (*samatha*) and insight (*vipassanā*) into the four truths. Quietude is the calm mental state which is, at one level, a necessary condition for insight, and at another level, an inseparable concomitant of insight. It thus results in an appeasement of the defilements (*kilesa*) obstructing the attainment of enlightenment. Insight prevents the defilements from arising again and can therefore be considered the last stage before enlightenment. For the attainment of enlightenment it is necessary that quietude and insight be brought into equilibrium; in this connection they are equated with concentration (*samādhi-samatha*) and wisdom (*paññā-vipassanā*).

Thus, having followed the noble eightfold way, the aspirant understands the conditionings (*saṅkhāra*). Having passed the four

Ways of the noble ones—the way of entrance into the stream, of once-return, of non-return and of arahantship—and attained the four corresponding fruits, the Paccekabodhisatta attains the knowledge of *Paccekabodhi*.

The self-enlightenment is called: "that which goes together with the state of a self-existent one" (Khp-a 229). "It means the knowledge of the four ways and wisdom. The Paccekabuddha realizes by means of this knowledge of enlightenment: 'All conditionings are impermanent.'" "All his defilements destroyed, their roots cut, like palm trees uprooted, conditionings that will not again exist in the future, in this way completely free from faults, he is solitary; being without a teacher, self-existent, perfectly enlightened by himself with regard to self-enlightenment" (Sn-a 64).

The enlightenment can only be described by means of relevant passages from the texts. But these very rarely refer to the experience as it is undergone by the Paccekabuddha himself because it surpasses all possibilities of verbal expression. A feeling of supramundane happiness has been connected with this enlightenment as well as serenity of senses and mind. The peace which results from the experience is called "not sown, not strewn, not explained, not taught, not made known, not established, not unveiled, not explained in detail, and not made manifest, nor shown" (Nidd II 350).

II.7. The Way towards Paccekabodhi: Nibbāna

The career of a *Sammāsambuddha*, Paccekabuddha and disciple ends in the state of *Nibbāna*. *Nibbāna* is attained first in their present lives, as the *Nibbāna* with a residue of substratum (*saupādisesa-nibbāna*), and then at the moment of death as the state of final *Nibbāna*, *Nibbāna* without a residue of substratum (*nirupādisesa-nibbāna*).

The attainment of final *Nibbāna* by five hundred Paccekabuddhas is described as follows: "Having played the game of the jhānas for three night-watches, taking hold of the plank of the meditation-support (*ālambana*) at the rise of dawn, based on this, the Paccekabuddha Mahāpaduma entered the sphere of the *Nibbāna* without residue of substratum. In this way all other (Paccekabuddhas) also entered *Nibbāna*" (A-a I 174). This closely resembles the description of the Buddha's last meditations (*Dīgha Nikāya* no. 16). The story continues to relate how, after the five hundred Paccekabuddhas had entered final *Nibbāna*, a servant of the king was sent to their huts to invite them for a meal. Seeing their dead bodies and thinking that they had fallen asleep, he touched their feet. The coolness of their feet then made it clear to him that they had entered final *Nibbāna*. Thereupon a funeral ceremony was ordered and their relics were placed in a sepulchral monument (*cetiya*). The Paccekabuddha Sunetta likewise entered final *Nibbāna* after he was killed by a stone from a sling.

The *Khuddakapāṭha* Commentary relates the story of the young brahmin Susīma, who, after having obtained instruction from Paccekabuddhas, attained *Paccekabodhi*. Famous and honoured, he soon entered final *Nibbāna* because (in the past) he had performed an act which had led to a short lifespan. The other Paccekabuddhas and the laymen then performed a funeral ceremony and placed his remains in a stupa, which thereafter was worshipped with flowers, processions, etc. (Khp-a I 198–200).

The entrance into final *Nibbāna* of the last Paccekabuddha of a period in which there is no Buddha takes place shortly before or after the descent of the future Buddha into the world. *Suttanipāta* verse 74 is ascribed to the last Paccekabuddha, Mātaṅga, who lived before the time of the Buddha. The commentator relates that, having heard from a Bodhisatta that a future Buddha had just been born, he went to Mount Mahāpapāta in the Himalayas, the mountain from which Paccekabuddhas can enter final *Nibbāna* when throwing themselves down from the rock. There he entered *Nibbāna*. Up to that moment he had been one who had attained the *Nibbāna* with a residue of substratum, but after uttering his verse and throwing himself down the precipice, he became one who attained *Nibbāna* without a residue of substratum.

III. The Paccekabuddha's Way of Life

III.1. The Paccekabuddha's way of life: solitary (*eka*)

One of the main characteristics of the Paccekabuddha's life is his solitariness. Although groups of Paccekabuddhas are mentioned as living together in a community, this communal living is confined to the practical aspects of their life. It is not connected with the practice of meditation and progress on the way towards enlightenment. Progress has to be acquired individually and cannot be made in communion with others.

A Paccekabuddha, according to the Cullaniddesa, is called solitary or alone in six respects: "1. He is alone in the entrance upon religious life; 2. he is alone in having no second, i.e., no companion; 3. he is alone in the annihilation of thirst; 4. he is alone, being absolutely free from passion, hatred and delusion, being free from defilements; 5. he is alone having gone the way which is to be gone alone; 6. he is alone being perfectly enlightened with regard to the highest unique self-enlightenment" (Nidd II 112–114).[12]

The text provides us with the following explanations of these six points:

"1. How is a Paccekabuddha alone in the entrance upon religious life? A Paccekabuddha, who is young, his hair very black, possessing auspicious youth, in the first part of his adult life, leaves the circle of his relatives, while his parents, unwilling to let him go, cry and complain with tearful faces. Having cut off entirely all the obstacles of living at home—wife and children, relatives, friends and comrades, and storage—he shaves off his hair and beard, puts on yellow robes and leaves home for homelessness. Undertaking the state of possessing nothing, he goes on alone.

"2. How is a Paccekabuddha alone in having no companion? Thus having entered upon religious life, he retires to the forest and goes on alone.

"3. How is a Paccekabuddha alone in the annihilation of thirst? Thus being alone, without companion, remaining zealous, ardent, of resolute will, ... exerting himself in the great exertion; having destroyed Māra and his army, Namuci, kinsman of the careless, he annihilates thirst, which is ensnaring and spreading, (and means) attachment ...

"4. How is a Paccekabuddha alone, being absolutely free from passion? By means of the destruction of passion, being absolutely

12. 1. *Pabbajjāsaṅkhātena eko;* 2. *adutiyaṭṭhena eko;* 3. *taṇhā-pahānaṭṭhena eko;* 4. *ekantavītarāgoti* (*-doso,-moho, nikkileso*) *ti eko;* 5. *ekāyanamaggaṃ gato ti eko;* 6. *ekaṃ anuttaraṃ paccekasambodhiṃ abhisambuddho ti eko.*

free from passion, he is alone; by means of the destruction of hatred, being absolutely free from hatred, he is alone; (by means of the destruction of) delusion ... (free) from delusion; (by means of the destruction of) defilements ... (free from) defilements.

"5. How is a Paccekabuddha alone, having gone the way which is to be gone alone?[13] The way which is to be gone alone means the four bases of mindfulness, the four right exertions, the four bases of supernatural power, the faculties, the five powers, the seven constituents of enlightenment, the noble eightfold way.

"6. How is a Paccekabuddha alone, being perfectly enlightened with regard to the highest unique self-enlightenment? Enlightenment (*bodhi*) means the knowledge of the four ways (of sanctity) and wisdom ... The Paccekabuddha realizes by this knowledge of enlightenment: 'All conditionings are impermanent' ..." (Nidd II 113–114).

The stories of the lives of Paccekabuddhas, especially those found in the *Suttanipāta* Commentary, again and again stress the importance of solitariness for their attainment of enlightenment. This need to retire from the world and from men is well known in the Indian religious tradition; but contrary to the practice of most Hindu and Buddhist ascetics, who leave the world but not necessarily their fellow-ascetics, the Paccekabodhisatta strives for insight in isolation. A community of fellow ascetics is felt by him to be an obstruction to his goal.

In connection with his solitariness the texts say that the Paccekabuddha is "like the horn of a rhinoceros" (*khaggavisāṇa-kappa*), comparing the one horn of the rhinoceros to the solitariness of the Paccekabuddha and the animal's solitary way of life to the way of life of the Paccekabuddha. This comparison, running throughout the *Suttanipāta* verses, is explained in Cullaniddesa as follows: "As the horn of the rhinoceros is alone and without a second, so too is the Paccekabuddha, ... who solitary, without a

13. *Ekāyana magga*: The Commentary on the *Majjhimanikāya* (M-a I 229) explains *ekāyana* with *ekamagga* and gives two meanings of the word *eka*. The first is related to the indivisibility of the way (*na dvedhāpathabhūtoti*); the second to the solitariness of the person following the way: it should be followed by a person alone (*ekena āyitabbo ti*), by someone who has abandoned communication with a crowd, who is withdrawn and separated.

second, goes on in the world being completely released from fetters" (Nidd II 129). The *Visuddhimagga* says: "(they) resemble the horn of the rhinoceros because of their solitary way of life" (Vism 234). And the commentary on the *Apadāna*: "as the horn of a rhinoceros is solitary and without a second, so is the Paccekabuddha ..." (Ap-a 133) "... because of his not being in contact with a crowd" (Ap-a 204). Although all commentaries take this comparison with reference to the horn of a rhinoceros, they combine this with an allusion to the Paccekabuddha's way of life. Since the rhino's way of life can equally be called solitary, it seems that in the comparison both aspects are intended: the one horn as well as the solitary life are compared to the way of life of the Paccekabuddha.

III.2. The Paccekabuddha's Way of Life: places of residence

Mount Gandhamādana, with its Nandamūlaka slope, situated in the northern Himalayas is mentioned as the favourite place of residence for Paccekabuddhas. Buddhaghosa says about them: "One should know that the Gandhamādana lies beyond the seven mountains, the Cullakāḷa, the Mahākāḷa, the Nāgapaliveṭhana, the Candagabbha, the Suriyagabbha, the Suvaṇṇapassa and the Himavanta. In that place there is a slope called Nandamūlaka, the dwelling place of the Paccekabuddhas and three caves: the Gold Cave (Suvaṇṇaguhā), the Jewel Cave (Maṇiguhā) and the Silver Cave (Rajataguhā). Here, in the opening of the Jewel Cave, is the tree called Mañjūsaka, which is one *yojana* high and one *yojana* wide. Whatever flowers there are in the water or on the ground, the tree makes them all flower together on the day a Paccekabuddha arrives. Around the tree there is a platform consisting of all sorts of jewels. There the Weeping-wind throws away the rubbish, the Even-making wind levels the sand, which is made of all sorts of jewels, the Sprinkling-wind sprinkles water brought from Lake Anotatta, the Sweet-fragrance-bringing-wind brings fragrances from all fragrant trees in the Himalayas, the Gathering-wind gathers and strews flowers, the Spreading-wind spreads them to all sides. There are always seats prepared, upon which—on the day of the arrival of a Paccekabuddha and on the day of *uposatha*—all Paccekabuddhas, having gathered, sit down.

"When a Paccekabuddha arrives there just after attaining enlightenment, he seats himself on the prepared seat. Then, if at the time other Paccekabuddhas are present, they also assemble at that same moment and sit down on the prepared seats. Having seated themselves, they enter an attainment and come out of it again. Then, in order to satisfy all, the eldest of the community inquires after the newly arrived Paccekabuddha's object of meditation: 'How was (this enlightenment of yours) attained?' And then he speaks his own verse, the solemn utterance (*udāna*) and its explanation. Later the Lord recited that same verse after being questioned by the Reverend Ānanda, and Ānanda recited it during the (first) Council as well. Each verse that was spoken in the place of those who are enlightened to self-enlightenment under the Mañjūsaka tree, was recited three or four times during the Council by Ānanda at the time he was questioned" (Sn-a 66–67).

The fact that Paccekabuddhas—as many of the Indian ascetics—prefer to reside in the North, in the Himalayan regions, is confirmed by other sources. The following fragment from the *Jātakas*, for example, relates the story of King Bharata (one of the former existences of the Buddha), who wished to present offerings to holy men and tried to find their whereabouts: "Standing in his royal court, having made the fivefold prostration with his face directed to the East he greeted (them) respectfully and said: 'I pay homage to the arahants in the eastern region. If we possess any virtue may you, out of compassion for us, receive our alms.' He then threw seven handfuls of jasmine flowers (into the air). But as there are no Paccekabuddhas in the East, they did not come on the following day. On the second day he paid homage to the South; from there they did not come either. On the third day he paid homage to the West; from there they did not come either. On the fourth day he paid homage to the North and said: 'May the Paccekabuddhas who live in the region of the northern Himalayas receive our alms.' He then threw seven handfuls of jasmine flowers (into the air). The flowers went to the Nandamūlaka slope and fell down upon the five hundred Paccekabuddhas. Reflecting on this, they knew the fact of the king's invitation. On the following day they addressed seven Paccekabuddhas and said: 'Sirs, the king invites you, show him (our) favour' ..." (J-a III 470–473).

A Paccekabuddha is able to go wherever he wishes and to live in any secluded, solitary place he likes. But from the texts it is clear that after his enlightenment he prefers to reside on Mount Gandhamādana, on the Nandamūlaka slope, in the Himalayas. Out of compassion he leaves this place to collect alms, to offer people an opportunity to increase their merit, or to help a Paccekabodhisatta, usually a former friend and companion on the way, to obtain his object of meditation.

Other places mentioned in connection with the Paccekabuddha's way of life are Isigili and Isipatana, the place usually called Migadāye, the Deer Park near Benares where the Buddha preached his first sermon and proclaimed the four noble truths. Isigili, one of the five mountains near Rājagaha, is mentioned in the *Majjhimanikāya* (M III 68–69), where it is related that five hundred Paccekabuddhas dwelt on the mountain in a cave. They were sometimes seen entering the cave after their almsround, whereupon people used to say: "The mountain swallows the seers" (*isī gilati*). This became the name of the place, Isigili. The *Papañcasūdanī* adds that when the seers returned from their almsround, the mountain would open like a huge pair of doors and let them enter.

The story which is connected with the name of Isipatana can be found in many texts, from the Pāli commentaries to the Sanskrit *Mahāvastu* and *Lalitavistara*: "After seven days these Paccekabuddhas come out of the attainment of suppression. (Coming) from the Nandamūlaka slope, they perform the (daily) duty of washing the mouth, etc., in Lake Anotatta, and having gone by air, these seers (*isi*) come down (*patanti*) there through the power of descending; they assemble there on *uposatha* days as well as other days. Leaving for the Gandhamādana it is said that they rise up (*uppatanti*) from there. Because of this power of coming down and rising up (*patan' uppatanavasa*) of the seers, this (place) is called Isipatana" (S-a III 296).

And: "Seers, who are called Buddhas and Paccekabuddhas, come (there), (the former) to turn the wheel of the *Dhamma* and (the latter) to celebrate *uposatha*. Instead of the word *patana* ('coming down') there should be (the word) *sannipāta* ('assembling'); this is the meaning (of Isipatana)" (A-a II 180).

The *Mahāvastu* explains this name in connection with the entrance into final *Nibbāna* of the five hundred Paccekabuddhas at the time of the birth of the Buddha, which was proclaimed to them by the gods. On this occasion the Paccekabuddhas gathered together at this place and, as related in the verses of the *Khaggavisāṇasutta* of the *Suttanipāta*, narrated their personal ways to enlightenment. Then they flew up into the air and consumed their bodies by fire, in this way entering final *Nibbāna*. After their death their bodily relics fell down (*sarīrāni patitāni*), which explains the name of the place.

In addition to these traditional residences of Paccekabuddhas there is also evidence that, like the early Buddhist monks, they wandered through the country. Again, like the early Buddhist monks, they were thought to spend the rainy season in one place in a hut built by laymen. This retreat during the rainy season is one of the traits common to most Indian ascetics and ascetic communities and is therefore also attributed to the Paccekabuddha. The *Manorathapurāṇī* relates the presentation of huts to Paccekabuddhas as a shelter for the rainy season by a pious woman, said to be a former existence of Mahā-gotamī: "Five Paccekabuddhas, (coming) from the Nandamūlaka slope, descended in Isipatana and walked for alms in the city. Then they came back to that same Isipatana. Saying: 'We shall ask for manual labour for the building of a hut in view of the approach of the rainy season,' they dressed in robes and entered the city in the evening ... At once they (i.e., Mahā-gotamī and her servants) entered the forest, put together the wooden material, were each of them thoughtful and made (for each of the Paccekabuddhas) a hut surrounded by a cloister-walk, etc. In it they placed a bed, a chair, drinking- and wash-water, etc., and having made the Paccekabuddhas consent to live there, they presented the excellent alms-gift" (A-a I 338–339).

On account of its quiet surroundings Isipatana was preferred by Paccekabuddhas as a place suitable for meditation. As such it was probably frequented before and also in the time of the Buddha.

III.3. The Paccekabuddha's Way of Life: behaviour (*cariyā*)

The commentaries distinguish eight aspects of a Buddhist ascetic's behaviour: "(i) the behaviour with regard to the ways of deportment (*iriyā-patha*)[14]—the four ways of deportment of those

14. I.e., the four bodily postures of walking, standing, sitting and lying down.

who are committed to resolve; (ii) behaviour with regard to the organs of sense (*āyatana*), with regard to the inner organs of sense, for those who guard the doors of the senses; (iii) behaviour with regard to mindfulness (*sati*), with regard to the four applications of mindfulness, for those who abide without negligence; (iv) behaviour with regard to concentration (*samādhi*), with regard to the four *jhānas*, for those who apply themselves to higher thought; (v) behaviour with regard to knowledge (*ñāṇa*), with regard to the four noble truths, for those who are endowed with intelligence; (vi) behaviour with regard to the way (*magga*), with regard to the four ways of the noble ones, for those who are rightly following this; (vii) behaviour with regard to the (supreme) attainment, with regard to the four fruits of asceticism, for those who have attained the fruitions; (viii) behaviour directed to the welfare of the world, with regard to all beings, (practised by) the three Buddhas,[15] but in this connection to a limited extent by the Paccekabuddha and the disciple" (Sn-a 64).

This passage shows that the Paccekabodhisatta's behaviour was considered to depend on the stage of his maturity and the level of his concentration. For example, shortly after having made the resolve, he is apt to direct his attention to the four ways of deportment, the approved behaviour of the pious. Then, controlling the sense faculties, he is able to concentrate upon mindfulness and to practise the four stages of *jhāna* with the aim of developing the knowledge of the four noble truths. Capable of going the way, he gradually passes the stages which lead him to his goal. Having attained the goal as a Paccekabuddha, he then is inclined to act, to a limited extent, for the welfare of other beings.

In section II. 5 we already mentioned the most important forms of meditation practised by the Paccekabuddha both during the time he is engaged in working for his salvation and after he has attained enlightenment. In this section we shall consider more closely his behaviour in the world, the way he is said to affect people and his surroundings and the way in which he is seen by those who meet him.

As an ascetic, the Paccekabuddha acts according to the rules traditionally followed by ascetics and monks, which had already

15. I.e., *Sammāsambuddha*, Paccekabuddha and *sāvaka*.

been developed before the Buddha's time by numerous individual religious men, ascetic communities and wandering monks. He is regarded by the people who meet him in a similar way as other ascetics and holy men and therefore to him are ascribed similar characteristics, rules of conduct and way of life. We have seen that the rules of conduct regarding his surroundings, his residence, the observance of *uposatha*, the sojourn in a fixed place during the rainy season, the way in which his hut was built and furnished, etc., have parallels in the monastic rules found in the Vinaya.

Parallel with the Buddhist monk and with other groups of ascetics, the Paccekabuddha's way of collecting alms is similarly bound to certain rules of conduct. These are described as follows: "The Paccekabuddha, having clothed himself in the morning, having taken bowl and robe, enters a village or hamlet for alms: his body controlled, his speech controlled, his mind controlled, his mindfulness fixed, his senses restrained, his eyes downcast, perfect with regard to the way of deportment, approaching high and low families, he walks to collect alms" (Nidd II 267).

When a Paccekabuddha resides on the Gandhamādana, he makes special preparations before he sets out to walk for alms: "The Paccekabuddha Tagarasikhin, third son of Padumavatī, spending his time on Mount Gandhamādana in the happiness resulting from the attainments of the fruit, rose in the morning. He washed his mouth in Lake Anotatta, clothed himself in Manosilātala, put on his waistband, took his bowl and upper robe and entered the fourth *jhāna*, which forms the basis for supernatural knowledge. He then flew through the air by means of higher power and came down at the city-gate. Having covered himself with his robe, he gradually reached the door of the house of a wealthy merchant with his bowl, ... with pleasing approach, etc." (S-a I 160). Having received alms, the Paccekabuddha usually recites a benediction expressing his hope that the donor's wish will be fulfilled, then he rises up into the air. He is sometimes said to deliver some teaching of *Dhamma* or some admonition on that occasion. Buddhaghosa mentions, as a condition for *Paccekabodhi*, the practice during almsround of the "duty of the one who has gone and has returned" (*gatapaccāgatavatta*),[16] which means the

16. A description can be found in the Commentary on the Satipaṭṭhānasutta.

keeping in mind of the object of reflection during the whole period of the almsround. It is not clear, however, whether he means that during a former existence as a monk the Paccekabodhisatta had to fulfil this duty, or whether Paccekabuddhas also are considered to observe this rule.

The result of insulting a Paccekabuddha is, in almost all the cases described in the canonical and commentarial literature, a lower and miserable form of existence in a following rebirth. The *Sāratthappakāsinī* relates how a Paccekabuddha was insulted by a king who felt jealous at the honour given to the old ascetic with his worn-out clothes: "One Paccekabuddha, having come from Mount Gandhamādana, was walking for alms in that city, his senses serene, his mind serene, endowed with the highest restraint. A great multitude looked at that Paccekabuddha, which, in doing so, diverted its devoted attendance to the king ... The Paccekabuddha was an old man, being in his last period of life. His robes, too, were worn-out; here and there threads unravelled. When the king saw the Paccekabuddha, who had fulfilled the perfections during two incalculable periods plus one hundred thousand *kalpas*, he did not have even a little serenity of mind, nor did he even show the slightest sign of respect by folding his hands to greet him. The king, thinking: 'This ascetic, methinks, does not look at me with envy,' became angry. Saying: 'Where does this leper dressed in leper's clothes come from?' he spat at him and went away. As a result of the ripening of this deed he was reborn in the great hell ..." (S-a I 349).

In the *Manorathapurāṇī*, a woman laughs at a humpbacked Paccekabuddha and as a result of her mockery is reborn as a humpbacked woman (A-a I 375). And in the commentary on the Dhammapada we find: "There was a Paccekabuddha who was a little humpbacked. Then one female servant took a gold drinking-vessel and hiding it under her woollen dress made herself look like a humpbacked woman. Imitating his way of moving she said: 'Thus moves our Paccekabuddha.' As a result of this she was reborn as a humpbacked woman" (Dhp-a I, II 226).

The scholiast of the *Jātakas* relates the story of Prince Duṭṭhakumāra. Since it was predicted: "This prince will die of

---

See Soma Thera, *The Way of Mindfulness*, 4th edition, BPS, p. 88 ff.

lack of drinking-water," the king ordered lakes and tanks to be made everywhere and water jars to be placed in every street or hall. "One day the prince, adorned and dressed, on a sudden inspiration went to the pleasure garden and on his way back saw a Paccekabuddha. A great multitude also saw the Paccekabuddha and honoured, praised and greeted him. The prince thought: 'Going with one like me, they honour, praise and greet this baldhead.' Angrily he descended from his elephant, went to the Paccekabuddha and said: 'Did you, ascetic, receive a meal?'—'Yes, prince,' he was answered. Then the prince took the bowl from his hand and threw it to the ground, crushing it together with the meal into dust by the force of his feet. The Paccekabuddha looked the prince in the face and said: 'Surely this being is lost.' Thereupon the prince said: 'I, ascetic, am the son of King Kitavāsa, Duṭṭhakumāra. What can you do being angry at me and looking at me with your eyes wide open?' The Paccekabuddha, having lost his meal, rose up into the air and went to the Nandamūlaka slope in the northern Himalayas. At that same moment the prince's bad deed ripened and screaming, 'I burn, I burn,' he fell down on the spot. A burning fire rose up in his body. All the drinking-water that had been stored disappeared; the conduits dried up and he, having reached the end of his life in the (same) place, was reborn in the Avīci hell" (J-a II 194–195).

In these cases the persons themselves are entirely responsible for their bad behaviour, but sometimes their act is prompted by Māra, the evil one, as is the story told before (Dhp-a I 2, 196. See above Section I.1).

III.4. The Paccekabuddha's Way of Life: walking for alms

A Paccekabuddha lives upon almsfood, like any other ascetic. He does not actually beg for alms; rather, in the same manner as ordained Buddhist monks, he walks silently among the houses with his alms bowl in his hands. According to the texts, he collects alms not primarily to obtain means of subsistence, but to offer people an opportunity to gain merit by giving him alms. The Indian doctrine of *kamma* taught that offerings made to an ascetic constitute a form of merit yielding favourable results to the giver; offerings made to a fully purified person—a Buddha, Paccekabuddha or *arahant*—produce the highest and most abundant merit.

The Paccekabuddha is especially concerned for those people who are in need of this merit because they live in bad forms of existence: "Paccekabuddhas are compassionate towards those who have entered a bad form of existence" (A-a I 185 ff.). The usual description of a Paccekabuddha's round of alms-gathering starts with his consideration of who would need the merit that can be obtained by the presentation of alms to him. Having found such a person, he then goes to him for alms. Most of the time that person is quite willing to present him with food, for, as can be gathered from the texts, it is considered quite natural for a lay person to supply an ascetic's needs. But there are different ways of giving and the merit depends on the perfection of this act of giving (*dāna*).

After having fulfilled his pious deed, the giver pronounces a wish (*paṭṭhāna*), sometimes more than one, which is always blessed by the Paccekabuddha. When the giving has been perfect, the wish comes to fulfilment. But if the way of giving was imperfect, usually only a part of the wish is fulfilled or it is realised to a limited extent. The wishes that occur in the texts range from riches and material possessions to a heavenly rebirth, insight and enlightenment. Having blessed the wish or wishes the Paccekabuddha then utters his thanks, and in some instances delivers a short teaching or incitement to act rightly. He then continues his almsround or goes through the air to his residence. Giving is considered a highly meritorious act for the laity. It can lead to arahantship, *Paccekabodhi* or Buddhahood, when the one who gives does so with the intention to attain one of these three forms of deliverance.

To receive the full results of giving, three "thoughts" should be perfect: the wish to give, the giving itself and the after-thought, i.e., the absence of subsequent regret. A *Jātaka* deals with the perfect way of giving alms and illustrates it with the story of an unbelieving wealthy merchant from Benares who, having ordered his own meal to be given to the Paccekabuddha Tagarasikhin, later regretted this.

"Once upon a time, when Brahmadatta was king of Benares, there was a rich merchant in Benares who was unbelieving and selfish. He did not give anything to anyone, he did not help with anything. One day while he was on his way to a royal audience, he saw the Paccekabuddha Tagarasikhin walking for alms and having respectfully saluted him he asked him: 'Reverend Sir, have you received alms?' Having received the answer 'Don't we walk on almsround, great merchant?' he ordered a servant: 'Go and bring this man to my home, make him sit down on my seat, fill his bowl with the meal that is prepared for me and order that it be given to him.' The servant brought the Paccekabuddha to the house, made him sit down and told the merchant's wife his master's order. She filled the bowl with a meal which tasted of all kinds of delicacies and gave it to the Paccekabuddha. He took the meal, left the merchant's house and went along the street. The merchant, coming back from the king's court, saw him, respectfully greeted him and asked him: 'Reverend Sir, did you receive a meal?'—'I did, O great merchant.' Having looked at the bowl he was not able to gladden his heart and he was not able to make the after-thought perfect, because he thought 'If slaves or servants had enjoyed this meal of mine they would have done even hard work. Ah! This is a loss for me!'" (J-a III 299–300). Therefore, because of his gift to the Paccekabuddha he acquired much wealth, but he was not capable of enjoying it because he could not make his after-thought perfect.

A similar example can be found in the *Saṃyutta-nikāya*, where it is told how a householder regrets his gift to the Paccekabuddha Tagarasikhin. As a result of this he fails to be reborn in heaven for seven times, as he would have been if he had given wholeheartedly. He does become a wealthy man as a result of his gift, but because of his regret, he cannot enjoy his clothes, cars and the pleasures of the senses.

He who gives perfectly is always protected from dangers. An example of this can be found in the story of the brahmin Saṃkha, famous for his generosity, who planned to go to the Gold-land (Suvaṇṇabhūmi) to acquire still more wealth to give to the poor and needy: "At that time a Paccekabuddha on the Gandhamādana noticed this and saw that he intended to go to acquire wealth. He reflected: 'The great man goes away to acquire wealth. Will there be any hindrance at sea for him or not?' and he knew: 'There will.' Then thinking: 'If he were to give me a sunshade and sandals, this man would find a refuge when his ship is wrecked at sea. He will find a refuge as a result of the presenting of sandals to me. I shall help him.' And having gone by air he came down not far from him (i.e., Saṃkha), and went towards him treading on the hot sand, which was like a layer of burning coal in the warm wind and sunshine. When Saṃkha saw him, his mind was pleased, and he thought: 'A field for merit has come to me; today the seed should be sown by me in this place.' He quickly went up to him and greeted him respectfully, saying: 'Reverend Sir, come from the road for a while out of compassion for me and come to the foot of this tree.' Having spoken in this way, while the Paccekabuddha went to the foot of the tree, he took away the sand from the foot of the tree, spread out his upper robe, and made the Paccekabuddha sit down. He then washed the Paccekabuddha's feet with scented and filtered water, anointed them with scented oil, took off his own sandals, and having cleaned and anointed them with scented oil, put them on his feet, saying: 'Reverend Sir, proceed with these sandals on, holding a sunshade over your head.' Thus he gave him a sunshade and the sandals. Having accepted these out of compassion for him, to increase his faith the Paccekabuddha rose up into the air before his very eyes and went back to the Gandhamādana" (J-a IV, 15–22). As a result of this gift Saṃkha was saved after a shipwreck and even presented with a heavenly ship filled with treasures.

The story of Padumavatī contains an unexpected element: she hesitates to present the gift consisting of a flower and after having presented it, takes it back again after which she gives it a second time. The *Mahāvastu* version of this story describes how the flower becomes very beautiful in the hand of the Paccekabuddha and radiates light. But when she takes it back, the lotus withers in her own hand, and she feels ashamed of her impudence (Ap I 555, verses 56–57; Mv III 170–171). The good results of the pious act of giving and the fulfilment of the wish uttered on that occasion are often mentioned as the starting-point of the way towards enlightenment. A woman who offered her own ivory bracelets to Paccekabuddhas was, as a result of her gift, reborn endowed with great wisdom, and became one who knows the *Tipiṭaka*, and who is endowed with great wisdom: "As a result of her help to the Paccekabuddhas, she attained the fruit of one who has entered the stream" (Dhp-a I 2, 226).

In the *Thera-apadāna* and *Therī-apadāna* various elder monks and nuns relate how, by helping a Paccekabuddha during a former life, they attained their present favourable state wherein they were able to know the *Dhamma* and to work for their own salvation. The style and content of these verses resemble closely those of the *Thera-* and *Therīgāthā* and of a corresponding passage in the *Netti-pakaraṇa*. In all cases these persons acquired merit by means of giving, even Pubbakammapiloti, who had wrongly accused the Paccekabuddha Surabhi during a former existence. The verses spoken by the nun Uppalavaṇṇā, who was Padumavatī, have previously been given. A few other examples follow here.

Vaṅgīsa said: "When the Leader showed me the head of a Paccekabuddha, then I, without effort, begged for *pabbajjā*." And Bhaddakāpilāni: "Having become Brahmadatta, Lord of the world, I served as long as I lived all the five hundred Paccekamunis, the sons of Padumavatī. I made them live in the royal gardens and worshipped them when they were extinguished. Having ordered sepulchral monuments (*cetiya*) to be made, we both (i.e., Nanda, king of Benares, and his queen) entered upon religious life and having practised the immeasurable states (*appamaññā* or *brahmavihārā*), we went to the world of Brahma" (Ap II 582, verses 53–55).

Owing to a perfect gift to a Paccekabuddha, a person is able to attain many happy rebirths and finally *Nibbāna*: "I gave a donation to a Paccekabuddha whose mind was released, who was free from obstructions, free from evil influences, dwelling in a passionless state, his thoughts without fetters..." And the wish: "May I be acquainted with those who live thus and may I surely be indifferent towards being ..." "By the ripening of this deed, I, my mind released, free from obstruction, free from evil influences, was acquainted with those who are bearing their last bodies, who are beyond right and wrong" (Nett 141).

The quality of the gift is not what counts most, but the intention with which it is given: the Paccekabuddha is called "one who enjoys blamelessly" (*anavajjabhojin*) and does not show any sign of like or dislike. The compassion which brings the Paccekabuddha to walk for alms is explained as: "the wish to bring happiness ... and the wish to remove suffering" (Sn-a 73–74).

III.5. The Paccekabuddha's Way of Life: instruction given by him

The *Manorathapurāṇī* states that in the time which lies between two Buddha-periods, a person receiving instruction from a Paccekabuddha can penetrate the knowledge of *Paccekabodhi*. The Commentary on the *Khuddakapāṭha* relates the story of the young brahmin Susīma. Desirous of learning, he wished to find "the end of learning" and was sent to the wise men in Isipatana. "Having gone to Isipatana he went to the Paccekabuddhas and asked: 'Do you know the beginning, middle and end (of learning)?'—'Yes, Sir, we know.'—'Please, teach that to me.'—'For this purpose, Sir, you should enter upon religious life, because it is not possible for someone who does not enter upon religious life to learn.'—'Very well, Reverend Sirs, make me enter upon religious life, and after this has been done, make known to me the end of learning.' Having made him enter upon religious life, they were not able to urge him to find an object of meditation and therefore they taught him what belongs to the practice of lesser ethics saying, 'Thus you should dress, in this way you should cover yourself' and similar ways of conduct. Being taught in this way he attained the (supportive) conditions and not long after that he was enlightened to *Paccekabodhi*" (Khp-a 198–199).

From this passage it is clear that even if a Paccekabuddha intends to teach, he is thought to be incapable of revealing the essence of teaching what he thinks is unteachable. In this respect one is reminded of the Buddha's hesitation to teach the *Dhamma* following his own attainment of enlightenment: "The *Dhamma* obtained by me is profound, of deep splendour, difficult to see, difficult to understand, incomprehensible, having the incomprehensible as its scope, fine, subtle, the sense of which can only be understood by the wise. If I were to explain this to other people, and if other people were not to understand it, that would mean distress and weariness for me and also depression of mind. Shall I retire, alone, to a forest hillside, practising the discipline of those who abide in happiness?" (*Catuṣpariṣatasūtra* 8, 2–3). However, the god Brahmā Sahampati approached the Buddha and appealed to his great compassion, urging him to teach. As a result of this request, the Buddha decided to abandon his unconcern and go forth to teach. This decision is characteristic only of a Buddha. A Paccekabuddha, unable to overcome the thought that the teaching will be too difficult for others to understand, is not prepared to take up the burdensome work of finding disciples and of inciting them to go against the stream. Thus he finds it difficult to come out from his concentration in order to establish contacts with other people (*Abhidharmakoṣa* III 196). But he does feel inclined to help those who would eventually attain insight by themselves. This he does by giving them advice on secondary issues, by inciting them indirectly with an object of meditation, or by instructing them in the ethics and way of life of those who enter upon religious life. As it has been said in the Commentary on the *Suttanipāta*: "Paccekabuddhas are enlightened by themselves (but) do not enlighten others: they comprehend only the essence of meaning (*attharasa*), not the essence of the idea (*dhammarasa*), they are not able to put the supramundane *Dhamma* into concepts and teach it" (Sn-a 51).

Pabbajjā, entrance upon religious life, is mentioned in many cases as a necessary condition for instruction, but elsewhere it is omitted. Here Paccekabuddhas urge persons to find an object of meditation to "cause their release" without being asked for instruction or advice. The way of instructing which is followed by Paccekabuddhas is typical: most times it is done indirectly by means of an example, a few clever remarks or a gesture, which helps the person able to understand the deeper meaning to take an object of meditation. In this connection the Paccekabuddha is said to teach "by means of the body" (*kāyikā*) and not "by means of words" (*vāciki*) (*Divyāvadāna* 83). A teaching of the *Dhamma* has been mentioned in a few places. The content of this teaching is not specified, except in one place where it is said: "He taught the *Dhamma*, saying: 'Be vigilant.'" Sn-a 110 mentions the Paccekabuddha's teaching as being very concise but to the point. However in all cases it is the person himself who has to accept or reject the teaching which is offered to him and has to make the decision whether or not to follow the way towards *Paccekabodhi*.

IV. The Khaggavisāṇasutta of the Suttanipāta

In this section the forty-one verses of the *Khaggavisāṇasutta* of the *Suttanipāta* have been translated, with a few excerpts from the Commentary of Buddhaghosa. This Commentary is very interesting for our subject, as it relates in detail the lives, behaviour and attainments of the Paccekabuddhas, who in the verses speak only briefly of their own way towards *Paccekabodhi*. In this it is comparable to the Commentary on the *Thera-* and *Therīgāthā*. The verses themselves do not mention the Paccekabuddha and their content conforms with the general ideal of the *muni* expressed in several other sections of the *Suttanipāta*. The verses appear to be more a composition than a collection of separate utterances spoken by different individual Paccekabuddhas. The attribution to individual Paccekabuddhas, however, goes back to the Mahāniddesa, which, together with the Cullaniddesa, is a part of the canonical *Suttapiṭaka*. These two books are Commentaries on parts of the *Suttanipāta*, and tradition ascribes them to the Venerable Sāriputta, though the books themselves do not support this.

The Khaggavisāṇa verses appear also in the *Apadāna* (Vol. I verses 9–49), which, though of later origin, is also a part of the *Suttapiṭaka*. A Sanskrit version of some of the verses is found in the *Mahāvastu* (I 357–369).

Buddhaghosa's Commentary supports the attribution of the verses to Paccekabuddhas through its stories about the origin (*uppatti*) of each verse. These stories relate the individual Paccekabodhisatta's life of the past, his aspiration for *Paccekabodhi* and his final attainment to which he gives utterance in the respective verse. Only four of these stories have been included here; the others may be found in the author's earlier book on the subject.[17]

The Commentary on verse 35 informs us that King Brahmadatta of Benares "even while exercising kingship, after having accomplished the preparations for the *kasiṇa*-meditations, realized the five higher knowledges and the eight attainments. Because a consecrated king inevitably has a duty to sit in court,

17. Ria Kloppenborg, *The* Paccekabuddha, *A Buddhist Ascetic*, Leiden, E. J. Brill, 1974.

having enjoyed these attainments, etc. only for one day, he sat down in the place of judgement. Then the people made a loud and great noise. Thinking: 'This noise is an obstruction for the attainment,' he ascended to the flat roof of the palace, and sat down there, thinking: 'I shall apply myself to the attainment.' But he was not able to apply himself to that: the attainment was lost because of the disturbance which resulted from kingship. Thereupon he thought: 'Which is better, kingship or the practice of an ascetic?' Then, having come to the insight: 'Happiness resulting from kingship is small, with various disadvantages; happiness resulting from the practice of an ascetic on the other hand is great, with various advantages and practised by the highest of men,' he ordered his minister: 'Rule this kingdom rightly and impartially, do not perform an unrighteous action' ..."

Thus having made circumstances suitable for the practice of meditation, he retired to the flat roof of the palace. But after a fortnight the king's wife threatened the minister into having sexual relations with her. Eventually, this was reported to the king, who left his rooftop meditation chamber to check up on what was going on during his absence.

Having convinced himself of the truth of the allegations, the king still did not consent to have the minister tortured and killed as the other court officials wanted, but had him expelled from the country, allowing him to take his family and property with him.

The expelled minister went to the kingdom of another king and entered his service. Having won the king's confidence, he persuaded him that he could capture King Brahmadatta's domain without resistance. King Brahmadatta repeatedly yielded to his enemy's demand for more and more territory, since he did not wish to become involved in violence, war and killing. Finally, when Benares itself was threatened, he agreed to go to war rather than surrender the city, but only on the condition that his own army would only be used to frighten the enemy and drive him away, without killing, injuring or plundering anyone.

"Then, having seen both armies standing together friendly, Brahmadatta thought: 'By only protecting my mind, not even such a small drop of blood as resulting from the bite of a little fly was shed among this great mass of people. Ah! That is good! Ah! That is well. All beings must be happy, they must be free of injury.'

Having thus produced the meditation on friendliness (*mettā*), having made this same the basis of further meditation, having comprehended the conditionings, he realized the knowledge of *Paccekabodhi* and attained the state of a self-existent one.

"The ministers prostrated themselves before him and said to him, while he was seated on his elephant's back, experiencing the happiness resulting from the attainment of the way and from fruition: 'It is time to go, great king, honour ought to be paid to the victorious army, food and wages ought to be given to the defeated army.'

"He said: 'Look hero, I am not a king, I am one who is called a Paccekabuddha.'—'What does the king say? Paccekabuddhas do not look like that!'—'How then, tell me, do Paccekabuddhas look?'—'Paccekabuddhas have their hair and beards two *aṅgulas* long, and are provided with the eight requisites.' He touched his head with his right hand: at once the characteristics of a householder disappeared, and the appearance of one who has entered upon religious life became manifest; his hair and beard were two *aṅgulas* long, he was provided with the eight requisites and looked like a senior monk of a hundred years. Having entered the fourth *jhāna* and having risen up into the air from his elephant's back, he was seated on a lotus-flower" (Sn-a 52–63).

35. Abandoning punishment for all living beings,
not hurting even a single one of them,
one should not wish for a son, not to mention a companion!
one should live alone, like the horn of a rhinoceros.

36. Affection arises in the one who has made (intimate) contact;
as a consequence of affection this suffering originates.
Considering the danger which comes from affection,
one should live alone, like the horn of a rhinoceros.

37. He who feels compassion towards friends or companions
neglects his aim, his mind being bound.
Considering this dread which lies in intimacy,
one should live alone, like the horn of a rhinoceros.

38. Like a spreading bamboo entwined
is regard for children and wife;
unattached like the top-sprout of a bamboo,
one should live alone, like the horn of a rhinoceros.

39. As an unbound deer in the forest
seeks a feeding-place when it wills,
wise, seeking independence,
one should live alone, like the horn of a rhinoceros.

40. When amidst companions one is approached with requests
in the house, and where one stands, walks or wanders.
Seeking independence which is undesired by others,
one should live alone, like the horn of a rhinoceros.

41. Play and enjoyment are there amidst companions,
and love for sons is great.
Feeling disgust at separation from the beloved,
one should live alone, like the horn of a rhinoceros.

42. In all four regions not obstructed,
content with anything,
fearless, enduring troubles,
one should live alone, like the horn of a rhinoceros.

43. Hard to please are even some ascetics,
and so are those who live the household life.
Being unconcerned with children of others,
one should live alone, like the horn of a rhinoceros.

44. Laying aside the marks of a householder
as the *kovilāra* sheds its leaves,
manly, having cut the householder's fetters,
one should live alone, like the horn of a rhinoceros.

45. If one finds a wise companion
with whom to live, virtuous and firm,
overcoming all troubles,
one should live with him, happily and mindful.

46. If one does not find a wise companion
with whom to live, virtuous and firm,
like a king leaving a conquered realm,
one should live alone, like the horn of a rhinoceros.

47. Truly let us praise the joy of companionship!
Better or equal ones should be chosen as friends.
If these are not found, living blamelessly,
one should live alone, like the horn of a rhinoceros.

48. Having seen the shining bracelets of gold,
well made by the goldsmith,
striking together, two on one arm,
one should live alone, like the horn of a rhinoceros.

49. "If with another I should live,
much idle talk or abuse would occur."
Considering this future risk,
one should live alone, like the horn of a rhinoceros.

(50. Commentary:) The son of a wealthy merchant in Benares, wishing to enter upon religious life, asked his parents for permission, which they refused to give. "You, dear, are delicate; difficult is *pabbajjā*, like walking up and down upon the edge of a razor." But he did not change his intention. "Then they thought, 'If he enters upon religious life, there will be distress for us; if we refuse him, there will be distress for him; yet, let there be distress for us, not for him,' and they gave permission. Thereupon, not taking notice of all his weeping home people, he went to Isipatana and entered upon religious life in the presence of the Paccekabuddhas. He did not obtain luxurious lodgings; he had to lie down on a mat of straw spread on the bed. As he was accustomed to a luxurious couch, he suffered much all night. In the morning, after having attended to the body's needs, he took his bowl and robe and entered the city for alms together with the Paccekabuddhas. Then the older ones obtained the best seats and the best almsfood. He, the newcomer, obtained a poor seat and lumpy food. He suffered much because of the coarse food, too. After only a few days he became pale and emaciated, and as a result he felt discouraged with religious life, as it happens when the *Dhamma* of an ascetic has not yet come to full development. Thereupon having sent a message to his parents, he left the religious life. But after a few days he regained his strength and again wished to re-enter the religious life. Then, in the same way, all happened again. But when for the third time he entered religious life, he practised in the right way and realized *Paccekabodhi* (Sn-a 98–99). He then uttered the following inspired verse, which he repeated in the midst of the Paccekabuddhas:

50. Truly, the varied objects of passion, sweet and delightful,
agitate the mind with manifold forms.
Having seen the danger lying in sensual pleasures,
one should live alone, like the horn of a rhinoceros.

51. "Illness and swelling and misfortune,
sickness and arrow and fear, that are mine."
Seeing this dread in sensual pleasures,
one should live alone, like the horn of a rhinoceros.

(52. Commentary:) "King Sitāluka[18] Brahmadatta of Benares entered upon religious life and lived in a hut in the forest. Experiencing there all kinds of difficulties—heat, cold, pain, hunger and thirst—he intended to move to a better place, but then he thought: 'Half a *yojana* from here, there is a place where none of these obstacles exists. Should I not better go there? By living in an easier way, one can win to a distinctive attainment.' But then it occurred to him: 'Homeless ones are not under the power of their requisites of life. They wield power over such thoughts and are not overpowered by them. I shall not go from here!' And he did not go. This same thought arose in him three times, but he always turned it down. Having lived at that very same place for seven years and practising the way rightly, he realized *Paccekabodhi* and uttered this verse" (Sn-a 101):

52. Cold and heat, hunger and thirst,
wind and sun, flies and serpents,
having endured all these without exception,
one should live alone, like the horn of a rhinoceros.

53. As an elephant of full-grown stature,
lotus-like and excellent abandons the herds
to live in the forest as he wishes,
one should live alone, like the horn of a rhinoceros.

54. It is impossible for one who is fond of society
to attain temporary[19] release,

---

18. The Buddha-word referred to is in the Greater Discourse on Voidness (Mahāsuññatā Sutta; MN 122).

19. "Temporary release" (*sāmayika-vimutti*) is reached by mundane meditative attainments (*lokiya-samāpatti*), for the duration of which the

Heeding the word of the sage of the solar race,[20]
one should live alone, like the horn of a rhinoceros.

55. Gone beyond distorting views,
right method reached, the way obtained,
thinking: "Knowledge has arisen, by others unguided,"
one should live alone, like the horn of a rhinoceros.

56. Having become free from greed, without deceit and thirst,
without hypocrisy, purified from faults and delusion,
without longing for anything in the entire world,
one should live alone, like the horn of a rhinoceros.

57. One should avoid an evil comrade,
who is not intent upon the good, who is intent upon wrong;
on one's own one should not associate with hankering and careless ones,
one should live alone, like the horn of a rhinoceros.

(58. Commentary:) "When eight Paccekabuddhas entered Benares on their almsround, the king saw them from his window and invited them for their meals. After having made them sit down, the king asked the Paccekabuddhas: "Who are you?' They answered: 'We, great king, are called "very learned" (*bahussuta*).' The king thought: 'I am called Sutabrahmadatta, Brahmadatta the learned, but I find no satisfaction in what I have learned. Well, in their presence I shall listen to an eloquent teaching of the good *Dhamma*.' Delighted, he gave them water to wash and offered them food. At the end of the meal, he took the bowl of the eldest of the group. Having honoured him, he sat down in front of him and said: 'Reverend Sirs, please, deliver a talk on the *Dhamma*.' The eldest said: 'Let one be happy, O great king, let there be destruction of passion,' and he rose. The king thought: 'This one is not very learned, the second will be learned; tomorrow

hindrances (*nivaraṇa*) and other mental defilements are in subsidence.

20. According to the Commentary, Ādiccabandhu is the name of the Paccekabuddha who spoke this verse. However, as the verses never mention Paccekabuddhas, it is more plausible that this is the ancient epithet of the Buddha himself.

I shall listen to an elaborated teaching of the dhamma,' and he invited him for the following day. In this way he invited them all, one after the other. They all changed only partly what they said, while the first words were always the same. In that way they said: 'Let there be destruction of hatred, destruction of delusion, destruction of the courses of existence, destruction of the round of rebirth, destruction of the substratum of rebirth, destruction of thirst,' and then they rose. Then the king started to investigate the meaning of their words, thinking; 'They say: "We are very learned," but their talk is not elaborated. What is the deeper meaning of what has been said by them?' Then investigating the saying: 'Let there be destruction of passion,' he came to know: 'When passion has been destroyed, hatred is also destroyed, also delusion, and all other kinds of defilements are destroyed!' He was delighted: 'These ascetics are very learned without explaining the teaching. As a man who points with his finger at the great earth or at the sky points out not only a spot the size of his finger, but the entire earth or sky, in the same way it is with these: while explaining one thing each, an immeasurable number of things has been explained.' Thereupon thinking: 'Should I not also become learned in the same way?' he abandoned kingship, entered upon religious life and attaining insight realized *Paccekabodhi*. He then uttered this verse" (Sn-a 109–110):

58. One should resort to a friend who is very learned, expert in the *Dhamma*,
who is excellent and intelligent;
knowing the advantages of it, one should remove doubt,
one should live alone, like the horn of a rhinoceros.

59. Not being content with play, pleasure and happiness arising from the objects of the senses in the world, not longing for these,
abstaining from adornment, speaking the truth,
one should live alone, like the horn of a rhinoceros.

60. Having abandoned child, wife, father and mother,
riches, wealth and relatives,
and the objects of the senses all together,
one should live alone, like the horn of a rhinoceros.

61. 'It is a bondage!, happiness in it is slight,
satisfaction is small, suffering is greater in it.
It is a baited hook.' Having come to know this,
being intelligent,
one should live alone, like the horn of a rhinoceros.

62. Having broken the fetters
like the fish in the water which has torn the net,
like the fire which does not return to the burnt place,
one should live alone, like the horn of a rhinoceros.

63. Walking with eyes cast down, without greed,
the senses guarded, the mind controlled,
free from lust, not burning (with passion),
one should live alone, like the horn of a rhinoceros.

(64. Commentary:) "A king of Benares used to enjoy himself in the pleasure garden every fourth month and was therefore called 'Four-month-Brahmadatta.' Entering the pleasure garden one day in the middle month of summer, he saw at the garden's gate a coral tree, full of leaves, with its branches adorned with flowers. Having taken one flower he entered the pleasure garden. Then a certain minister thought: 'A superb flower has been taken by the king,' and while sitting on his elephant's back, he also took one flower. In this way each member of the whole entourage took a flower. Those who could not lay hands on a flower took a leaf. Thus the tree became bare of leaves and flowers, and only its trunk was left. When the king left the pleasure garden in the evening, he saw this and thought: 'What has happened to this tree? At the time of my arrival it was adorned with coral-like flowers amidst branches the colour of jewels, now it is empty of leaves and flowers.' Then he saw, not far from this tree, another tree which was not in bloom but full of leaves. Having seen it he realized: 'The other tree was desirable for many people because its branches were heavy with flowers; therefore within a short time it came to destruction. But this tree here is still the same because it is not desirable. This kingdom of mine is also desirable like the tree in bloom, while the state of a monk is not desirable, like the tree which is not in bloom. Therefore, as long as this kingdom is not plundered like that tree, so long this other is covered with leaves (gains). Like the coral tree, I should cover myself with the yellow

robe and enter upon religious life (giving up the householder's marks).' Having then abandoned kingship and entered upon religious life, he attained insight and realized *Paccekabodhi*. He then uttered these verses":

64. Having given up the marks of a householder
like the coral tree deprived of leaves,
having gone forth dressed in yellow robes,
one should live alone, like the horn of a rhinoceros.

65. Not fond of flavours, free from eager longings,
no feeder of others, house by house he walks for alms;
the mind not attached to any family at all,
one should live alone, like the horn of a rhinoceros.

66. Having eliminated the five hindrances of the mind,
having expelled all minor faults,
not dependent, having cut the blemish of affection,
one should live alone, like the horn of a rhinoceros.

67. Having left behind happiness and suffering
and mental joy and distress, even from the past,
attaining equanimity, quietude, the pure,
one should live alone, like the horn of a rhinoceros.

68. Whose energy is bent on the attainment of the highest good,
whose mind is sincere, who acts without indolence,
of strong exertion, possessing firmness and power,
he should live alone, like the horn of a rhinoceros.

69. Not abandoning solitude, and *jhāna*,
always living according to the *Dhamma* with regard to the teachings,
being one who clearly sees the danger which lies in existence,
one should live alone, like the horn of a rhinoceros.

70. Wishing for the destruction of thirst, zealous, not foolish, learned, mindful,
having examined the *Dhamma*, restrained, full of energy,
one should live alone, like the horn of a rhinoceros.

71. Like the lion, not afraid of sounds,
like the wind, not caught in a net,

like the lotus-flower, not defiled by the water,
one should live alone, like the horn of a rhinoceros.

72. Like the lion, powerful in his teeth, using force,
king of wild animals, living as a conqueror,
using solitary bed-and-seat,
one should live alone, like the horn of a rhinoceros.

73. Friendliness, equanimity, compassion, release,
and sympathy, practising these in time,
not being disturbed by the whole world,
one should live alone, like the horn of a rhinoceros.

74. Having eliminated passion, hatred and delusion,
having broken the fetters,
not frightened by the dissolution of life,
one should live alone, like the horn of a rhinoceros.

75. People follow and serve for selfish reasons,
unselfish friends are hard to find today;
they understand their own advantage, the impure people.
One should live alone, like the horn of a rhinoceros.

The Noble Eightfold Path

The Way to the End of Suffering

by

Bhikkhu Bodhi

WHEEL PUBLICATION NO. 308/309/310/311

Preface

The essence of the Buddha's teaching can be summed up in two principles: the Four Noble Truths and the Noble Eightfold Path. The first covers the side of doctrine, and the primary response it elicits is understanding; the second covers the side of discipline, in the broadest sense of that word, and the primary response it calls for is practice. In the structure of the teaching these two principles lock together into an indivisible unity called the *dhamma-vinaya*, the doctrine-and-discipline, or, in brief, the Dhamma. The internal unity of the Dhamma is guaranteed by the fact that the last of the Four Noble Truths, the truth of the way, is the Noble Eightfold Path, while the first factor of the Noble Eightfold Path, right view, is the understanding of the Four Noble Truths. Thus the two principles penetrate and include one another, the formula of the Four Noble Truths containing the Eightfold Path and the Noble Eightfold Path containing the Four Truths.

Given this integral unity, it would be pointless to pose the question which of the two aspects of the Dhamma has greater value, the doctrine or the path. But if we did risk the pointless by asking that question, the answer would have to be the path. The path claims primacy because it is precisely this that brings the teaching to life. The path translates the Dhamma from a collection of abstract formulas into a continually unfolding disclosure of truth. It gives an outlet from the problem of suffering with which the teaching starts. And it makes the teaching's goal, liberation from suffering, accessible to us in our own experience, where alone it takes on authentic meaning.

To follow the Noble Eightfold Path is a matter of practice rather than intellectual knowledge, but to apply the path correctly it has to be properly understood. In fact, right understanding of the path is itself a part of the practice. It is a facet of right view, the first path factor, the forerunner and guide for the rest of the path. Thus, though initial enthusiasm might suggest that the task of intellectual comprehension may be shelved as a bothersome distraction, mature consideration reveals it to be quite essential to ultimate success in the practice.

The present book aims at contributing towards a proper understanding of the Noble Eightfold Path by investigating its eight factors and their components to determine exactly what they involve. I have attempted to be concise, using as the framework for exposition the Buddha's own words in explanation of the path factors, as found in the Sutta Piṭaka of the Pāli Canon. To assist the reader with limited access to primary sources even in translation, I have tried to confine my selection of quotations as much as possible (but not completely) to those found in Venerable Nyanatiloka's classic anthology, *The Word of the Buddha*. In some cases passages taken from that work have been slightly modified, to accord with my own preferred renderings. For further amplification of meaning I have sometimes drawn upon the commentaries; especially in my accounts of concentration and wisdom (Chapters VII and VIII) I have relied heavily on the *Visuddhimagga* (*The Path of Purification*), a vast encyclopedic work which systematizes the practice of the path in a detailed and comprehensive manner. Limitations of space prevent an exhaustive treatment of each factor. To compensate for this deficiency I have included a list of recommended readings at the end, which the reader may consult for more detailed explanations of individual path factors. For full commitment to the practice of the path, however, especially in its advanced stages of concentration and insight, it will be extremely helpful to have contact with a properly qualified teacher.

Bhikkhu Bodhi

I. The Way to the End of Suffering

The search for a spiritual path is born out of suffering. It does not start with lights and ecstasy, but with the hard tacks of pain, disappointment, and confusion. However, for suffering to give birth to a genuine spiritual search, it must amount to more than something passively received from without. It has to trigger an inner realization, a perception which pierces through the facile complacency of our usual encounter with the world to glimpse the insecurity perpetually gaping underfoot. When this insight dawns, even if only momentarily, it can precipitate a profound personal crisis. It overturns accustomed goals and values, mocks our routine preoccupations, leaves old enjoyments stubbornly unsatisfying.

At first such changes generally are not welcome. We try to deny our vision and to smother our doubts; we struggle to drive away the discontent with new pursuits. But the flame of inquiry, once lit, continues to burn, and if we do not let ourselves be swept away by superficial readjustments or slouch back into a patched up version of our natural optimism, eventually the original glimmering of insight will again flare up, again confront us with our essential plight. It is precisely at that point, with all escape routes blocked, that we are ready to seek a way to bring our disquietude to an end. No longer can we continue to drift complacently through life, driven blindly by our hunger for sense pleasures and by the pressure of prevailing social norms. A deeper reality beckons us; we have heard the call of a more stable, more authentic happiness, and until we arrive at our destination we cannot rest content.

But it is just then that we find ourselves facing a new difficulty. Once we come to recognize the need for a spiritual path we discover that spiritual teachings are by no means homogeneous and mutually compatible. When we browse through the shelves of humanity's spiritual heritage, both ancient and contemporary, we do not find a single tidy volume but a veritable bazaar of spiritual systems and disciplines each offering itself to us as the highest, the fastest, the most powerful, or the most profound solution to our quest for the Ultimate.

Confronted with this melange, we fall into confusion trying to size them up—to decide which is truly liberative, a real solution to our needs, and which is a sidetrack beset with hidden flaws.

One approach to resolving this problem that is popular today is the eclectic one: to pick and choose from the various traditions whatever seems amenable to our needs, welding together different practices and techniques into a synthetic whole that is personally satisfying. Thus one may combine Buddhist mindfulness meditation with sessions of Hindu mantra recitation, Christian prayer with Sufi dancing, Jewish Kabbala with Tibetan visualization exercises. Eclecticism, however, though sometimes helpful in making a transition from a predominantly worldly and materialistic way of life to one that takes on a spiritual hue, eventually wears thin. While it makes a comfortable halfway house, it is not comfortable as a final vehicle.

There are two interrelated flaws in eclecticism that account for its ultimate inadequacy. One is that eclecticism compromises the very traditions it draws upon. The great spiritual traditions themselves do not propose their disciplines as independent techniques that may be excised from their setting and freely recombined to enhance the felt quality of our lives. They present them, rather, as parts of an integral whole, of a coherent vision regarding the fundamental nature of reality and the final goal of the spiritual quest. A spiritual tradition is not a shallow stream in which one can wet one's feet and then beat a quick retreat to the shore. It is a mighty, tumultuous river which would rush through the entire landscape of one's life, and if one truly wishes to travel on it, one must be courageous enough to launch one's boat and head out for the depths.

The second defect in eclecticism follows from the first. As spiritual practices are built upon visions regarding the nature of reality and the final good, these visions are not mutually compatible. When we honestly examine the teachings of these traditions, we will find that major differences in perspective reveal themselves to our sight, differences which cannot be easily dismissed as alternative ways of saying the same thing. Rather, they point to very different experiences constituting the supreme goal and the path that must be trodden to reach that goal.

Hence, because of the differences in perspectives and practices that the different spiritual traditions propose, once we decide that we have outgrown eclecticism and feel that we are ready to make a serious commitment to one particular path, we find ourselves confronted with the challenge of choosing a path that will lead us to true enlightenment and liberation. One cue to resolving this dilemma is to clarify to ourselves our fundamental aim, to determine what we seek in a genuinely liberative path. If we reflect carefully, it will become clear that the prime requirement is a way to the end of suffering. All problems ultimately can be reduced to the problem of suffering; thus what we need is a way that will end this problem finally and completely. Both these qualifying words are important. The path has to lead to a *complete* end of suffering, to an end of suffering in all its forms, and to a *final* end of suffering, to bring suffering to an irreversible stop.

But here we run up against another question. How are we to find such a path—a path which has the capacity to lead us to the full and final end of suffering? Until we actually follow a path to its goal we cannot know with certainty where it leads, and in order to follow a path to its goal we must place complete trust in the efficacy of the path. The pursuit of a spiritual path is not like selecting a new suit of clothes. To select a new suit one need only try on a number of suits, inspect oneself in the mirror, and select the suit in which one appears most attractive. The choice of a spiritual path is closer to marriage: one wants a partner for life, one whose companionship will prove as trustworthy and durable as the pole star in the night sky.

Faced with this new dilemma, we may think that we have reached a dead end and conclude that we have nothing to guide us but personal inclination, if not a flip of the coin. However, our selection need not be as blind and uninformed as we imagine, for we do have a guideline to help us. Since spiritual paths are generally presented in the framework of a total teaching, we can evaluate the effectiveness of any particular path by investigating the teaching which expounds it.

In making this investigation we can look to three criteria as standards for evaluation:

(1) *First*, the teaching has to give a full and accurate picture of the range of suffering. If the picture of suffering it gives is

incomplete or defective, then the path it sets forth will most likely be flawed, unable to yield a satisfactory solution. Just as an ailing patient needs a doctor who can make a full and correct diagnosis of his illness, so in seeking release from suffering we need a teaching that presents a reliable account of our condition.

(2) The *second* criterion calls for a correct analysis of the causes giving rise to suffering. The teaching cannot stop with a survey of the outward symptoms. It has to penetrate beneath the symptoms to the level of causes, and to describe those causes accurately. If a teaching makes a faulty causal analysis, there is little likelihood that its treatment will succeed.

(3) The *third* criterion pertains directly to the path itself. It stipulates that the path which the teaching offers has to remove suffering at its source. This means it must provide a method to cut off suffering by eradicating its causes. If it fails to bring about this root-level solution, its value is ultimately nil. The path it prescribes might help to remove symptoms and make us feel that all is well; but one afflicted with a fatal disease cannot afford to settle for cosmetic surgery when below the surface the cause of his malady continues to thrive.

To sum up, we find three requirements for a teaching proposing to offer a true path to the end of suffering: first, it has to set forth a full and accurate picture of the range of suffering; second, it must present a correct analysis of the causes of suffering; and third, it must give us the means to eradicate the causes of suffering.

This is not the place to evaluate the various spiritual disciplines in terms of these criteria. Our concern is only with the Dhamma, the teaching of the Buddha, and with the solution this teaching offers to the problem of suffering. That the teaching should be relevant to this problem is evident from its very nature; for it is formulated, not as a set of doctrines about the origin and end of things commanding belief, but as a message of deliverance from suffering claiming to be verifiable in our own experience. Along with that message there comes a method of practice, a way leading to the end of suffering. This way is the Noble Eightfold Path (*ariya aṭṭhaṅgika magga*). The Eightfold Path stands at the very heart of the Buddha's teaching. It was the discovery of the path that gave the Buddha's own enlightenment a universal significance and elevated him from the status of a wise and benevolent sage to that of a world teacher. To his own disciples he was pre-eminently "the arouser of the path unarisen before, the producer of the path not produced before, the declarer of the path not declared before, the knower of the path, the seer of the path, the guide along the path" (MN 108). And he himself invites the seeker with the promise and challenge: "You yourselves must strive. The Buddhas are only teachers. The meditative ones who practice the path are released from the bonds of evil" (Dhp 276).

To see the Noble Eightfold Path as a viable vehicle to liberation, we have to check it out against our three criteria: to look at the Buddha's account of the range of suffering, his analysis of its causes, and the program he offers as a remedy.

The Range of Suffering

The Buddha does not merely touch the problem of suffering tangentially; he makes it, rather, the very cornerstone of his teaching. He starts the Four Noble Truths that sum up his message with the announcement that life is inseparably tied to something he calls *dukkha*. The Pāli word is often translated as suffering, but it means something deeper than pain and misery. It refers to a basic unsatisfactoriness running through our lives, the lives of all but the enlightened. Sometimes this unsatisfactoriness erupts into the open as sorrow, grief, disappointment, or despair; but usually it hovers at the edge of our awareness as a vague unlocalized sense that things are never quite perfect, never fully adequate to our expectations of what they should be. This fact of *dukkha*, the Buddha says, is the only real spiritual problem. The other problems—the theological and metaphysical questions that have taunted religious thinkers through the centuries—he gently waves aside as "matters not tending to liberation." What he teaches, he says, is just suffering and the ending of suffering, *dukkha* and its cessation.

The Buddha does not stop with generalities. He goes on to expose the different forms that *dukkha* takes, both the evident and the subtle. He starts with what is close at hand, with the suffering inherent in the physical process of life itself. Here *dukkha* shows up in the events of birth, aging, and death, in our susceptibility to sickness, accidents, and injuries, even in hunger and thirst. It appears again in our inner reactions to disagreeable situations and events: in the sorrow, anger, frustration, and fear aroused by painful separations, by unpleasant encounters, by the failure to get what we want. Even our pleasures, the Buddha says, are not immune from *dukkha.* They give us happiness while they last, but they do not last forever; eventually they must pass away, and when they go the loss leaves us feeling deprived. Our lives, for the most part, are strung out between the thirst for pleasure and the fear of pain. We pass our days running after the one and running away from the other, seldom enjoying the peace of contentment; real satisfaction seems somehow always out of reach, just beyond the next horizon. Then in the end we have to die: to give up the identity we spent our whole life building, to leave behind everything and everyone we love.

But even death, the Buddha teaches, does not bring us to the end of *dukkha*, for the life process does not stop with death. When life ends in one place, with one body, the "mental continuum," the individual stream of consciousness, springs up again elsewhere with a new body as its physical support. Thus the cycle goes on over and over—birth, aging, and death—driven by the thirst for more existence. The Buddha declares that this round of rebirths—called *saṃsāra*, "the wandering"—has been turning through beginningless time. It is without a first point, without temporal origin. No matter how far back in time we go we always find living beings—ourselves in previous lives—wandering from one state of existence to another. The Buddha describes various realms where rebirth can take place: realms of torment, the animal realm, the human realm, realms of celestial bliss. But none of these realms can offer a final refuge. Life in any plane must come to an end. It is impermanent and thus marked with that insecurity which is the deepest meaning of *dukkha*. For this reason one aspiring to the complete end of *dukkha* cannot rest content with any mundane achievement, with any status, but must win emancipation from the entire unstable whirl.

The Causes of Suffering

A teaching proposing to lead to the end of suffering must, as we said, give a reliable account of its causal origination. For if we want to put a stop to suffering, we have to stop it where it begins, with its causes. To stop the causes requires a thorough knowledge of what they are and how they work; thus the Buddha devotes a sizeable section of his teaching to laying bare "the truth of the origin of *dukkha*." The origin he locates within ourselves, in a fundamental malady that permeates our being, causing disorder in our own minds and vitiating our relationships with others and with the world. The sign of this malady can be seen in our proclivity to certain unwholesome mental states called in Pāli *kilesas*, usually translated "defilements." The most basic defilements are the triad of greed, aversion, and delusion. Greed (*lobha*) is self-centered desire: the desire for pleasure and possessions, the drive for survival, the urge to bolster the sense of ego with power, status, and prestige. Aversion (*dosa*) signifies the response of negation, expressed as rejection, irritation, condemnation, hatred, enmity, anger, and violence. Delusion (*moha*) means mental darkness: the thick coat of insensitivity which blocks out clear understanding.

From these three roots emerge the various other defilements—conceit, jealousy, ambition, lethargy, arrogance, and the rest—and from all these defilements together, the roots and the branches, comes *dukkha* in its diverse forms: as pain and sorrow, as fear and discontent, as the aimless drifting through the round of birth and death. To gain freedom from suffering, therefore, we have to eliminate the defilements. But the work of removing the defilements has to proceed in a methodical way. It cannot be accomplished simply by an act of will, by wanting them to go away. The work must be guided by investigation. We have to find out what the defilements depend upon and then see how it lies within our power to remove their support.

The Buddha teaches that there is one defilement which gives rise to all the others, one root which holds them all in place. This root is ignorance (*avijjā*).[1] Ignorance is not mere absence of knowledge, a lack of knowing particular pieces of information. Ignorance can co-exist with a vast accumulation of itemized knowledge, and in its own way it can be tremendously shrewd and resourceful. As the basic root of *dukkha*, ignorance is a fundamental darkness shrouding the mind. Sometimes this

1. Ignorance is actually identical in nature with the unwholesome root "delusion" (*moha*). When the Buddha speaks in a psychological context about mental factors, he generally uses the word "delusion"; when he speaks about the causal basis of *saṃsāra*, he uses the word "ignorance" (*avijjā*).

ignorance operates in a passive manner, merely obscuring correct understanding. At other times it takes on an active role: it becomes the great deceiver, conjuring up a mass of distorted perceptions and conceptions which the mind grasps as attributes of the world, unaware that they are its own deluded constructs.

In these erroneous perceptions and ideas we find the soil that nurtures the defilements. The mind catches sight of some possibility of pleasure, accepts it at face value, and the result is greed. Our hunger for gratification is thwarted, obstacles appear, and up spring anger and aversion. Or we struggle over ambiguities, our sight clouds, and we become lost in delusion. With this we discover the breeding ground of *dukkha*: ignorance issuing in the defilements, the defilements issuing in suffering. As long as this causal matrix stands we are not yet beyond danger. We might still find pleasure and enjoyment—sense pleasures, social pleasures, pleasures of the mind and heart. But no matter how much pleasure we might experience, no matter how successful we might be at dodging pain, the basic problem remains at the core of our being and we continue to move within the bounds of *dukkha*.

Cutting Off the Causes of Suffering

To free ourselves from suffering fully and finally we have to eliminate it by the root, and that means to eliminate ignorance. But how does one go about eliminating ignorance? The answer follows clearly from the nature of the adversary. Since ignorance is a state of not knowing things as they really are, what is needed is knowledge of things as they really are. Not merely conceptual knowledge, knowledge as idea, but perceptual knowledge, a knowing which is also a seeing. This kind of knowing is called wisdom (*paññā*). Wisdom helps to correct the distorting work of ignorance. It enables us to grasp things as they are in actuality, directly and immediately, free from the screen of ideas, views, and assumptions our minds ordinarily set up between themselves and the real.

To eliminate ignorance we need wisdom, but how is wisdom to be acquired? As indubitable knowledge of the ultimate nature of things, wisdom cannot be gained by mere learning, by gathering and accumulating a battery of facts. However, the Buddha says, wisdom can be cultivated. It comes into being through a set of conditions, conditions which we have the power to develop.

These conditions are actually mental factors, components of consciousness, which fit together into a systematic structure that can be called a path in the word's essential meaning: a course or way for movement leading to a goal. The goal here is the end of suffering, and the path leading to it is the Noble Eightfold Path with its eight factors: right view, right intention, right speech, right action, right livelihood, right effort, right mindfulness, and right concentration.

The Buddha calls this path the middle way (*majjhimā paṭipadā*). It is the middle way because it steers clear of two extremes, two misguided attempts to gain release from suffering. One is the extreme of indulgence in sense pleasures, the attempt to extinguish dissatisfaction by gratifying desire. This approach gives pleasure, but the enjoyment won is gross, transitory, and devoid of deep contentment. The Buddha recognized that sensual desire can exercise a tight grip over the minds of human beings, and he was keenly aware of how ardently attached people become to the pleasures of the senses. But he also knew that this pleasure is far inferior to the happiness that arises from renunciation, and therefore he repeatedly taught that the way to the Ultimate eventually requires the relinquishment of sensual desire. Thus the Buddha describes the indulgence in sense pleasures as "low, common, worldly, ignoble, not leading to the goal."

The other extreme is the practice of self-mortification, the attempt to gain liberation by afflicting the body. This approach may stem from a genuine aspiration for deliverance, but it works within the compass of a wrong assumption that renders the energy expended barren of results. The error is taking the body to be the cause of bondage, when the real source of trouble lies in the mind—the mind obsessed by greed, aversion, and delusion. To rid the mind of these defilements the affliction of the body is not only useless but self-defeating, for it is the impairment of a necessary instrument. Thus the Buddha describes this second extreme as "painful, ignoble, not leading to the goal."[2]

Aloof from these two extreme approaches is the Noble Eightfold Path, called the middle way, not in the sense that it effects a compromise between the extremes, but in the sense that

2. SN 56:11; *Word of the Buddha*, p. 26.

it transcends them both by avoiding the errors that each involves. The path avoids the extreme of sense indulgence by its recognition of the futility of desire and its stress on renunciation. Desire and sensuality, far from being means to happiness, are springs of suffering to be abandoned as the requisite of deliverance. But the practice of renunciation does not entail the tormenting of the body. It consists in mental training, and for this the body must be fit, a sturdy support for the inward work. Thus the body is to be looked after well, kept in good health, while the mental faculties are trained to generate the liberating wisdom. That is the middle way, the Noble Eightfold Path, which "gives rise to vision, gives rise to knowledge, and leads to peace, to direct knowledge, to enlightenment, to *Nibbāna*."[3]

II. Right View
(*Sammā Diṭṭhi*)

The eight factors of the Noble Eightfold Path are not steps to be followed in sequence, one after another. They can be more aptly described as components rather than as steps, comparable to the intertwining strands of a single cable that requires the contributions of all the strands for maximum strength. With a certain degree of progress all eight factors can be present simultaneously, each supporting the others. However, until that point is reached, some sequence in the unfolding of the path is inevitable. Considered from the standpoint of practical training, the eight path factors divide into three groups: (i) the moral discipline group (*sīlakkhandha*), made up of right speech, right action, and right livelihood; (ii) the concentration group (*samādhikkhandha*), made up of right effort, right mindfulness, and right concentration; and (iii) the wisdom group (*paññākkhandha*), made up of right view and right intention. These three groups represent three stages of training: the training in the higher moral discipline, the training in the higher consciousness, and the training in the higher wisdom.[4]

3. Ibid.
4. *Adhisīlasikkhā, adhicittasikkhā, adhipaññāsikkhā.*

The order of the three trainings is determined by the overall aim and direction of the path. Since the final goal to which the path leads, liberation from suffering, depends ultimately on uprooting ignorance, the climax of the path must be the training directly opposed to ignorance. This is the training in wisdom, designed to awaken the faculty of penetrative understanding which sees things "as they really are." Wisdom unfolds by degrees, but even the faintest flashes of insight presuppose as their basis a mind that has been concentrated, cleared of disturbance and distraction. Concentration is achieved through the training in the higher consciousness, the second division of the path, which brings the calm and collectedness needed to develop wisdom. But in order for the mind to be unified in concentration, a check must be placed on the unwholesome dispositions which ordinarily dominate its workings, since these dispositions disperse the beam of attention and scatter it among a multitude of concerns. The unwholesome dispositions continue to rule as long as they are permitted to gain expression through the channels of body and speech as bodily and verbal deeds. Therefore, at the very outset of training, it is necessary to restrain the faculties of action, to prevent them from becoming tools of the defilements. This task is accomplished by the first division of the path, the training in moral discipline. Thus the path evolves through its three stages, with moral discipline as the foundation for concentration, concentration the foundation for wisdom, and wisdom the direct instrument for reaching liberation.

Perplexity sometimes arises over an apparent inconsistency in the arrangement of the path factors and the threefold training. Wisdom—which includes right view and right intention—is the last stage in the threefold training, yet its factors are placed at the beginning of the path rather than at its end, as might be expected according to the canon of strict consistency. The sequence of the path factors, however, is not the result of a careless slip, but is determined by an important logistical consideration, namely, that right view and right intention of a preliminary type are called for at the outset as the spur for entering the threefold training. Right view provides the perspective for practice, right intention the sense of direction. But the two do not expire in this preparatory role. For when the mind has been refined by the training in moral discipline and concentration, it arrives at a superior right view and right intention, which now form the proper training in the higher wisdom.

Right view is the forerunner of the entire path, the guide for all the other factors. It enables us to understand our starting point, our destination, and the successive landmarks to pass as practice advances. To attempt to engage in the practice without a foundation of right view is to risk getting lost in the futility of undirected movement. Doing so might be compared to wanting to drive someplace without consulting a road map or listening to the suggestions of an experienced driver. One might get into the car and start to drive, but rather than approaching closer to one's destination, one is more likely to move farther away from it. To arrive at the desired place one has to have some idea of its general direction and of the roads leading to it. Analogous considerations apply to the practice of the path, which takes place in a framework of understanding established by right view.

The importance of right view can be gauged from the fact that our perspectives on the crucial issues of reality and value have a bearing that goes beyond mere theoretical convictions. They govern our attitudes, our actions, our whole orientation to existence. Our views might not be clearly formulated in our mind; we might have only a hazy conceptual grasp of our beliefs. But whether formulated or not, expressed or maintained in silence, these views have a far-reaching influence. They structure our perceptions, order our values, crystallize into the ideational framework through which we interpret to ourselves the meaning of our being in the world.

These views then condition action. They lie behind our choices and goals, and our efforts to turn these goals from ideals into actuality. The actions themselves might determine consequences, but the actions along with their consequences hinge on the views from which they spring. Since views imply an "ontological commitment," a decision on the question of what is real and true, it follows that views divide into two classes, right views and wrong views. The former correspond to what is real, the latter deviate from the real and confirm the false in its place. These two different kinds of views, the Buddha teaches, lead to radically disparate lines of action, and thence to opposite results. If we hold a wrong view, even if that view is vague, it will lead us towards courses of action that eventuate in suffering. On the other hand, if we adopt a right view, that view will steer us towards right action, and thereby towards freedom from suffering. Though our conceptual orientation towards the world might seem innocuous and inconsequential, when looked at closely it reveals itself to be the decisive determinant of our whole course of future development. The Buddha himself says that he sees no single factor so responsible for the arising of unwholesome states of mind as wrong view, and no factor so helpful for the arising of wholesome states of mind as right view. Again, he says that there is no single factor so responsible for the suffering of living beings as wrong view, and no factor so potent in promoting the good of living beings as right view (AN 1:16.2).

In its fullest measure right view involves a correct understanding of the entire Dhamma or teaching of the Buddha, and thus its scope is equal to the range of the Dhamma itself. But for practical purposes two kinds of right view stand out as primary. One is mundane right view, right view which operates within the confines of the world. The other is supramundane right view, the superior right view which leads to liberation from the world. The first is concerned with the laws governing material and spiritual progress within the round of becoming, with the principles that lead to higher and lower states of existence, to mundane happiness and suffering. The second is concerned with the principles essential to liberation. It does not aim merely at spiritual progress from life to life, but at emancipation from the cycle of recurring lives and deaths.

Mundane Right View

Mundane right view involves a correct grasp of the law of *kamma*, the moral efficacy of action. Its literal name is "right view of the ownership of action" (*kammassakatā sammādiṭṭhi*), and it finds its standard formulation in the statement: "Beings are the owners of their actions, the heirs of their actions; they spring from their actions, are bound to their actions, and are supported by their actions. Whatever deeds they do, good or bad, of those they shall be heirs."[5] More specific formulations have also come down in

5. AN 3:33; *Word of the Buddha*, p. 19.

the texts. One stock passage, for example, affirms that virtuous actions such as giving and offering alms have moral significance, that good and bad deeds produce corresponding fruits, that one has a duty to serve mother and father, that there is rebirth and a world beyond the visible one, and that religious teachers of high attainment can be found who expound the truth about the world on the basis of their own superior realization.[6]

To understand the implications of this form of right view we first have to examine the meaning of its key term, *kamma*. The word *kamma* means action. For Buddhism the relevant kind of action is volitional action, deeds expressive of morally determinate volition, since it is volition that gives the action ethical significance. Thus the Buddha expressly identifies action with volition. In a discourse on the analysis of *kamma* he says: "Monks, it is volition that I call action (*kamma*). Having willed, one performs an action through body, speech, or mind."[7] The identification of *kamma* with volition makes *kamma* essentially a mental event, a factor originating in the mind which seeks to actualize the mind's drives, dispositions, and purposes. Volition comes into being through any of three channels—body, speech, or mind—called the three doors of action (*kammadvāra*). A volition expressed through the body is a bodily action; a volition expressed through speech is a verbal action; and a volition that issues in thoughts, plans, ideas, and other mental states without gaining outer expression is a mental action. Thus the one factor of volition differentiates into three types of *kamma* according to the channel through which it becomes manifest.

Right view requires more than a simple knowledge of the general meaning of *kamma*. It is also necessary to understand: (i) the ethical distinction of *kamma* into the unwholesome and the wholesome; (ii) the principal cases of each type; and (iii) the roots from which these actions spring. As expressed in a *sutta*: "When a noble disciple understands what is kammically unwholesome, and the root of unwholesome *kamma*, what is kammically wholesome, and the root of wholesome *kamma*, then he has right view."[8]

---

6. MN 117; *Word of the Buddha*, p. 36.
7. AN 6:63; *Word of the Buddha*, p. 19.
8. MN 9; *Word of the Buddha*, p. 29.

(i) Taking these points in order, we find that *kamma* is first distinguished as unwholesome (*akusala*) and wholesome (*kusala*). Unwholesome *kamma* is action that is morally blameworthy, detrimental to spiritual development, and conducive to suffering for oneself and others. Wholesome *kamma*, on the other hand, is action that is morally commendable, helpful to spiritual growth, and productive of benefits for oneself and others.

(ii) Innumerable instances of unwholesome and wholesome *kamma* can be cited, but the Buddha selects ten of each as primary. These he calls the ten courses of unwholesome and wholesome action. Among the ten in the two sets, three are bodily, four are verbal, and three are mental. The ten courses of unwholesome *kamma* may be listed as follows, divided by way of their doors of expression:

1. Destroying life 2. Taking what is not given 3. Wrong conduct in regard to sense pleasures	Bodily action (*kāyakamma*)
4. False speech 5. Slanderous speech 6. Harsh speech 7. Idle chatter	Verbal action (*vacīkamma*)
8. Covetousness 9. Ill will 10. Wrong view	Mental action (*manokamma*)

The ten courses of wholesome *kamma* are the opposites of these: abstaining from the first seven courses of unwholesome *kamma*, being free from covetousness and ill will, and holding right view. Though the seven cases of abstinence are exercised entirely by the mind and do not necessarily entail overt action, they are still designated wholesome bodily and verbal action because they centre on the control of the faculties of body and speech.

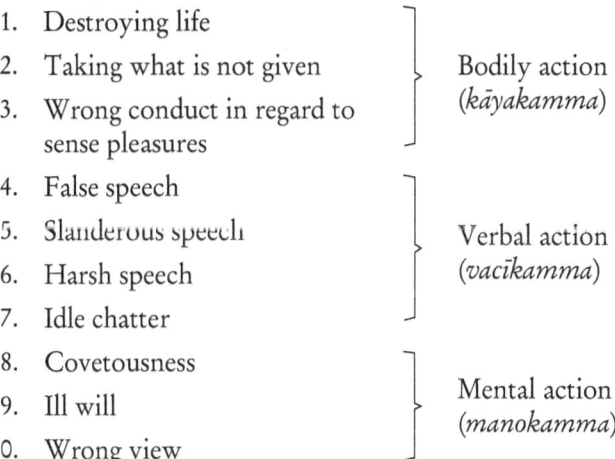

(iii) Actions are distinguished as wholesome and unwholesome on the basis of their underlying motives, called "roots" (*mūla*), which impart their moral quality to the volitions concomitant with themselves. Thus *kamma* is wholesome or unwholesome according to whether its roots are wholesome or unwholesome. The roots are threefold for each set. The unwholesome roots are the three defilements we already mentioned—greed, aversion, and delusion. Any action originating from these is an unwholesome *kamma*. The three wholesome roots are their opposites, expressed negatively in the old Indian fashion as non-greed (*alobha*), non-aversion (*adosa*), and non-delusion (*amoha*). Though these are negatively designated, they signify not merely the absence of defilements but the corresponding virtues. Non-greed implies renunciation, detachment, and generosity; non-aversion implies loving-kindness, sympathy, and gentleness; and non-delusion implies wisdom. Any action originating from these roots is a wholesome *kamma*.

The most important feature of *kamma* is its capacity to produce results corresponding to the ethical quality of the action. An immanent universal law holds sway over volitional actions, bringing it about that these actions issue in retributive consequences, called *vipāka*, "ripenings," or *phala*, "fruits." The law connecting actions with their fruits works on the simple principle that unwholesome actions ripen in suffering, wholesome actions in happiness. The ripening need not come right away; it need not come in the present life at all. Kamma can operate across the succession of lifetimes; it can even remain dormant for aeons into the future. But whenever we perform a volitional action, the volition leaves its imprint on the mental continuum, where it remains as a stored up potency. When the stored up *kamma* meets with conditions favorable to its maturation, it awakens from its dormant state and triggers off some effect that brings due compensation for the original action. The ripening may take place in the present life, in the next life, or in some life subsequent to the next. A *kamma* may ripen by producing rebirth into the next existence, thus determining the basic form of life; or it may ripen in the course of a lifetime, issuing in our varied experiences of happiness and pain, success and failure, progress and decline. But whenever it ripens and in whatever way, the same principle invariably holds: wholesome actions yield favorable results, unwholesome actions yield unfavorable results.

To recognize this principle is to hold right view of the mundane kind. This view at once excludes the multiple forms of wrong view with which it is incompatible. As it affirms that our actions have an influence on our destiny continuing into future lives, it opposes the nihilistic view which regards this life as our only existence and holds that consciousness terminates with death. As it grounds the distinction between good and evil, right and wrong, in an objective universal principle, it opposes the ethical subjectivism which asserts that good and evil are only postulations of personal opinion or means to social control. As it affirms that people can choose their actions freely, within limits set by their conditions, it opposes the "hard deterministic" line that our choices are always made subject to necessitation, and hence that free volition is unreal and moral responsibility untenable.

Some of the implications of the Buddha's teaching on the right view of *kamma* and its fruits run counter to popular trends in present-day thought, and it is helpful to make these differences explicit. The teaching on right view makes it known that good and bad, right and wrong, transcend conventional opinions about what is good and bad, what is right and wrong. An entire society may be predicated upon a confusion of correct moral values, and even though everyone within that society may applaud one particular kind of action as right and condemn another kind as wrong, this does not make them validly right and wrong. For the Buddha moral standards are objective and invariable. While the moral character of deeds is doubtlessly conditioned by the circumstances under which they are performed, there are objective criteria of morality against which any action, or any comprehensive moral code, can be evaluated. This objective standard of morality is integral to the Dhamma, the cosmic law of truth and righteousness. Its transpersonal ground of validation is the fact that deeds, as expressions of the volitions that engender them, produce consequences for the agent, and that the correlations between deeds and their consequences are intrinsic to the volitions themselves. There is no divine judge standing above the cosmic process who assigns rewards and punishments. Nevertheless, the deeds themselves, through their inherent moral or immoral nature, generate the appropriate results.

For most people, the vast majority, the right view of *kamma* and its results is held out of confidence, accepted on faith from an eminent spiritual teacher who proclaims the moral efficacy of action. But even when the principle of *kamma* is not personally seen, *it still remains a facet of right view.* It is part and parcel of right view because right view is concerned with understanding—with understanding our place in the total scheme of things—and one who accepts the principle that our volitional actions possess a moral potency has, to that extent, grasped an important fact pertaining to the nature of our existence. However, the right view of the kammic efficacy of action need not remain exclusively an article of belief screened behind an impenetrable barrier. It can become a matter of direct seeing. Through the attainment of certain states of deep concentration it is possible to develop a special faculty called the "divine eye" (*dibbacakkhu*), a super-sensory power of vision that reveals things hidden from the eyes of flesh. When this faculty is developed, it can be directed out upon the world of living beings to investigate the workings of the kammic law. With the special vision it confers one can then see for oneself, with immediate perception, how beings pass away and re-arise according to their *kamma*, how they meet happiness and suffering through the maturation of their good and evil deeds.[9]

Superior Right View

The right view of *kamma* and its fruits provides a rationale for engaging in wholesome actions and attaining high status within the round of rebirths, but by itself it does not lead to liberation. It is possible for someone to accept the law of *kamma* yet still limit his aims to mundane achievements. One's motive for performing noble deeds might be the accumulation of meritorious *kamma* leading to prosperity and success here and now, a fortunate rebirth as a human being, or the enjoyment of celestial bliss in the heavenly worlds. There is nothing within the logic of kammic causality to impel the urge to transcend the cycle of *kamma* and its fruit. The impulse to deliverance from the entire round of becoming depends upon the acquisition of a different and deeper perspective, one which yields insight into the inherent defectiveness of all forms of saṃsāric existence, even the most exalted.

This superior right view leading to liberation is the understanding of the Four Noble Truths. It is this right view that

9. See DN 2, MN 27, etc. For details, see Vism XIII, 72–101.

figures as the first factor of the Noble Eightfold Path in the proper sense: as the *noble* right view. Thus the Buddha defines the path factor of right view expressly in terms of the four truths: "What now is right view? It is understanding of suffering (*dukkha*), understanding of the origin of suffering, understanding of the cessation of suffering, understanding of the way leading to the cessation to suffering."[10] The Eightfold Path starts with a conceptual understanding of the Four Noble Truths apprehended only obscurely through the media of thought and reflection. It reaches its climax in a direct intuition of those same truths, penetrated with a clarity tantamount to enlightenment. Thus it can be said that the right view of the Four Noble Truths forms both the beginning and the culmination of the way to the end of suffering.

The first noble truth is the truth of suffering (*dukkha*), the inherent unsatisfactoriness of existence, revealed in the impermanence, pain, and perpetual incompleteness intrinsic to all forms of life.

> This is the noble truth of suffering. Birth is suffering; aging is suffering; sickness is suffering; death is suffering; sorrow, lamentation, pain, grief, and despair are suffering; association with the unpleasant is suffering; separation from the pleasant is suffering; not to get what one wants is suffering; in brief, the five aggregates of clinging are suffering.[11]

The last statement makes a comprehensive claim that calls for some attention. The five aggregates of clinging (*pañcupādānakkhandhā*) are a classificatory scheme for understanding the nature of our being. What we are, the Buddha teaches, is a set of five aggregates—material form, feelings, perceptions, mental formations, and consciousness—all connected with clinging. We are the five and the five are us. Whatever we identify with, whatever we hold to as our self, falls within the set of five aggregates. Together these five aggregates generate the whole array of thoughts, emotions, ideas, and dispositions in which we dwell, "our world." Thus the Buddha's declaration that

---

10. DN 22; *Word of the Buddha*, p. 29.
11. DN 22; SN 56:11; *Word of the Buddha*, p. 3.

the five aggregates are *dukkha* in effect brings all experience, our entire existence, into the range of suffering.

But here the question arises: Why should the Buddha say that the five aggregates are *dukkha*? The reason he says that the five aggregates are *dukkha* is that they are impermanent. They change from moment to moment, arise and fall away, without anything substantial behind them persisting through the change. Since the constituent factors of our being are always changing, utterly devoid of a permanent core, there is nothing we can cling to in them as a basis for security. There is only a constantly disintegrating flux which, when clung to in the desire for permanence, brings a plunge into suffering.

The second noble truth points out the cause of *dukkha*. From the set of defilements which eventuate in suffering, the Buddha singles out craving (*taṇhā*) as the dominant and most pervasive cause, "the origin of suffering."

> This is the noble truth of the origin of suffering. It is this craving which produces repeated existence, is bound up with delight and lust, and seeks pleasure here and there, namely, craving for sense pleasures, craving for existence, and craving for non-existence.[12]

The third noble truth simply reverses this relationship of origination. If craving is the cause of *dukkha*, then to be free from *dukkha* we have to eliminate craving. Thus the Buddha says:

> This is the noble truth of the cessation of suffering. It is the complete fading away and cessation of this craving, its forsaking and abandonment, liberation and detachment from it.[13]

The state of perfect peace that comes when craving is eliminated is *Nibbāna* (*Nirvana*), the unconditioned state experienced while alive with the extinguishing of the flames of greed, aversion, and delusion. The fourth noble truth shows the way to reach the end of *dukkha*, the way to the realization of *Nibbāna*. That way is the Noble Eightfold Path itself.

12. Ibid.; *Word of the Buddha*, p. 16.
13. Ibid.; *Word of the Buddha*, p. 22.

The right view of the Four Noble Truths develops in two stages. The first is called the right view that accords with the truths (*saccānulomika sammā diṭṭhi*); the second, the right view that penetrates the truths (*saccapaṭivedha sammā diṭṭhi*). To acquire the right view that accords with the truths requires a clear understanding of their meaning and significance in our lives. Such an understanding arises first by learning the truths and studying them. Subsequently it is deepened by reflecting upon them in the light of experience until one gains a strong conviction as to their veracity.

But even at this point the truths have not been penetrated, and thus the understanding achieved is still defective, a matter of concept rather than perception. To arrive at the experiential realization of the truths it is necessary to take up the practice of meditation—first to strengthen the capacity for sustained concentration, then to develop insight. Insight arises by contemplating the five aggregates, the factors of existence, in order to discern their real characteristics. At the climax of such contemplation the mental eye turns away from the conditioned phenomena comprised in the aggregates and shifts its focus to the unconditioned state, *Nibbāna*, which becomes accessible through the deepened faculty of insight. With this shift, when the mind's eye sees *Nibbāna*, there takes place a simultaneous penetration of all Four Noble Truths. By seeing *Nibbāna*, the state beyond *dukkha*, one gains a perspective from which to view the five aggregates and see that they are *dukkha* simply because they are conditioned, subject to ceaseless change. At the same moment *Nibbāna* is realized, craving stops; the understanding then dawns that craving is the true origin of *dukkha*. When *Nibbāna* is seen, it is realized to be the state of peace, free from the turmoil of becoming. And because this experience has been reached by practicing the Noble Eightfold Path, one knows for oneself that the Noble Eightfold Path is truly the way to the end of *dukkha*.

This right view that penetrates the Four Noble Truths comes at the end of the path, not at the beginning. We have to start with the right view conforming to the truths, acquired through learning and fortified through reflection. This view inspires us to take up the practice, to embark on the threefold training in moral discipline, concentration, and wisdom. When the training matures, the eye of wisdom opens by itself, penetrating the truths and freeing the mind from bondage.

III. Right Intention
(*Sammā Saṅkappa*)

The second factor of the path is called in Pāli *sammā saṅkappa*, which we will translate as "right intention." The term is sometimes translated as "right thought," a rendering that can be accepted if we add the proviso that in the present context the word "thought" refers specifically to the purposive or conative aspect of mental activity, the cognitive aspect being covered by the first factor, right view. It would be artificial, however, to insist too strongly on the division between these two functions. From the Buddhist perspective, the cognitive and purposive sides of the mind do not remain isolated in separate compartments but intertwine and interact in close correlation. Emotional predilections influence views, and views determine predilections. Thus a penetrating view of the nature of existence, gained through deep reflection and validated through investigation, brings with it a restructuring of values which sets the mind moving towards goals commensurate with the new vision. The application of mind needed to achieve those goals is what is meant by right intention.

The Buddha explains right intention as threefold: the intention of renunciation, the intention of good will, and the intention of harmlessness.[14] The three are opposed to three parallel kinds of wrong intention: intention governed by desire, intention governed by ill will, and intention governed by harmfulness.[15] Each kind of right intention counters the corresponding kind of wrong intention. The intention of renunciation counters the intention of desire, the intention of good will counters the intention of ill will, and the intention of harmlessness counters the intention of harmfulness.

---

14. *Nekkhammasaṅkappa, abyāpādasaṅkappa, avihiṃsāsaṅkappa.*

15. *Kāmasaṅkappa, byāpādasaṅkappa, vihiṃsāsaṅkappa.* Though *kāma* usually means sensual desire, the context seems to allow a wider interpretation, as self-seeking desire in all its forms.

The Buddha discovered this twofold division of thought in the period prior to his Enlightenment (see MN 19). While he was striving for deliverance, meditating in the forest, he found that his thoughts could be distributed into two different classes. In one he put thoughts of desire, ill will, and harmfulness, in the other thoughts of renunciation, good will, and harmlessness. Whenever he noticed thoughts of the first kind arise in him, he understood that those thoughts lead to harm for oneself and others, obstruct wisdom, and lead away from *Nibbāna*. Reflecting in this way he expelled such thoughts from his mind and brought them to an end. But whenever thoughts of the second kind arose, he understood those thoughts to be beneficial, conducive to the growth of wisdom, aids to the attainment of *Nibbāna*. Thus he strengthened those thoughts and brought them to completion.

Right intention claims the second place in the path, between right view and the triad of moral factors that begins with right speech, because the mind's intentional function forms the crucial link connecting our cognitive perspective with our modes of active engagement in the world. On the one side actions always point back to the thoughts from which they spring. Thought is the forerunner of action, directing body and speech, stirring them into activity, using them as its instruments for expressing its aims and ideals. These aims and ideals, our intentions, in turn point back a further step to the prevailing views. When wrong views prevail, the outcome is wrong intention giving rise to unwholesome actions. Thus one who denies the moral efficacy of action and measures achievement in terms of gain and status will aspire to nothing but gain and status, using whatever means he can to acquire them. When such pursuits become widespread, the result is suffering, the tremendous suffering of individuals, social groups, and nations out to gain wealth, position, and power without regard for consequences. The cause for the endless competition, conflict, injustice, and oppression does not lie outside the mind. These are all just manifestations of intentions, outcroppings of thoughts driven by greed, by hatred, by delusion.

But when the intentions are right, the actions will be right, and for the intentions to be right the surest guarantee is right views. One who recognizes the law of *kamma*, that actions bring retributive consequences, will frame his pursuits to accord with this law; thus his actions, expressive of his intentions, will conform to the canons of right conduct. The Buddha succinctly sums up the matter when he says that for a person who holds a wrong view, his deeds, words, plans, and purposes grounded in that view will lead to suffering, while for a person who holds right view, his deeds, words, plans, and purposes grounded in that view will lead to happiness.[16]

Since the most important formulation of right view is the understanding of the Four Noble Truths, it follows that this view should be in some way determinative of the content of right intention. This we find to be in fact the case. Understanding the four truths in relation to one's own life gives rise to the intention of renunciation; understanding them in relation to other beings gives rise to the other two right intentions. When we see how our own lives are pervaded by *dukkha*, and how this *dukkha* derives from craving, the mind inclines to renunciation—to abandoning craving and the objects to which it binds us. Then, when we apply the truths in an analogous way to other living beings, the contemplation nurtures the growth of good will and harmlessness. We see that, like ourselves, all other living beings want to be happy, and again that, like ourselves, they are subject to suffering. The consideration that all beings seek happiness causes thoughts of good will to arise—the loving wish that they be well, happy, and peaceful. The consideration that beings are exposed to suffering causes thoughts of harmlessness to arise—the compassionate wish that they be free from suffering.

The moment the cultivation of the Noble Eightfold Path begins, the factors of right view and right intention together start to counteract the three unwholesome roots. Delusion, the primary cognitive defilement, is opposed by right view, the nascent seed of wisdom. The complete eradication of delusion will only take place when right view is developed to the stage of full realization, but every flickering of correct understanding contributes to its eventual destruction. The other two roots, being emotive defilements, require opposition through the redirecting of intention, and thus meet their antidotes in thoughts of renunciation, good will, and harmlessness.

16. AN 1:16.2.

Since greed and aversion are deeply grounded, they do not yield easily; however, the work of overcoming them is not impossible if an effective strategy is employed. The path devised by the Buddha makes use of an indirect approach: it proceeds by tackling the thoughts to which these defilements give rise. Greed and aversion surface in the form of thoughts, and thus can be eroded by a process of "thought substitution," by replacing them with the thoughts opposed to them. The intention of renunciation provides the remedy to greed. Greed comes to manifestation in thoughts of desire—as sensual, acquisitive, and possessive thoughts. Thoughts of renunciation spring from the wholesome root of non-greed, which they activate whenever they are cultivated. Since contrary thoughts cannot coexist, when thoughts of renunciation are roused, they dislodge thoughts of desire, thus causing non-greed to replace greed. Similarly, the intentions of good will and harmlessness offer the antidote to aversion. Aversion comes to manifestation either in thoughts of ill will—as angry, hostile, or resentful thoughts; or in thoughts of harming—as the impulses to cruelty, aggression, and destruction. Thoughts of good will counter the former outflow of aversion, thoughts of harmlessness the latter outflow, in this way excising the unwholesome root of aversion itself.

The Intention of Renunciation

The Buddha describes his teaching as running contrary to the way of the world. The way of the world is the way of desire, and the unenlightened who follow this way flow with the current of desire, seeking happiness by pursuing the objects in which they imagine they will find fulfilment. The Buddha's message of renunciation states exactly the opposite: the pull of desire is to be resisted and eventually abandoned. Desire is to be abandoned not because it is morally evil but because it is a root of suffering.[17]

17. Strictly speaking, greed or desire (*rāga*) becomes immoral only when it impels actions violating the basic principles of ethics, such as killing, stealing, adultery, etc. When it remains merely as a mental factor or issues in actions not inherently immoral—e.g., the enjoyment of good food, the desire for recognition, sexual relations that do not hurt others—it is not immoral but is still a form of craving causing bondage to suffering.

Thus renunciation, turning away from craving and its drive for gratification, becomes the key to happiness, to freedom from the hold of attachment.

The Buddha does not demand that everyone leave the household life for the monastery or ask his followers to discard all sense enjoyments on the spot. The degree to which a person renounces depends on his or her disposition and situation. But what remains as a guiding principle is this: that the attainment of deliverance requires the complete eradication of craving, and progress along the path is accelerated to the extent that one overcomes craving. Breaking free from domination by desire may not be easy, but the difficulty does not abrogate the necessity. Since craving is the origin of *dukkha*, putting an end to *dukkha* depends on eliminating craving, and that involves directing the mind to renunciation.

But it is just at this point, when one tries to let go of attachment, that one encounters a powerful inner resistance. The mind does not want to relinquish its hold on the objects to which it has become attached. For such a long time it has been accustomed to gaining, grasping, and holding, that it seems impossible to break these habits by an act of will. One might agree to the need for renunciation, might want to leave attachment behind, but when the call is actually sounded the mind recoils and continues to move in the grip of its desires.

So the problem arises of how to break the shackles of desire. The Buddha does not offer as a solution the method of repression—the attempt to drive desire away with a mind full of fear and loathing. This approach does not resolve the problem but only pushes it below the surface, where it continues to thrive. The tool the Buddha holds out to free the mind from desire is understanding. Real renunciation is not a matter of compelling ourselves to give up things still inwardly cherished, but of changing our perspective on them so that they no longer bind us. When we understand the nature of desire, when we investigate it closely with keen attention, desire falls away by itself, without need for struggle.

To understand desire in such a way that we can loosen its hold, we need to see that desire is invariably bound up with *dukkha*. The whole phenomenon of desire, with its cycle of wanting and gratification, hangs on our way of seeing things. We remain in bondage to desire because we see it as our means to happiness. If we can look at desire from a different angle, its force will be abated, resulting in the move towards renunciation. What is needed to alter perception is something called "wise consideration" (*yoniso manasikāra*). Just as perception influences thought, so thought can influence perception. Our usual perceptions are tinged with "unwise consideration" (*ayoniso manasikāra*). We ordinarily look only at the surfaces of things, scan them in terms of our immediate interests and wants; only rarely do we dig into the roots of our involvements or explore their long-range consequences. To set this straight calls for wise consideration: looking into the hidden undertones to our actions, exploring their results, evaluating the worthiness of our goals. In this investigation our concern must not be with what is pleasant but with what is true. We have to be prepared and willing to discover what is true even at the cost of our comfort. For real security always lies on the side of truth, not on the side of comfort.

When desire is scrutinized closely, we find that it is constantly shadowed by *dukkha*. Sometimes *dukkha* appears as pain or irritation; often it lies low as a constant strain of discontent. But the two—desire and *dukkha*—are inseparable concomitants. We can confirm this for ourselves by considering the whole cycle of desire. At the moment desire springs up it creates in us a sense of lack, the pain of want. To end this pain we struggle to fulfil the desire. If our effort fails, we experience frustration, disappointment, sometimes despair. But even the pleasure of success is not unqualified. We worry that we might lose the ground we have gained. We feel driven to secure our position, to safeguard our territory, to gain more, to rise higher, to establish tighter controls. The demands of desire seem endless, and each desire demands the eternal: it wants the things we get to last forever. But all the objects of desire are impermanent. Whether it be wealth, power, position, or other persons, separation is inevitable, and the pain that accompanies separation is proportional to the force of attachment: strong attachment brings much suffering; little attachment brings little suffering; no attachment brings no suffering.[18]

18. For a full account of the *dukkha* tied up with sensual desire, see MN 13.

Contemplating the *dukkha* inherent in desire is one way to incline the mind to renunciation. Another way is to contemplate directly the benefits flowing from renunciation. To move from desire to renunciation is not, as might be imagined, to move from happiness to grief, from abundance to destitution. It is to pass from gross, entangling pleasures to an exalted happiness and peace, from a condition of servitude to one of self-mastery. Desire ultimately breeds fear and sorrow, but renunciation gives fearlessness and joy. It promotes the accomplishment of all three stages of the threefold training: it purifies conduct, aids concentration, and nourishes the seed of wisdom. The entire course of practice from start to finish can in fact be seen as an evolving process of renunciation culminating in *Nibbāna* as the ultimate stage of relinquishment, "the relinquishing of all foundations of existence" (*sabb'ūpadhipaṭinissagga*).

When we methodically contemplate the dangers of desire and the benefits of renunciation, gradually we steer our mind away from the domination of desire. Attachments are shed like the leaves of a tree, naturally and spontaneously. The changes do not come suddenly, but when there is persistent practice, there is no doubt that they will come. Through repeated contemplation one thought knocks away another, the intention of renunciation dislodges the intention of desire.

The Intention of Good Will

The intention of good will opposes the intention of ill will, thoughts governed by anger and aversion. As in the case of desire, there are two ineffective ways of handling ill will. One is to yield to it, to express the aversion by bodily or verbal action. This approach releases the tension, helps drive the anger "out of one's system," but it also poses certain dangers. It breeds resentment, provokes retaliation, creates enemies, poisons relationships, and generates unwholesome *kamma*; in the end, the ill will does not leave the "system" after all, but instead is driven down to a deeper level where it continues to vitiate one's thoughts and conduct. The other approach, repression, also fails to dispel the destructive force of ill will. It merely turns that force around and pushes it inward, where it becomes transmogrified into self-contempt, chronic depression, or a tendency to irrational outbursts of violence.

The remedy the Buddha recommends to counteract ill will, especially when the object is another person, is a quality called in Pāli *mettā*. This word derives from another word meaning "friend," but *mettā* signifies much more than ordinary friendliness. I prefer to translate it by the compound "loving kindness," which best captures the intended sense: an intense feeling of selfless love for other beings radiating outwards as a heartfelt concern for their well-being and happiness. *Mettā* is not just sentimental good will, nor is it a conscientious response to a moral imperative or divine command. It must become a deep inner feeling, characterized by spontaneous warmth rather than by a sense of obligation. At its peak *mettā* rises to the heights of a *brahmavihāra*, a "divine dwelling," a total way of being centred on the radiant wish for the welfare of all living beings.

The kind of love implied by *mettā* should be distinguished from sensual love as well as from the love involved in personal affection. The first is a form of craving, necessarily self-directed, while the second still includes a degree of attachment: we love a person because that person gives us pleasure, belongs to our family or group, or reinforces our own self-image. Only rarely does the feeling of affection transcend all traces of ego-reference, and even then its scope is limited. It applies only to a certain person or group of people while excluding others.

The love involved in *mettā*, in contrast, does not hinge on particular relations to particular persons. Here the reference point of self is utterly omitted. We are concerned only with suffusing others with a mind of loving kindness, which ideally is to be developed into a universal state, extended to all living beings without discriminations or reservations. The way to impart to *mettā* this universal scope is to cultivate it as an exercise in meditation. Spontaneous feelings of good will occur too sporadically and are too limited in range to be relied on as the remedy for aversion. The idea of deliberately developing love has been criticized as contrived, mechanical, and calculated. Love, it is said, can only be genuine when it is spontaneous, arisen without inner prompting or effort. But it is a Buddhist thesis that the mind cannot be commanded to love spontaneously; it can only be shown the means to develop love and enjoined to practice accordingly. At first the means has to be employed with some deliberation, but through practice the feeling of love becomes ingrained, grafted onto the mind as a natural and spontaneous tendency.

The method of development is *mettā-bhāvanā*, the meditation on loving kindness, one of the most important kinds of Buddhist meditation. The meditation begins with the development of loving kindness towards oneself.[19] It is suggested that one take oneself as the first object of *mettā* because true loving kindness for others only becomes possible when one is able to feel genuine loving kindness for oneself. Probably most of the anger and hostility we direct to others springs from negative attitudes we hold towards ourselves. When *mettā* is directed inwards towards oneself, it helps to melt down the hardened crust created by these negative attitudes, permitting a fluid diffusion of kindness and sympathy outwards.

Once one has learned to kindle the feeling of *mettā* towards oneself, the next step is to extend it to others. The extension of *mettā* hinges on a shift in the sense of identity, on expanding the sense of identity beyond its ordinary confines and learning to identify with others. The shift is purely psychological in method, entirely free from theological and metaphysical postulates, such as that of a universal self immanent in all beings. Instead, it proceeds from a simple, straightforward course of reflection which enables us to share the subjectivity of others and experience the world (at least imaginatively) from the standpoint of their own inwardness. The procedure starts with oneself. If we look into our own mind, we find that the basic urge of our being is the wish to be happy and free from suffering. Now, as soon as we see this in ourselves, we can immediately understand that all living beings share the same basic wish. All want to be well, happy, and secure. To develop *mettā* towards others, what is to be done is to imaginatively share their own innate wish for happiness. We use our own desire for happiness as the key, experience this desire as the basic urge of others, then come back to our own position and extend to them

19. This might appear to contradict what we said earlier, that *mettā* is free from self-reference. The contradiction is only apparent, however, for in developing *mettā* towards oneself one regards oneself objectively, as a third person. Further, the kind of love developed is not self-cherishing but a detached altruistic wish for one's own well-being.

the wish that they may achieve their ultimate objective, that they may be well and happy.

The methodical radiation of *mettā* is practiced first by directing *mettā* to individuals representing certain groups. These groups are set in an order of progressive remoteness from oneself. The radiation begins with a dear person, such as a parent or teacher, then moves on to a friend, then to a neutral person, then finally to a hostile person. Though the types are defined by their relation to oneself, the love to be developed is not based on that relation but on each person's common aspiration for happiness. With each individual one has to bring his (or her) image into focus and radiate the thought: "May he (she) be well! May he (she) be happy! May he (she) be peaceful!"[20] Only when one succeeds in generating a warm feeling of good will and kindness towards that person should one turn to the next. Once one gains some success with individuals, one can then work with larger units. One can try developing *mettā* towards all friends, all neutral persons, all hostile persons. Then *mettā* can be widened by directional suffusion, proceeding in the various directions—east, south, west, north, above, below—then it can be extended to all beings without distinction. In the end one suffuses the entire world with a mind of loving kindness "vast, sublime, and immeasurable, without enmity, without aversion."

The Intention of Harmlessness

The intention of harmlessness is thought guided by compassion (*karuṇā*), aroused in opposition to cruel, aggressive, and violent thoughts. Compassion supplies the complement to loving kindness. Whereas loving kindness has the characteristic of wishing for the happiness and welfare of others, compassion has the characteristic of wishing that others be free from suffering, a wish to be extended without limits to all living beings. Like *mettā*, compassion arises by entering into the subjectivity of others, by sharing their interiority in a deep and total way. It springs up by considering that all beings, like ourselves, wish to be free from

20. Any other formula found to be effective may be used in place of the formula given here. For a full treatment, see Ñāṇamoli Thera, *The Practice of Loving Kindness,* Wheel No. 7.

suffering, yet despite their wishes continue to be harassed by pain, fear, sorrow, and other forms of *dukkha*.

To develop compassion as a meditative exercise, it is most effective to start with somebody who is actually undergoing suffering, since this provides the natural object for compassion. One contemplates this person's suffering, either directly or imaginatively, then reflects that, like oneself, he (she) also wants to be free from suffering. The thought should be repeated, and contemplation continually exercised, until a strong feeling of compassion swells up in the heart. Then, using that feeling as a standard, one turns to different individuals, considers how they are each exposed to suffering, and radiates the gentle feeling of compassion out to them. To increase the breadth and intensity of compassion it is helpful to contemplate the various sufferings to which living beings are susceptible. A useful guideline to this extension is provided by the first noble truth, with its enumeration of the different aspects of *dukkha*. One contemplates beings as subject to old age, then as subject to sickness, then to death, then to sorrow, lamentation, pain, grief, and despair, and so forth.

When a high level of success has been achieved in generating compassion by the contemplation of beings who are directly afflicted by suffering, one can then move on to consider people who are presently enjoying happiness which they have acquired by immoral means. One might reflect that such people, despite their superficial fortune, are doubtlessly troubled deep within by the pangs of conscience. Even if they display no outward signs of inner distress, one knows that they will eventually reap the bitter fruits of their evil deeds, which will bring them intense suffering. Finally, one can widen the scope of one's contemplation to include all living beings. One should contemplate all beings as subject to the universal suffering of *saṃsāra*, driven by their greed, aversion, and delusion through the round of repeated birth and death. If compassion is initially difficult to arouse towards beings who are total strangers, one can strengthen it by reflecting on the Buddha's dictum that in this beginningless cycle of rebirths, it is hard to find even a single being who has not at some time been one's own mother or father, sister or brother, son or daughter.

To sum up, we see that the three kinds of right intention—of renunciation, good will, and harmlessness—counteract the three wrong intentions of desire, ill will, and harmfulness. The importance of putting into practice the contemplations leading to the arising of these thoughts cannot be overemphasized. The contemplations have been taught as methods for cultivation, not mere theoretical excursions. To develop the intention of renunciation we have to contemplate the suffering tied up with the quest for worldly enjoyment; to develop the intention of good will we have to consider how all beings desire happiness; to develop the intention of harmlessness we have to consider how all beings wish to be free from suffering. The unwholesome thought is like a rotten peg lodged in the mind; the wholesome thought is like a new peg suitable to replace it. The actual contemplation functions as the hammer used to drive out the old peg with the new one. The work of driving in the new peg is practice—practising again and again, as often as is necessary to reach success. The Buddha gives us his assurance that the victory can be achieved. He says that whatever one reflects upon frequently becomes the inclination of the mind. If one frequently thinks sensual, hostile, or harmful thoughts, desire, ill will, and harmfulness become the inclination of the mind. If one frequently thinks in the opposite way, renunciation, good will, and harmlessness become the inclination of the mind (MN 19). The direction we take always comes back to ourselves, to the intentions we generate moment by moment in the course of our lives.

IV. Right Speech, Right Action, Right Livelihood

(*Sammā Vācā, Sammā Kammanta, Sammā Ājīva*)

The next three path factors—right speech, right action, and right livelihood—may be treated together, as collectively they make up the first of the three divisions of the path, the division of moral discipline (*sīlakkhandha*). Though the principles laid down in this section restrain immoral actions and promote good conduct, their ultimate purpose is not so much ethical as spiritual. They are not prescribed merely as guides to action, but primarily as aids to mental purification. As a necessary measure for human well-being, ethics has its own justification in the Buddha's teaching and its importance cannot be underrated. But in the special context of the Noble Eightfold Path ethical principles are subordinate to the path's governing goal, final deliverance from suffering. Thus for the moral training to become a proper part of the path, it has to be taken up under the tutelage of the first two factors, right view and right intention, and to lead beyond to the trainings in concentration and wisdom.

Though the training in moral discipline is listed first among the three groups of practices, it should not be regarded lightly. It is the foundation for the entire path, essential for the success of the other trainings. The Buddha himself frequently urged his disciples to adhere to the rules of discipline, "seeing danger in the slightest fault." One time, when a monk approached the Buddha and asked for the training in brief, the Buddha told him: "First establish yourself in the starting point of wholesome states, that is, in purified moral discipline and in right view. Then, when your moral discipline is purified and your view straight, you should practice the four foundations of mindfulness" (SN 47:3).

The Pāli word we have been translating as "moral discipline," *sīla*, appears in the texts with several overlapping meanings all connected with right conduct. In some contexts it means action conforming to moral principles, in others the principles themselves, in still others the virtuous qualities of character that result from the observance of moral principles. *Sīla* in the sense of precepts or principles represents the formalistic side of the ethical training, *sīla* as virtue the animating spirit, and *sīla* as right conduct the expression of virtue in real-life situations. Often *sīla* is formally defined as abstinence from unwholesome bodily and verbal action. This definition, with its stress on outer action, appears superficial. Other explanations, however, make up for the deficiency and reveal that there is more to *sīla* than is evident at first glance. The *Abhidhamma*, for example, equates *sīla* with the mental factors of abstinence (*viratiyo*)—right speech, right action, and right livelihood—an equation which makes it clear that what is really being cultivated through the observance of moral precepts is the mind. Thus while the training in *sīla* brings the "public" benefit of inhibiting socially detrimental actions, it entails the personal benefit of mental purification, preventing the defilements from dictating to us what lines of conduct we should follow.

The English word "morality" and its derivatives suggest a sense of obligation and constraint quite foreign to the Buddhist conception of *sīla*; this connotation probably enters from the theistic background to Western ethics. Buddhism, with its non-theistic framework, grounds its ethics, not on the notion of obedience, but on that of harmony. In fact, the commentaries explain the word *sīla* by another word, *samādhāna*, meaning "harmony" or "coordination."

The observance of *sīla* leads to harmony at several levels—social, psychological, kammic, and contemplative. At the social level the principles of *sīla* help to establish harmonious interpersonal relations, welding the mass of differently constituted members of society with their own private interests and goals into a cohesive social order in which conflict, if not utterly eliminated, is at least reduced. At the psychological level *sīla* brings harmony to the mind, protection from the inner split caused by guilt and remorse over moral transgressions. At the kammic level the observance of *sīla* ensures harmony with the cosmic law of *kamma*, hence favorable results in the course of future movement through the round of repeated birth and death. And at the fourth level, the contemplative, *sīla* helps establish the preliminary purification of mind to be completed, in a deeper and more thorough way, by the methodical development of serenity and insight.

When briefly defined, the factors of moral training are usually worded negatively, in terms of abstinence. But there is more to *sīla* than refraining from what is wrong. Each principle embedded in the precepts, as we will see, actually has two aspects, both essential to the training as a whole. One is abstinence from the unwholesome, the other commitment to the wholesome; the former is called "avoidance" (*vāritta*) and the latter "performance" (*cāritta*). At the outset of training the Buddha stresses the aspect of avoidance. He does so, not because abstinence from the unwholesome is sufficient in itself, but to establish the steps of practice in proper sequence. The steps are set out in their natural order (more logical than temporal) in the famous dictum of the

Dhammapada: "To abstain from all evil, to cultivate the good, and to purify one's mind—this is the teaching of the Buddhas" (v. 183). The other two steps—cultivating the good and purifying the mind—also receive their due, but to ensure their success, a resolve to avoid the unwholesome is a necessity. Without such a resolve the attempt to develop wholesome qualities is bound to issue in a warped and stunted pattern of growth.

The training in moral discipline governs the two principal channels of outer action, speech and body, as well as another area of vital concern—one's way of earning a living. Thus the training contains three factors: right speech, right action, and right livelihood. These we will now examine individually, following the order in which they are set forth in the usual exposition of the path.

Right Speech (*Sammā Vācā*)

The Buddha divides right speech into four components: abstaining from false speech, abstaining from slanderous speech, abstaining from harsh speech, and abstaining from idle chatter. Because the effects of speech are not as immediately evident as those of bodily action, its importance and potential are easily overlooked. But a little reflection will show that speech and its offshoot, the written word, can have enormous consequences for good or for harm. In fact, whereas for beings such as animals who live at the preverbal level physical action is of dominant concern, for humans immersed in verbal communication speech gains the ascendancy. Speech can break lives, create enemies, and start wars, or it can give wisdom, heal divisions, and create peace. This has always been so, yet in the modern age the positive and negative potentials of speech have been vastly multiplied by the tremendous increase in the means, speed, and range of communications. The capacity for verbal expression, oral and written, has often been regarded as the distinguishing mark of the human species. From this we can appreciate the need to make this capacity the means to human excellence rather than, as too often has been the case, the sign of human degradation.

(1) Abstaining from false speech (*musāvādā veramaṇī*)

> Herein someone avoids false speech and abstains from it. He speaks the truth, is devoted to truth, reliable, worthy of confidence, not a deceiver of people. Being at a meeting, or amongst people, or in the midst of his relatives, or in a society, or in the king's court, and called upon and asked as witness to tell what he knows, he answers, if he knows nothing: "I know nothing," and if he knows, he answers: "I know"; if he has seen nothing, he answers: "I have seen nothing," and if he has seen, he answers: "I have seen." Thus he never knowingly speaks a lie, either for the sake of his own advantage, or for the sake of another person's advantage, or for the sake of any advantage whatsoever.[21]

This statement of the Buddha discloses both the negative and the positive sides to the precept. The negative side is abstaining from lying, the positive side speaking the truth. The determinative factor behind the transgression is the intention to deceive. If one speaks something false believing it to be true, there is no breach of the precept as the intention to deceive is absent. Though the deceptive intention is common to all cases of false speech, lies can appear in different guises depending on the motivating root, whether greed, hatred, or delusion. Greed as the chief motive results in the lie aimed at gaining some personal advantage for oneself or for those close to oneself—material wealth, position, respect, or admiration. With hatred as the motive, false speech takes the form of the malicious lie, the lie intended to hurt and damage others. When delusion is the principal motive, the result is a less pernicious type of falsehood: the irrational lie, the compulsive lie, the interesting exaggeration, lying for the sake of a joke.

The Buddha's stricture against lying rests upon several reasons. For one thing, lying is disruptive to social cohesion. People can live together in society only in an atmosphere of mutual trust, where they have reason to believe that others will speak the truth; by destroying the grounds for trust and inducing mass suspicion, widespread lying becomes the harbinger signalling the fall from social solidarity to chaos. But lying has other consequences of a

21. AN 10:176; *Word of the Buddha*, p. 50.

deeply personal nature at least equally disastrous. By their very nature lies tend to proliferate. Lying once and finding our word suspect, we feel compelled to lie again to defend our credibility, to paint a consistent picture of events. So the process repeats itself: the lies stretch, multiply, and connect until they lock us into a cage of falsehoods from which it is difficult to escape. The lie is thus a miniature paradigm for the whole process of subjective illusion. In each case the self-assured creator, sucked in by his own deceptions, eventually winds up their victim.

Such considerations probably lie behind the words of counsel the Buddha spoke to his son, the young novice Rāhula, soon after the boy was ordained. One day the Buddha came to Rāhula, pointed to a bowl with a little bit of water in it, and asked: "Rāhula, do you see this bit of water left in the bowl?" Rāhula answered: "Yes, sir." "So little, Rāhula, is the spiritual achievement (*sāmañña*, lit. "recluseship") of one who is not afraid to speak a deliberate lie." Then the Buddha threw the water away, put the bowl down, and said: "Do you see, Rāhula, how that water has been discarded? In the same way one who tells a deliberate lie discards whatever spiritual achievement he has made." Again he asked: "Do you see how this bowl is now empty? In the same way one who has no shame in speaking lies is empty of spiritual achievement." Then the Buddha turned the bowl upside down and said: "Do you see, Rāhula, how this bowl has been turned upside down? In the same way one who tells a deliberate lie turns his spiritual achievements upside down and becomes incapable of progress." Therefore, the Buddha concluded, one should not speak a deliberate lie even in jest.[22]

It is said that in the course of his long training for enlightenment over many lives, a bodhisatta can break all the moral precepts except the pledge to speak the truth. The reason for this is very profound, and reveals that the commitment to truth has a significance transcending the domain of ethics and even mental purification, taking us to the domains of knowledge and being. Truthful speech provides, in the sphere of interpersonal communication, a parallel to wisdom in the sphere of private understanding. The two are respectively the outward and inward

---

22. MN 61.

modalities of the same commitment to what is real. Wisdom consists in the realization of truth, and truth (*sacca*) is not just a verbal proposition but the nature of things as they are. To realize truth our whole being has to be brought into accord with actuality, with things as they are, which requires that in communications with others we respect things as they are by speaking the truth. Truthful speech establishes a correspondence between our own inner being and the real nature of phenomena, allowing wisdom to rise up and fathom their real nature. Thus, much more than an ethical principle, devotion to truthful speech is a matter of taking our stand on reality rather than illusion, on the truth grasped by wisdom rather than the fantasies woven by desire.

(2) Abstaining from slanderous speech (*pisuṇāya vācāya veramaṇī*)

> He avoids slanderous speech and abstains from it. What he has heard here he does not repeat there, so as to cause dissension there; and what he has heard there he does not repeat here, so as to cause dissension here. Thus he unites those that are divided; and those that are united he encourages. Concord gladdens him, he delights and rejoices in concord; and it is concord that he spreads by his words.[23]

Slanderous speech is speech intended to create enmity and division, to alienate one person or group from another. The motive behind such speech is generally aversion, resentment of a rival's success or virtues, the intention to tear down others by verbal denigrations. Other motives may enter the picture as well: the cruel intention of causing hurt to others, the evil desire to win affection for oneself, the perverse delight in seeing friends divided.

Slanderous speech is one of the most serious moral transgressions. The root of hate makes the unwholesome *kamma* already heavy enough, but since the action usually occurs after deliberation, the negative force becomes even stronger because premeditation adds to its gravity. When the slanderous statement is false, the two wrongs of falsehood and slander combine to produce an extremely powerful unwholesome *kamma*. The

23. AN 10:176; *Word of the Buddha*, p. 50.

canonical texts record several cases in which the calumny of an innocent party led to an immediate rebirth in the plane of misery.

The opposite of slander, as the Buddha indicates, is speech that promotes friendship and harmony. Such speech originates from a mind of loving kindness and sympathy. It wins the trust and affection of others, who feel they can confide in one without fear that their disclosures will be used against them. Beyond the obvious benefits that such speech brings in this present life, it is said that abstaining from slander has as its kammic result the gain of a retinue of friends who can never be turned against one by the slanderous words of others.[24]

(3) Abstaining from harsh speech (*pharusāya vācāya veramaṇī*)

> He avoids harsh language and abstains from it. He speaks such words as are gentle, soothing to the ear, loving, such words as go to the heart, and are courteous, friendly, and agreeable to many.[25]

Harsh speech is speech uttered in anger, intended to cause the hearer pain. Such speech can assume different forms, of which we might mention three. One is *abusive speech*: scolding, reviling, or reproving another angrily with bitter words. A second is *insult*: hurting another by ascribing to him some offensive quality which detracts from his dignity. A third is *sarcasm*: speaking to someone in a way which ostensibly lauds him, but with such a tone or twist of phrasing that the ironic intent becomes clear and causes pain.

The main root of harsh speech is aversion, assuming the form of anger. Since the defilement in this case tends to work impulsively, without deliberation, the transgression is less serious than slander and the kammic consequence generally less severe. Still, harsh speech is an unwholesome action with disagreeable results for oneself and others, both now and in the future, so it has to be restrained. The ideal antidote is patience—learning to tolerate blame and criticism from others, to sympathize with their shortcomings, to respect differences in viewpoint, to endure abuse without feeling compelled to retaliate. The Buddha calls for patience even under the most trying conditions:

24. Subcommentary to Dīgha Nikāya.

25. AN 10:176; *Word of the Buddha*, pp. 50–51.

> Even if, monks, robbers and murderers saw through your limbs and joints, whosoever should give way to anger thereat would not be following my advice. For thus ought you to train yourselves: "Undisturbed shall our mind remain, with heart full of love, and free from any hidden malice; and that person shall we penetrate with loving thoughts, wide, deep, boundless, freed from anger and hatred."[26]

(4) Abstaining from idle chatter (*samphappalāpā veramaṇī*)

> He avoids idle chatter and abstains from it. He speaks at the right time, in accordance with facts, speaks what is useful, speaks of the Dhamma and the discipline; his speech is like a treasure, uttered at the right moment, accompanied by reason, moderate and full of sense.[27]

Idle chatter is pointless talk, speech that lacks purpose or depth. Such speech communicates nothing of value, but only stirs up the defilements in one's own mind and in others. The Buddha advises that idle talk should be curbed and speech restricted as much as possible to matters of genuine importance. In the case of a monk, the typical subject of the passage just quoted, his words should be selective and concerned primarily with the Dhamma. Lay persons will have more need for affectionate small talk with friends and family, polite conversation with acquaintances, and talk in connection with their line of work. But even then they should be mindful not to let the conversation stray into pastures where the restless mind, always eager for something sweet or spicy to feed on, might find the chance to indulge its defiling propensities.

The traditional exegesis of abstaining from idle chatter refers only to avoiding engagement in such talk oneself. But today it might be of value to give this factor a different slant, made imperative by certain developments peculiar to our own time, unknown in the days of the Buddha and the ancient commentators. This is avoiding exposure to the idle chatter constantly bombarding us through the new media of communication created by modern technology. An incredible array of devices—television, radio,

26. MN 21; *Word of the Buddha*, p. 51.
27. AN 10:176; *Word of the Buddha*, p. 51.

newspapers, pulp journals, the cinema—turns out a continuous stream of needless information and distracting entertainment the net effect of which is to leave the mind passive, vacant, and sterile. All these developments, naively accepted as "progress," threaten to blunt our aesthetic and spiritual sensitivities and deafen us to the higher call of the contemplative life. Serious aspirants on the path to liberation have to be extremely discerning in what they allow themselves to be exposed to. They would greatly serve their aspirations by including these sources of amusement and needless information in the category of idle chatter and making an effort to avoid them.

Right Action (*Sammā Kammanta*)

Right action means refraining from unwholesome deeds that occur with the body as their natural means of expression. The pivotal element in this path factor is the mental factor of abstinence, but because this abstinence applies to actions performed through the body, it is called "right action." The Buddha mentions three components of right action: abstaining from taking life, abstaining from taking what is not given, and abstaining from sexual misconduct. These we will briefly discuss in order.

> (1) Abstaining from taking life (*pāṇātipātā veramaṇī*)
>
> Herein someone avoids the taking of life and abstains from it. Without stick or sword, conscientious, full of sympathy, he is desirous of the welfare of all sentient beings.[28]

"Abstaining from taking life" has a wider application than simply refraining from killing other human beings. The precept enjoins abstaining from killing any sentient being. A "sentient being" (*pāṇī, satta*) is a living being endowed with mind or consciousness; for practical purposes, this means human beings, animals, and insects. Plants are not considered to be sentient beings; though they exhibit some degree of sensitivity, they lack full-fledged consciousness, the defining attribute of a sentient being.

The "taking of life" that is to be avoided is *intentional* killing, the deliberate destruction of life of a being endowed with

---

28. AN 10:176; *Word of the Buddha*, p. 53.

consciousness. The principle is grounded in the consideration that all beings love life and fear death, that all seek happiness and are averse to pain. The essential determinant of transgression is the volition to kill, issuing in an action that deprives a being of life. Suicide is also generally regarded as a violation, but not accidental killing as the intention to destroy life is absent. The abstinence may be taken to apply to two kinds of action, the primary and the secondary. The primary is the actual destruction of life; the secondary is deliberately harming or torturing another being without killing it.

While the Buddha's statement on non-injury is quite simple and straightforward, later commentaries give a detailed analysis of the principle. A treatise from Thailand, written by an erudite Thai patriarch, collates a mass of earlier material into an especially thorough treatment, which we shall briefly summarize here.[29] The treatise points out that the taking of life may have varying degrees of moral weight entailing different consequences. The three primary variables governing moral weight are the object, the motive, and the effort. With regard to the object there is a difference in seriousness between killing a human being and killing an animal, the former being kammically heavier since man has a more highly developed moral sense and greater spiritual potential than animals. Among human beings, the degree of kammic weight depends on the qualities of the person killed and his relation to the killer; thus killing a person of superior spiritual qualities or a personal benefactor, such as a parent or a teacher, is an especially grave act.

The motive for killing also influences moral weight. Acts of killing can be driven by greed, hatred, or delusion. Of the three, killing motivated by hatred is the most serious, and the weight increases to the degree that the killing is premeditated. The force of effort involved also contributes, the unwholesome *kamma* being proportional to the force and the strength of the defilements.

The positive counterpart to abstaining from taking life, as the Buddha indicates, is the development of kindness and compassion for other beings. The disciple not only avoids

29. HRH Prince Vajirañāṇavarorasa, *The Five Precepts and the Five Ennoblers* (Bangkok, 1975), pp. 1–9.

destroying life; he dwells with a heart full of sympathy, desiring the welfare of all beings. The commitment to non-injury and concern for the welfare of others represent the practical application of the second path factor, right intention, in the form of good will and harmlessness.

> (2) Abstaining from taking what is not given (*adinnādānā veramaṇī*)
>
> He avoids taking what is not given and abstains from it; what another person possesses of goods and chattel in the village or in the wood, that he does not take away with thievish intent.[30]

"Taking what is not given" means appropriating the rightful belongings of others with thievish intent. If one takes something that has no owner, such as unclaimed stones, wood, or even gems extracted from the earth, the act does not count as a violation even though these objects have not been given. But also implied as a transgression, though not expressly stated, is withholding from others what should rightfully be given to them.

Commentaries mention a number of ways in which "taking what is not given" can be committed. Some of the most common may be enumerated:

(1) *stealing*: taking the belongings of others secretly, as in house-breaking, picking pockets, etc.;
(2) *robbery*: taking what belongs to others openly by force or threats;
(3) *snatching*: suddenly pulling away another's possession before he has time to resist;
(4) *fraudulence*: gaining possession of another's belongings by falsely claiming them as one's own;
(5) *deceitfulness*: using false weights and measures to cheat customers.[31]

The degree of moral weight that attaches to the action is determined by three factors: the value of the object taken; the qualities of the victim of the theft; and the subjective state of the

30. AN 10:176; *Word of the Buddha*, p. 53.

31. *The Five Precepts and the Five Ennoblers* gives a fuller list, pp. 10–13.

thief. Regarding the first, moral weight is directly proportional to the value of the object. Regarding the second, the weight varies according to the moral qualities of the deprived individual. Regarding the third, acts of theft may be motivated either by greed or hatred. While greed is the most common cause, hatred may also be responsible as when one person deprives another of his belongings not so much because he wants them for himself as because he wants to harm the latter. Between the two, acts motivated by hatred are kammically heavier than acts motivated by sheer greed.

The positive counterpart to abstaining from stealing is honesty, which implies respect for the belongings of others and for their right to use their belongings as they wish. Another related virtue is contentment, being satisfied with what one has without being inclined to increase one's wealth by unscrupulous means. The most eminent opposite virtue is generosity, giving away one's own wealth and possessions in order to benefit others.

> (3) Abstaining from sexual misconduct (*kāmesu micchā-cārā veramaṇī*)
>
> He avoids sexual misconduct and abstains from it. He has no intercourse with such persons as are still under the protection of father, mother, brother, sister or relatives, nor with married women, nor with female convicts, nor lastly, with betrothed girls.[32]

The guiding purposes of this precept, from the ethical standpoint, are to protect marital relations from outside disruption and to promote trust and fidelity within the marital union. From the spiritual standpoint it helps curb the expansive tendency of sexual desire and thus is a step in the direction of renunciation, which reaches its consummation in the observance of celibacy (*brahmacariya*) binding on monks and nuns. But for the laity the precept enjoins abstaining from sexual relations with an illicit partner. The primary transgression is entering into full sexual union, but all other sexual involvements of a less complete kind may be considered secondary infringements.

---

32. AN 10:176; *Word of the Buddha*, p. 53.

The main question raised by the precept concerns who is to count as an illicit partner. The Buddha's statement defines the illicit partner from the perspective of the man, but later treatises elaborate the matter for both sexes.[33]

For a man, three kinds of women are considered illicit partners:

(1) A woman who is married to another man. This includes, besides a woman already married to a man, a woman who is not his legal wife but is generally recognized as his consort, who lives with him or is kept by him or is in some way acknowledged as his partner. All these women are illicit partners for men other than their own husbands. This class would also include a woman engaged to another man. But a widow or divorced woman is not out of bounds, provided she is not excluded for other reasons.

(2) A woman still under protection. This is a girl or woman who is under the protection of her mother, father, relatives, or others rightfully entitled to be her guardians. This provision rules out elopements or secret marriages contrary to the wishes of the protecting party.

(3) A woman prohibited by convention. This includes close female relatives forbidden as partners by social tradition, nuns and other women under a vow of celibacy, and those prohibited as partners by the law of the land.

From the standpoint of a woman, two kinds of men are considered illicit partners:

(1) For a married woman any man other than her husband is out of bounds. Thus a married woman violates the precept if she breaks her vow of fidelity to her husband. But a widow or divorcee is free to remarry.

(2) For any woman any man forbidden by convention, such as close relatives and those under a vow of celibacy, is an illicit partner.

Besides these, any case of forced, violent, or coercive sexual union constitutes a transgression. But in such a case the violation falls only on the offender, not on the one compelled to submit.

---

33. The following is summarized from *The Five Precepts and the Five Ennoblers*, pp. 16–18.

The positive virtue corresponding to the abstinence is, for the laity, marital fidelity. Husband and wife should each be faithful and devoted to the other, content with the relationship, and should not risk a breakup to the union by seeking outside partners. The principle does not, however, confine sexual relations to the marital union. It is flexible enough to allow for variations depending on social convention. The essential purpose, as was said, is to prevent sexual relations which are hurtful to others. When mature independent people, though unmarried, enter into a sexual relationship through free consent, so long as no other person is intentionally harmed, no breach of the training factor is involved.

Ordained monks and nuns, including men and women who have undertaken the eight or ten precepts, are obliged to observe celibacy. They must abstain not only from sexual misconduct, but from all sexual involvements, at least during the period of their vows. The holy life at its highest aims at complete purity in thought, word, and deed, and this requires turning back the tide of sexual desire.

Right Livelihood (*Sammā Ājīva*)

Right livelihood is concerned with ensuring that one earns one's living in a righteous way. For a lay disciple the Buddha teaches that wealth should be gained in accordance with certain standards. One should acquire it only by legal means, not illegally; one should acquire it peacefully, without coercion or violence; one should acquire it honestly, not by trickery or deceit; and one should acquire it in ways which do not entail harm and suffering for others.[34] The Buddha mentions five specific kinds of livelihood which bring harm to others and are therefore to be avoided: dealing in weapons, in living beings (including raising animals for slaughter as well as slave trade and prostitution), in meat production and butchery, in poisons, and in intoxicants (AN 5:177). He further names several dishonest means of gaining wealth which fall under wrong livelihood: practising deceit, treachery, soothsaying, trickery, and usury (MN 117). Obviously any occupation that requires violation of right speech and right

34. See AN 4:62; AN 5:41; AN 8:54.

action is a wrong form of livelihood, but other occupations, such as selling weapons or intoxicants, may not violate those factors and yet be wrong because of their consequences for others.

The Thai treatise discusses the positive aspects of right livelihood under the three convenient headings of rightness regarding actions, rightness regarding persons, and rightness regarding objects.[35] "Rightness regarding actions" means that workers should fulfil their duties diligently and conscientiously, not idling away time, claiming to have worked longer hours than they did, or pocketing the company's goods. "Rightness regarding persons" means that due respect and consideration should be shown to employers, employees, colleagues, and customers. An employer, for example, should assign his workers chores according to their ability, pay them adequately, promote them when they deserve a promotion and give them occasional vacations and bonuses. Colleagues should try to cooperate rather than compete, while merchants should be equitable in their dealings with customers. "Rightness regarding objects" means that in business transactions and sales the articles to be sold should be presented truthfully. There should be no deceptive advertising, misrepresentations of quality or quantity, or dishonest maneuvers.

V. Right Effort
(*Sammā Vāyāma*)

The purification of conduct established by the prior three factors serves as the basis for the next division of the path, the division of concentration (*samādhi-kkhandha*). This present phase of practice, which advances from moral restraint to direct mental training, comprises the three factors of right effort, right mindfulness, and right concentration. It gains its name from the goal to which it aspires, the power of sustained concentration, itself required as the support for insight-wisdom. Wisdom is the primary tool for deliverance, but the penetrating vision it yields can only open up when the mind has been composed and collected.

35. *The Five Precepts and the Five Ennoblers*, pp. 45–47.

Right concentration brings the requisite stillness to the mind by unifying it with undistracted focus on a suitable object. To do so, however, the factor of concentration needs the aid of effort and mindfulness. Right effort provides the energy demanded by the task, right mindfulness the steadying points for awareness.

The commentators illustrate the interdependence of the three factors within the concentration group with a simple simile. Three boys go to a park to play. While walking along they see a tree with flowering tops and decide they want to gather the flowers. But the flowers are beyond the reach even of the tallest boy. Then one friend bends down and offers his back. The tall boy climbs up, but still hesitates to reach for the flowers from fear of falling. So the third boy comes over and offers his shoulder for support. The first boy, standing on the back of the second boy, then leans on the shoulder of the third boy, reaches up, and gathers the flowers.[36]

In this simile the tall boy who picks the flowers represents concentration with its function of unifying the mind. But to unify the mind concentration needs support: the energy provided by right effort, which is like the boy who offers his back. It also requires the stabilizing awareness provided by mindfulness, which is like the boy who offers his shoulder. When right concentration receives this support, then empowered by right effort and balanced by right mindfulness it can draw in the scattered strands of thought and fix the mind firmly on its object.

Energy (*viriya*), the mental factor behind right effort, can appear in either wholesome or unwholesome forms. The same factor fuels desire, aggression, violence, and ambition on the one hand, and generosity, self-discipline, kindness, concentration, and understanding on the other. The exertion involved in right effort is a wholesome form of energy, but it is something more specific, namely, the energy in wholesome states of consciousness directed to liberation from suffering. This last qualifying phrase is especially important. For wholesome energy to become a contributor to the path it has to be guided by right view and right intention, and to work in association with the other path factors. Otherwise, as the energy in ordinary wholesome states of mind, it merely engenders

36. *Papañcasūdanī* (Commentary to Majjhima Nikāya).

an accumulation of merit that ripens within the round of birth and death; it does not issue in liberation from the round.

Time and again the Buddha has stressed the need for effort, for diligence, exertion, and unflagging perseverance. The reason why effort is so crucial is that each person has to work out his or her own deliverance. The Buddha does what he can by pointing out the path to liberation; the rest involves putting the path into practice, a task that demands energy. This energy is to be applied to the cultivation of the mind, which forms the focus of the entire path. The starting point is the defiled mind, afflicted and deluded; the goal is the liberated mind, purified and illuminated by wisdom. What comes in between is the unremitting effort to transform the defiled mind into the liberated mind. The work of self-cultivation is not easy—there is no one who can do it for us but ourselves—but it is not impossible. The Buddha himself and his accomplished disciples provide the living proof that the task is not beyond our reach. They assure us, too, that anyone who follows the path can accomplish the same goal. But what is needed is effort, the work of practice taken up with the determination: "I shall not give up my efforts until I have attained whatever is attainable by manly perseverance, energy, and endeavor."[37]

The nature of the mental process effects a division of right effort into four "great endeavors":

(1) to prevent the arising of unarisen unwholesome states;
(2) to abandon unwholesome states that have already arisen;
(3) to arouse wholesome states that have not yet arisen;
(4) to maintain and perfect wholesome states already arisen.

The unwholesome states (*akusalā dhammā*) are the defilements, and the thoughts, emotions, and intentions derived from them, whether breaking forth into action or remaining confined within. The wholesome states (*kusalā dhammā*) are states of mind untainted by defilements, especially those conducing to deliverance. Each of the two kinds of mental states imposes a double task. The unwholesome side requires that the defilements lying dormant be prevented from erupting and that the active defilements already present be expelled. The wholesome side

37. MN 70; *Word of the Buddha*, pp. 59–60.

requires that the undeveloped liberating factors first be brought into being, then persistently developed to the point of full maturity. Now we will examine each of these four divisions of right effort, giving special attention to their most fertile field of application, the cultivation of the mind through meditation.

Prevent the Arising of Unarisen Unwholesome States

> Herein the disciple rouses his will to avoid the arising of evil, unwholesome states that have not yet arisen; and he makes effort, stirs up his energy, exerts his mind and strives.[38]

The first side of right effort aims at overcoming unwholesome states, states of mind tainted by defilements. Insofar as they impede concentration the defilements are usually presented in a fivefold set called the "five hindrances" (*pañcanīvaraṇā*): sensual desire, ill will, dullness and drowsiness, restlessness and worry, and doubt.[39] They receive the name "hindrances" because they block the path to liberation; they grow up and over the mind preventing calm and insight, the primary instruments for progress. The first two hindrances, sensual desire and ill will, are the strongest of the set, the most formidable barriers to meditative growth, representing, respectively, the unwholesome roots of greed and aversion. The other three hindrances, less toxic but still obstructive, are offshoots of delusion, usually in association with other defilements.

Sensual desire is interpreted in two ways. Sometimes it is understood in a narrow sense as lust for the "five strands of sense pleasure," i.e., agreeable sights, sounds, smells, tastes, and touches; sometimes a broader interpretation is given, by which the term becomes inclusive of craving in all its modes, whether for sense pleasures, wealth, power, position, fame, or anything else it can settle upon. The second hindrance, *ill will*, is a synonym for aversion. It comprises hatred, anger, resentment, repulsion of every shade, whether directed towards other people, towards oneself, towards objects, or towards situations. The third hindrance, *dullness and drowsiness*, is a compound of two factors linked together by their common feature of mental unwieldiness.

38. AN 4:13; *Word of the Buddha*, p. 57.

39. *Kāmacchanda, byāpāda, thīna-middha, uddhacca-kukkucca, vicikicchā.*

One is dullness (*thīna*), manifest as mental inertia; the other is drowsiness (*middha*), seen in mental sinking, heaviness of mind, or excessive inclination to sleep. At the opposite extreme is the fourth hindrance, *restlessness and worry*. This too is a compound with its two members linked by their common feature of disquietude. Restlessness (*uddhacca*) is agitation or excitement, which drives the mind from thought to thought with speed and frenzy; worry (*kukkucca*) is remorse over past mistakes and anxiety about their possible undesired consequences. The fifth hindrance, *doubt*, signifies a chronic indecisiveness and lack of resolution: not the probing of critical intelligence, an attitude encouraged by the Buddha, but a persistent inability to commit oneself to the course of spiritual training due to lingering doubts concerning the Buddha, his doctrine, and his path.

The first effort to be made regarding the hindrances is the effort to prevent the unarisen hindrances from arising; this is also called the endeavor to restrain (*saṃvarappadhāna*). The effort to hold the hindrances in check is imperative both at the start of meditative training and throughout the course of its development. For when the hindrances arise, they disperse attention and darken the quality of awareness, to the detriment of calm and clarity. The hindrances do not come from outside the mind but from within. They appear through the activation of certain tendencies constantly lying dormant in the deep recesses of the mental continuum, awaiting the opportunity to surface.

Generally what sparks the hindrances into activity is the input afforded by sense experience. The physical organism is equipped with five sense faculties each receptive to its own specific kind of data—the eye to forms, the ear to sounds, the nose to smells, the tongue to tastes, the body to tangibles. Sense objects continuously impinge on the senses, which relay the information they receive to the mind, where it is processed, evaluated, and accorded an appropriate response. But the mind can deal with the impressions it receives in different ways, governed in the first place by the manner in which it attends to them. When the mind adverts to the incoming data carelessly, with unwise consideration (*ayoniso manasikāra*), the sense objects tend to stir up unwholesome states. They do this either directly, through their immediate impact, or else indirectly by depositing memory traces which later may swell up as the objects of defiled thoughts, images, and fantasies. As a general rule the defilement that is activated corresponds to the object: attractive objects provoke desire, disagreeable objects provoke ill will, and indeterminate objects provoke the defilements connected with delusion.

Since an uncontrolled response to the sensory input stimulates the latent defilements, what is evidently needed to prevent them from arising is control over the senses. Thus the Buddha teaches, as the discipline for keeping the hindrances in check, an exercise called the restraint of the sense faculties (*indriya-saṃvara*):

> When he perceives a form with the eye, a sound with the ear, an odor with the nose, a taste with the tongue, an impression with the body, or an object with the mind, he apprehends neither the sign nor the particulars. And he strives to ward off that through which evil and unwholesome states, greed and sorrow, would arise, if he remained with unguarded senses; and he watches over his senses, restrains his senses.[40]

Restraint of the senses does not mean denial of the senses, retreating into a total withdrawal from the sensory world. This is impossible, and even if it could be achieved, the real problem would still not be solved; for the defilements lie in the mind, not in the sense organs or objects. The key to sense control is indicated by the phrase "not apprehending the sign or the particulars." The "sign" (*nimitta*) is the object's general appearance insofar as this appearance is grasped as the basis for defiled thoughts; the "particulars" (*anubyañjana*) are its less conspicuous features. If sense control is lacking, the mind roams recklessly over the sense fields. First it grasps the sign, which sets the defilements into motion, then it explores the particulars, which permits them to multiply and thrive.

To restrain the senses requires that mindfulness and clear understanding be applied to the encounter with the sense fields. Sense consciousness occurs in a series, as a sequence of momentary cognitive acts each having its own special task. The initial stages in the series occur as automatic functions: first the mind adverts to the object, then apprehends it, then admits the percept, examines

40. AN 4:14; *Word of the Buddha*, p. 57.

it, and identifies it. Immediately following the identification a space opens up in which there occurs a free evaluation of the object leading to the choice of a response. When mindfulness is absent the latent defilements, pushing for an opportunity to emerge, will motivate a wrong consideration. One will grasp the sign of the object, explore its details, and thereby give the defilements their opportunity: on account of greed one will become fascinated by an agreeable object, on account of aversion one will be repelled by a disagreeable object. But when one applies mindfulness to the sensory encounter, one nips the cognitive process in the bud before it can evolve into the stages that stimulate the dormant taints. Mindfulness holds the hindrances in check by keeping the mind at the level of what is sensed. It rivets awareness on the given, preventing the mind from embellishing the datum with ideas born of greed, aversion, and delusion. Then, with this lucent awareness as a guide, the mind can proceed to comprehend the object as it is, without being led astray.

Abandon the Arisen Unwholesome States

> Herein the disciple rouses his will to overcome the evil, unwholesome states that have already arisen and he makes effort, stirs up his energy, exerts his mind and strives.[41]

Despite the effort at sense control the defilements may still surface. They swell up from the depths of the mental continuum, from the buried strata of past accumulations, to congeal into unwholesome thoughts and emotions. When this happens a new kind of effort becomes necessary, the effort to abandon arisen unwholesome states, called for short the endeavor to abandon (*pahānappadhāna*):

> He does not retain any thought of sensual lust, ill will, or harmfulness, or any other evil and unwholesome states that may have arisen; he abandons them, dispels them, destroys them, causes them to disappear.[42]

41. AN 4:13; *Word of the Buddha*, p. 58.
42. AN 4:14; *Word of the Buddha*, p. 58.

Just as a skilled physician has different medicines for different ailments, so the Buddha has different antidotes for the different hindrances, some equally applicable to all, some geared to a particular hindrance. In an important discourse the Buddha explains five techniques for expelling distracting thoughts.[43] The first is to expel the defiled thought with a wholesome thought which is its exact opposite, analogous to the way a carpenter might use a new peg to drive out an old one. For each of the five hindrances there is a specific remedy, a line of meditation designed expressly to deflate it and destroy it. This remedy can be applied intermittently, when a hindrance springs up and disrupts meditation on the primary subject; or it can be taken as a primary subject itself, used to counter a defilement repeatedly seen to be a persistent obstacle to one's practice. But for the antidote to become effective in the first role, as a temporary expedient required by the upsurge of a hindrance, it is best to gain some familiarity with it by making it a primary object, at least for short periods.

For desire a remedy of general application is the meditation on impermanence, which knocks away the underlying prop of clinging, the implicit assumption that the objects clung to are stable and durable. For desire in the specific form of sensual lust the most potent antidote is the contemplation of the unattractive nature of the body, to be dealt with at greater length in the next chapter. Ill will meets its proper remedy in the meditation on loving kindness (*mettā*), which banishes all traces of hatred and anger through the methodical radiation of the altruistic wish that all beings be well and happy. The dispelling of dullness and drowsiness calls for a special effort to arouse energy, for which several methods are suggested: the visualization of a brilliant ball of light, getting up and doing a period of brisk walking meditation, reflection on death, or simply making a firm determination to continue striving. Restlessness and worry are most effectively countered by turning the mind to a simple object that tends to calm it down; the method usually recommended is mindfulness of breathing, attention to the in-and-out flow of the breath. In the case of doubt the special remedy is investigation: to make

43. MN 20; *Word of the Buddha*, p. 58.

inquiries, ask questions, and study the teachings until the obscure points become clear.[44]

Whereas this first of the five methods for expelling the hindrances involves a one-to-one alignment between a hindrance and its remedy, the other four utilize general approaches. The second marshals the forces of shame (*hiri*) and moral dread (*ottappa*) to abandon the unwanted thought: one reflects on the thought as vile and ignoble or considers its undesirable consequences until an inner revulsion sets in which drives the thought away. The third method involves a deliberate diversion of attention. When an unwholesome thought arises and clamors to be noticed, instead of indulging it one simply shuts it out by redirecting one's attention elsewhere, as if closing one's eyes or looking away to avoid an unpleasant sight. The fourth method uses the opposite approach. Instead of turning away from the unwanted thought, one confronts it directly as an object, scrutinizes its features, and investigates its source. When this is done the thought quiets down and eventually disappears. For an unwholesome thought is like a thief: it only creates trouble when its operation is concealed, but put under observation it becomes tame. The fifth method, to be used only as a last resort, is suppression—vigorously restraining the unwholesome thought with the power of the will in the way a strong man might throw a weaker man to the ground and keep him pinned there with his weight.

By applying these five methods with skill and discretion, the Buddha says, one becomes a master of all the pathways of thought. One is no longer the subject of the mind but its master. Whatever thought one wants to think, that one will think. Whatever thought one does not want to think, that one will not think. Even if unwholesome thoughts occasionally arise, one can dispel them immediately, just as quickly as a red-hot pan will turn to steam a few chance drops of water.

44. For a full treatment of the methods for dealing with the hindrances individually, consult the commentary to the Satipaṭṭhāna Sutta (DN 22, MN 10). A translation of the relevant passages, with further extracts from the subcommentary, can be found in Soma Thera, *The Way of Mindfulness*, pp. 116–26.

Arouse Unarisen Wholesome States

> Herein the disciple rouses his will to arouse wholesome states that have not yet arisen; and he makes effort, stirs up his energy, exerts his mind and strives.[45]

Simultaneously with the removal of defilements, right effort also imposes the task of cultivating wholesome states of mind. This involves two divisions: the arousing of wholesome states not yet arisen and the maturation of wholesome states already arisen.

The first of the two divisions is also known as the endeavor to develop (*bhāvanāppadhāna*). Though the wholesome states to be developed can be grouped in various ways—serenity and insight, the four foundations of mindfulness, the eight factors of the path, etc.—the Buddha lays special stress on a set called the seven factors of enlightenment (*satta bojjhaṅgā*): mindfulness, investigation of phenomena, energy, rapture, tranquillity, concentration, and equanimity.

> Thus he develops the factors of enlightenment, based on solitude, on detachment, on cessation, and ending in deliverance, namely: the enlightenment factors of mindfulness, investigation of phenomena, energy, rapture, tranquillity, concentration, and equanimity.[46]

The seven states are grouped together as "enlightenment factors" both because they lead to enlightenment and because they constitute enlightenment. In the preliminary stages of the path they prepare the way for the great realization; in the end they remain as its components. The experience of enlightenment, perfect and complete understanding, is just these seven components working in unison to break all shackles and bring final release from sorrow.

The way to enlightenment starts with *mindfulness*. Mindfulness clears the ground for insight into the nature of things by bringing to light phenomena in the now, the present moment,

---

45. AN 4:13; *Word of the Buddha*, pp. 58–59.

46. AN 4:14; *Word of the Buddha*, p. 59. The Pāli names for the seven are: *satisambojjhaṅga, dhammavicaya-sambojjhaṅga, viriyasambojjhaṅga, pītisam-bojjhaṅga, passaddhisambojjhaṅga, samādhisambojjhaṅga, upekkhāsam-bojjhaṅga.*

stripped of all subjective commentary, interpretations, and projections. Then, when mindfulness has brought the bare phenomena into focus, the factor of *investigation* steps in to search out their characteristics, conditions, and consequences. Whereas mindfulness is basically receptive, investigation is an active factor which unflinchingly probes, analyzes, and dissects phenomena to uncover their fundamental structures.

The work of investigation requires *energy*, the third factor of enlightenment, which mounts in three stages. The first, inceptive energy, shakes off lethargy and arouses initial enthusiasm. As the work of contemplation advances, energy gathers momentum and enters the second stage, perseverance, wherein it propels the practice without slackening. Finally, at the peak, energy reaches the third stage, invincibility, where it drives contemplation forward leaving the hindrances powerless to stop it.

As energy increases, the fourth factor of enlightenment is quickened. This is *rapture*, a pleasurable interest in the object. Rapture gradually builds up, ascending to ecstatic heights: waves of bliss run through the body, the mind glows with joy, fervor and confidence intensify. But these experiences, as encouraging as they are, still contain a flaw: they create an excitation verging on restlessness. With further practice, however, rapture subsides and a tone of quietness sets in signalling the rise of the fifth factor, *tranquillity*. Rapture remains present, but it is now subdued, and the work of contemplation proceeds with self-possessed serenity.

Tranquillity brings to ripeness *concentration*, the sixth factor, one-pointed unification of mind. Then, with the deepening of concentration, the last enlightenment factor comes into dominance. This is *equanimity*, inward poise and balance free from the two defects of excitement and inertia. When inertia prevails, energy must be aroused; when excitement prevails, it is necessary to exercise restraint. But when both defects have been vanquished the practice can unfold evenly without need for concern. The mind of equanimity is compared to the driver of a chariot when the horses are moving at a steady pace: he neither has to urge them forward nor to hold them back, but can just sit comfortably and watch the scenery go by. Equanimity has the same "on-looking" quality. When the other factors are balanced the mind remains poised watching the play of phenomena.

Maintain Arisen Wholesome States

> Herein the disciple rouses his will to maintain the wholesome things that have already arisen, and not to allow them to disappear, but to bring them to growth, to maturity, and to the full perfection of development; and he makes effort, stirs up his energy, exerts his mind and strives.[47]

This last of the four right efforts aims at maintaining the arisen wholesome factors and bringing them to maturity. Called the "endeavor to maintain" (*anurakkhaṇappadhāna*), it is explained as the effort to "keep firmly in the mind a favorable object of concentration that has arisen."[48] The work of guarding the object causes the seven enlightenment factors to gain stability and gradually increase in strength until they issue in the liberating realization. This marks the culmination of right effort, the goal in which the countless individual acts of exertion finally reach fulfilment.

VI. Right Mindfulness
(*Sammā Sati*)

The Buddha says that the Dhamma, the ultimate truth of things, is directly visible, timeless, calling out to be approached and seen. He says further that it is always available to us, and that the place where it is to be realized is within oneself.[49] The ultimate truth, the Dhamma, is not something mysterious and remote, but the truth of our own experience. It can be reached only by understanding our experience, by penetrating it right through to its foundations. This truth, in order to become liberating truth, has to be known directly. It is not enough merely to accept it on faith, to believe it on the authority of books or a teacher, or to think it out through deductions and inferences. It has to be known by insight, grasped and absorbed by a kind of knowing which is also an immediate seeing.

---

47. AN 4:13; *Word of the Buddha*, p. 59.
48. AN 4:14; *Word of the Buddha*, p. 59.
49. *Dhammo sandiṭṭhiko akāliko ehipassiko opanayiko paccattaṃ veditabbo viññūhi* (MN 7, etc.).

What brings the field of experience into focus and makes it accessible to insight is a mental faculty called in Pāli *sati*, usually translated as "mindfulness." Mindfulness is presence of mind, attentiveness or awareness. Yet the kind of awareness involved in mindfulness differs profoundly from the kind of awareness at work in our usual mode of consciousness. All consciousness involves awareness in the sense of a knowing or experiencing of an object. But with the practice of mindfulness awareness is applied at a special pitch. The mind is deliberately kept at the level of *bare attention*, a detached observation of what is happening within us and around us in the present moment. In the practice of right mindfulness the mind is trained to remain in the present, open, quiet, and alert, contemplating the present event. All judgements and interpretations have to be suspended, or if they occur, just registered and dropped. The task is simply to note whatever comes up just as it is occurring, riding the changes of events in the way a surfer rides the waves on the sea. The whole process is a way of coming back into the present, of standing in the here and now without slipping away, without getting swept away by the tides of distracting thoughts.

It might be assumed that we are always aware of the present, but this is a mirage. Only seldom do we become aware of the present in the precise way required by the practice of mindfulness. In ordinary consciousness the mind begins a cognitive process with some impression given in the present, but it does not stay with it. Instead it uses the immediate impression as a springboard for building blocks of mental constructs which remove it from the sheer facticity of the datum. The cognitive process is generally interpretative. The mind perceives its object free from conceptualization only briefly. Then, immediately after grasping the initial impression, it launches on a course of ideation by which it seeks to interpret the object to itself, to make it intelligible in terms of its own categories and assumptions. To bring this about the mind posits concepts, joins the concepts into constructs—sets of mutually corroborative concepts—then weaves the constructs together into complex interpretative schemes. In the end the original direct experience has been overrun by ideation and the presented object appears only dimly through dense layers of ideas and views, like the moon through a layer of clouds.

The Buddha calls this process of mental construction *papañca*, "elaboration," "embellishment," or "conceptual proliferation." The elaborations block out the presentational immediacy of phenomena; they let us know the object only "at a distance," not as it really is. But the elaborations do not only screen cognition; they also serve as a basis for projections. The deluded mind, cloaked in ignorance, projects its own internal constructs outwardly, ascribing them to the object as if they really belonged to it. As a result, what we know as the final object of cognition, what we use as the basis for our values, plans, and actions, is a patchwork product, not the original article. To be sure, the product is not wholly illusion, not sheer fantasy. It takes what is given in immediate experience as its groundwork and raw material, but along with this it includes something else: the embellishments fabricated by the mind.

The springs for this process of fabrication, hidden from view, are the latent defilements. The defilements create the embellishments, project them outwardly, and use them as hooks for coming to the surface, where they cause further distortion. To correct the erroneous notions is the task of wisdom, but for wisdom to discharge its work effectively, it needs direct access to the object as it is in itself, uncluttered by the conceptual elaborations. The task of right mindfulness is to clear up the cognitive field. Mindfulness brings to light experience in its pure immediacy. It reveals the object as it is before it has been plastered over with conceptual paint, overlaid with interpretations. To practice mindfulness is thus a matter not so much of doing but of undoing: not thinking, not judging, not associating, not planning, not imagining, not wishing. All these "doings" of ours are modes of interference, ways the mind manipulates experience and tries to establish its dominance. Mindfulness undoes the knots and tangles of these "doings" by simply noting. It does nothing but note, watching each occasion of experience as it arises, stands, and passes away. In the watching there is no room for clinging, no compulsion to saddle things with our desires. There is only a sustained contemplation of experience in its bare immediacy, carefully and precisely and persistently.

Mindfulness exercises a powerful grounding function. It anchors the mind securely in the present, so it does not float away into the past and future with their memories, regrets, fears, and hopes. The mind without mindfulness is sometimes compared to a pumpkin, the mind established in mindfulness to a stone.[50] A pumpkin placed on the surface of a pond soon floats away and always remains on the water's surface. But a stone does not float away; it stays where it is put and at once sinks into the water until it reaches bottom. Similarly, when mindfulness is strong, the mind stays with its object and penetrates its characteristics deeply. It does not wander and merely skim the surface as the mind destitute of mindfulness does.

Mindfulness facilitates the achievement of both serenity and insight. It can lead to either deep concentration or wisdom, depending on the mode in which it is applied. Merely a slight shift in the mode of application can spell the difference between the course the contemplative process takes, whether it descends to deeper levels of inner calm culminating in the stages of absorption, the *jhānas*, or whether instead it strips away the veils of delusion to arrive at penetrating insight. To lead to the stages of serenity the primary chore of mindfulness is to keep the mind on the object, free from straying. Mindfulness serves as the guard charged with the responsibility of making sure that the mind does not slip away from the object to lose itself in random undirected thoughts. It also keeps watch over the factors stirring in the mind, catching the hindrances beneath their camouflages and expelling them before they can cause harm. To lead to insight and the realizations of wisdom, mindfulness is exercised in a more differentiated manner. Its task, in this phase of practice, is to observe, to note, to discern phenomena with utmost precision until their fundamental characteristics are brought to light.

Right mindfulness is cultivated through a practice called "the four foundations of mindfulness" (*cattāro satipaṭṭhānā*), the mindful contemplation of four objective spheres: the body, feelings, states of mind, and phenomena.[51] As the Buddha explains:

50. Commentary to Vism. See Vism XIV, n. 64.

51. Sometimes the word *satipaṭṭhāna* is translated "foundation of mindfulness," with emphasis on the objective side, sometimes "application of mindfulness," with emphasis on the subjective side. Both explanations are allowed by the texts and commentaries.

> And what, monks, is right mindfulness? Herein, a monk dwells contemplating the body in the body, ardent, clearly comprehending and mindful, having put away covetousness and grief concerning the world. He dwells contemplating feelings in feelings ... states of mind in states of mind ... phenomena in phenomena, ardent, clearly comprehending and mindful, having put away covetousness and grief concerning the world.[52]

The Buddha says that the four foundations of mindfulness form "the only way that leads to the attainment of purity, to the overcoming of sorrow and lamentation, to the end of pain and grief, to the entering upon the right path and the realization of *Nibbāna*."[53] They are called "the only way" (*ekāyano maggo*), not for the purpose of setting forth a narrow dogmatism, but to indicate that the attainment of liberation can only issue from the penetrating contemplation of the field of experience undertaken in the practice of right mindfulness.

Of the four applications of mindfulness, the contemplation of the body is concerned with the material side of existence; the other three are concerned principally (though not solely) with the mental side. The completion of the practice requires all four contemplations. Though no fixed order is laid down in which they are to be taken up, the body is generally taken first as the basic sphere of contemplation; the others come into view later, when mindfulness has gained in strength and clarity. Limitations of space do not allow for a complete explanation of all four foundations. Here we have to settle for a brief synopsis.

Contemplation of the Body (*kāyānupassanā*)

The Buddha begins his exposition of the body with contemplation of the mindfulness of breathing (*ānāpānasati*). Though not required as a starting point for meditation, in actual practice mindfulness of breathing usually serves as the "root meditation subject" (*mūlakammaṭṭhāna*), the foundation for the entire course of contemplation. It would be a mistake, however, to consider this subject merely an exercise for neophytes. By itself mindfulness of

52. DN 22; *Word of the Buddha*, p. 61.
53. Ibid.; *Word of the Buddha*, p. 61.

breathing can lead to all the stages of the path culminating in full awakening. In fact it was this meditation subject that the Buddha used on the night of his own enlightenment. He also reverted to it throughout the years during his solitary retreats, and constantly recommended it to the monks, praising it as "peaceful and sublime, an unadulterated blissful abiding, which banishes at once and stills evil unwholesome thoughts as soon as they arise" (MN 118).

Mindfulness of breathing can function so effectively as a subject of meditation because it works with a process that is always available to us, the process of respiration. What it does to turn this process into a basis for meditation is simply to bring it into the range of awareness by making the breath an object of observation. The meditation requires no special intellectual sophistication, only awareness of the breath. One merely breathes naturally through the nostrils keeping the breath in mind at the contact point around the nostrils or upper lip, where the sensation of breath can be felt as the air moves in and out. There should be no attempt to control the breath or to force it into predetermined rhythms, only a mindful contemplation of the natural process of breathing in and out. The awareness of breath cuts through the complexities of discursive thinking, rescues us from pointless wandering in the labyrinth of vain imaginings, and grounds us solidly in the present. For whenever we become aware of breathing, really aware of it, we can be aware of it only in the present, never in the past or the future.

The Buddha's exposition of mindfulness of breathing involves four basic steps. The first two (which are not necessarily sequential) require that a long inhalation or exhalation be noted as it occurs, and that a short inhalation or exhalation be noted as it occurs. One simply observes the breath moving in and out, observing it as closely as possible, noting whether the breath is long or short. As mindfulness grows sharper, the breath can be followed through the entire course of its movement, from the beginning of an inhalation through its intermediary stages to its end, then from the beginning of an exhalation through its intermediary stages to its end. This third step is called "clearly perceiving the entire (breath) body." The fourth step, "calming the bodily function," involves a progressive quieting down of the breath and its associated bodily functions until they become extremely fine and subtle. Beyond these four basic steps lie more advanced practices which direct mindfulness of breathing towards deep concentration and insight.[54]

Another practice in the contemplation of the body, which extends meditation outwards from the confines of a single fixed position, is mindfulness of the postures. The body can assume four basic postures—walking, standing, sitting, and lying down—and a variety of other positions marking the change from one posture to another. Mindfulness of the postures focuses full attention on the body in whatever position it assumes: when walking one is aware of walking, when standing one is aware of standing, when sitting one is aware of sitting, when lying down one is aware of lying down, when changing postures one is aware of changing postures. The contemplation of the postures illuminates the impersonal nature of the body. It reveals that the body is not a self or the belonging of a self, but merely a configuration of living matter subject to the directing influence of volition.

The next exercise carries the extension of mindfulness a step further. This exercise, called "mindfulness and clear comprehension" (*satisampajañña*), adds to the bare awareness an element of understanding. When performing any action, one performs it with full awareness or clear comprehension. Going and coming, looking ahead and looking aside, bending and stretching, dressing, eating, drinking, urinating, defecating, falling asleep, waking up, speaking, remaining silent—all become occasions for the progress of meditation when done with clear comprehension. In the commentaries clear comprehension is explained as fourfold: (1) understanding the purpose of the action, i.e., recognizing its aim and determining whether that aim accords with the Dhamma; (2) understanding suitability, i.e., knowing the most efficient means to achieve one's aim; (3) understanding the range of meditation, i.e., keeping the mind constantly in a meditative frame even when engaged in action; and (4) understanding without delusion, i.e., seeing the action as an impersonal process devoid of a controlling ego-entity.[55] This last aspect will be explored more thoroughly in the last chapter, on the development of wisdom.

54. For details, see Vism VIII, 145–244.

55. See Soma Thera, *The Way of Mindfulness*, pp. 58–97.

The next two sections on mindfulness of the body present analytical contemplations intended to expose the body's real nature. One of these is the meditation on the body's unattractiveness, already touched on in connection with right effort; the other, the analysis of the body into the four primary elements. The first, the meditation on unattractiveness,[56] is designed to counter infatuation with the body, especially in its form of sexual desire. The Buddha teaches that the sexual drive is a manifestation of craving, thus a cause of *dukkha* that has to be reduced and extricated as a precondition for bringing *dukkha* to an end. The meditation aims at weakening sexual desire by depriving the sexual urge of its cognitive underpinning, the perception of the body as sensually alluring. Sensual desire rises and falls together with this perception. It springs up because we view the body as attractive; it declines when this perception of beauty is removed. The perception of bodily attractiveness in turn lasts only so long as the body is looked at superficially, grasped in terms of selected impressions. To counter that perception we have to refuse to stop with these impressions but proceed to inspect the body at a deeper level, with a probing scrutiny grounded in dispassion.

Precisely this is what is undertaken in the meditation on unattractiveness, which turns back the tide of sensuality by pulling away its perceptual prop. The meditation takes one's own body as object, since for a neophyte to start off with the body of another, especially a member of the opposite sex, might fail to accomplish the desired result. Using visualization as an aid, one mentally dissects the body into its components and investigates them one by one, bringing their repulsive nature to light. The texts mention thirty-two parts: head-hairs, body-hairs, nails, teeth, skin, flesh, sinews, bones, marrow, kidneys, heart, liver, diaphragm, spleen, lungs, large intestines, small intestines, stomach contents, excrement, brain, bile, phlegm, pus, blood, sweat, fat, tears, grease, snot, spittle, synovial fluid, and urine. The repulsiveness of the parts implies the same for the whole: the body seen close-up is truly unattractive, its beautiful appearance a mirage. But the aim

---

56. *Asubha-bhāvanā.* The same subject is also called the perception of repulsiveness (*paṭikkūlasaññā*) and mindfulness concerning the body (*kāyagatā sati*).

of this meditation must not be misapprehended. The aim is not to produce aversion and disgust but detachment, to extinguish the fire of lust by removing its fuel.[57]

The other analytical contemplation deals with the body in a different way. This meditation, called the analysis into elements (*dhātuvavatthāna*), sets out to counter our innate tendency to identify with the body by exposing the body's essentially impersonal nature. The means it employs, as its name indicates, is the mental dissection of the body into the four primary elements, referred to by the archaic names earth, water, fire, and air, but actually signifying the four principal behavioral modes of matter: solidity, fluidity, heat, and oscillation. The solid element is seen most clearly in the body's solid parts—the organs, tissues, and bones; the fluid element, in the bodily fluids; the heat element, in the body's temperature; the oscillation element, in the respiratory process. The break with the identification of the body as "I" or "my self" is effected by a widening of perspective after the elements have come into view. Having analyzed the body into the elements, one then considers that all four elements, the chief aspects of bodily existence, are essentially identical with the chief aspects of external matter, with which the body is in constant interchange. When one vividly realizes this through prolonged meditation, one ceases to identify with the body, ceases to cling to it. One sees that the body is nothing more than a particular configuration of changing material processes which support a stream of changing mental processes. There is nothing here that can be considered a truly existent self, nothing that can provide a substantial basis for the sense of personal identity.[58]

The last exercise in mindfulness of the body is a series of "cemetery meditations," contemplations of the body's disintegration after death, which may be performed either imaginatively, with the aid of pictures, or through direct confrontation with a corpse. By any of these means one obtains a clear mental image of a decomposing body, then applies the process to one's own body, considering: "This body, now so full of life, has the same nature and is subject to the same fate. It cannot escape death, cannot

57. For details, see Vism VIII, 42–144.

58. For details, see Vism XI, 27–117.

escape disintegration, but must eventually die and decompose." Again, the purpose of this meditation should not be misunderstood. The aim is not to indulge in a morbid fascination with death and corpses, but to sunder our egoistic clinging to existence with a contemplation sufficiently powerful to break its hold. The clinging to existence subsists through the implicit assumption of permanence. In the sight of a corpse we meet the teacher who proclaims unambiguously: "Everything formed is impermanent."

Contemplation of Feeling (*vedanānupassanā*)

The next foundation of mindfulness is feeling (*vedanā*). The word "feeling" is used here, not in the sense of emotion (a complex phenomenon best subsumed under the third and fourth foundations of mindfulness), but in the narrower sense of the affective tone or "hedonic quality" of experience. This may be of three kinds, yielding three principal types of feeling: pleasant feeling, painful feeling, and neutral feeling. The Buddha teaches that feeling is an inseparable concomitant of consciousness, since every act of knowing is colored by some affective tone. Thus feeling is present at every moment of experience; it may be strong or weak, clear or indistinct, but some feeling must accompany the cognition.

Feeling arises in dependence on a mental event called "contact" (*phassa*). Contact marks the "coming together" of consciousness with the object via a sense faculty; it is the factor by virtue of which consciousness "touches" the object presenting itself to the mind through the sense organ. Thus there are six kinds of contact distinguished by the six sense faculties—eye-contact, ear-contact, nose-contact, tongue-contact, body-contact, and mind-contact—and six kinds of feeling distinguished by the contact from which they spring.

Feeling acquires special importance as an object of contemplation because it is feeling that usually triggers the latent defilements into activity. The feelings may not be clearly registered, but in subtle ways they nourish and sustain the dispositions to unwholesome states. Thus when a pleasant feeling arises, we fall under the influence of the defilement greed and cling to it. When a painful feeling occurs, we respond with displeasure, hate, and fear, which are aspects of aversion. And when a neutral feeling occurs, we generally do not notice it, or let it lull us into a false sense of security—states of mind governed by delusion. From this it can be seen that each of the root defilements is conditioned by a particular kind of feeling: greed by pleasant feeling, aversion by painful feeling, delusion by neutral feeling.

But the link between feelings and the defilements is not a necessary one. Pleasure does not always have to lead to greed, pain to aversion, neutral feeling to delusion. The tie between them can be snapped, and one essential means for snapping it is mindfulness. Feeling will stir up a defilement only when it is not noticed, when it is indulged rather than observed. By turning it into an object of observation, mindfulness defuses the feeling so that it cannot provoke an unwholesome response. Then, instead of relating to the feeling by way of habit through attachment, repulsion, or apathy, we relate by way of contemplation, using the feeling as a springboard for understanding the nature of experience.

In the early stages the contemplation of feeling involves attending to the arisen feelings, noting their distinctive qualities: pleasant, painful, neutral. The feeling is noted without identifying with it, without taking it to be "I" or "mine" or something happening "to me." Awareness is kept at the level of bare attention: one watches each feeling that arises, seeing it as merely a feeling, a bare mental event shorn of all subjective references, all pointers to an ego. The task is simply to note the feeling's quality, its tone of pleasure, pain, or neutrality.

But as practice advances, as one goes on noting each feeling, letting it go and noting the next, the focus of attention shifts from the qualities of feelings to the process of feeling itself. The process reveals a ceaseless flux of feelings arising and dissolving, succeeding one another without a halt. Within the process there is nothing lasting. Feeling itself is only a stream of events, occasions of feeling flashing into being moment by moment, dissolving as soon as they arise. Thus begins the insight into impermanence, which, as it evolves, overturns the three unwholesome roots. There is no greed for pleasant feelings, no aversion for painful feelings, no delusion over neutral feelings. All are seen as merely fleeting and substanceless events devoid of any true enjoyment or basis for involvement.

Contemplation of the State of Mind (*cittānupassanā*)

With this foundation of mindfulness we turn from a particular mental factor, feeling, to the general state of mind to which that factor belongs. To understand what is entailed by this contemplation it is helpful to look at the Buddhist conception of the mind. Usually we think of the mind as an enduring faculty remaining identical with itself through the succession of experiences. Though experience changes, the mind which undergoes the changing experience seems to remain the same, perhaps modified in certain ways but still retaining its identity. However, in the Buddha's teaching the notion of a permanent mental organ is rejected. The mind is regarded, not as a lasting subject of thought, feeling, and volition, but as a sequence of momentary mental acts, each distinct and discrete, their connections with one another causal rather than substantial.

A single act of consciousness is called a *citta*, which we shall render "a state of mind." Each *citta* consists of many components, the chief of which is consciousness itself, the basic experiencing of the object; consciousness is also called *citta*, the name for the whole being given to its principal part. Along with consciousness every *citta* contains a set of concomitants called *cetasikas*, mental factors. These include feeling, perception, volition, the emotions, etc.; in short, all the mental functions except the primary knowing of the object, which is *citta* or consciousness.

Since consciousness in itself is just a bare experiencing of an object, it cannot be differentiated through its own nature but only by way of its associated factors, the *cetasikas*. The *cetasikas* color the *citta* and give it its distinctive character; thus when we want to pinpoint the *citta* as an object of contemplation, we have to do so by using the *cetasikas* as indicators. In his exposition of the contemplation of the state of mind, the Buddha mentions, by reference to *cetasikas*, sixteen kinds of *citta* to be noted: the mind with lust, the mind without lust, the mind with aversion, the mind without aversion, the mind with delusion, the mind without delusion, the cramped mind, the scattered mind, the developed mind, the undeveloped mind, the surpassable mind, the unsurpassable mind, the concentrated mind, the unconcentrated mind, the freed mind, the unfreed mind. For practical purposes it is sufficient at the start to focus solely on the first six states, noting whether the mind is associated with any of the unwholesome roots or free from them. When a particular *citta* is present, it is contemplated merely as a *citta*, a state of mind. It is not identified with as "I" or "mine," not taken as a self or as something belonging to a self. Whether it is a pure state of mind or a defiled state, a lofty state or a low one, there should be no elation or dejection, only a clear recognition of the state. The state is simply noted, then allowed to pass without clinging to the desired ones or resenting the undesired ones.

As contemplation deepens, the contents of the mind become increasingly rarefied. Irrelevant flights of thought, imagination, and emotion subside, mindfulness becomes clearer, the mind remains intently aware, watching its own process of becoming. At times there might appear to be a persisting observer behind the process, but with continued practice even this apparent observer disappears. The mind itself—the seemingly solid, stable mind—dissolves into a stream of *cittas* flashing in and out of being moment by moment, coming from nowhere and going nowhere, yet continuing in sequence without pause.

Contemplation of Phenomena (*dhammānupassanā*)

In the context of the fourth foundation of mindfulness, the multivalent word *dhammā* (here intended in the plural) has two interconnected meanings, as the account in the *sutta* shows. One meaning is *cetasikas*, the mental factors, which are now attended to in their own right apart from their role as coloring the state of mind, as was done in the previous contemplation. The other meaning is the elements of actuality, the ultimate constituents of experience as structured in the Buddha's teaching. To convey both senses we render *dhammā* as "phenomena," for lack of a better alternative. But when we do so this should not be taken to imply the existence of some *noumenon* or substance behind the phenomena. The point of the Buddha's teaching of *anattā*, egolessness, is that the basic constituents of actuality are bare phenomena (*suddha-dhammā*) occurring without any noumenal support.

The *sutta* section on the contemplation of phenomena is divided into five sub-sections, each devoted to a different set of phenomena: the five hindrances, the five aggregates, the six inner and outer sense bases, the seven factors of enlightenment, and the Four Noble Truths. Among these, the five hindrances and the seven enlightenment factors are *dhammā* in the narrower sense of mental factors, the others are *dhammā* in the broader sense of constituents of actuality. (In the third section, however, on the sense bases, there is a reference to the fetters that arise through the senses; these can also be included among the mental factors.) In the present chapter we shall deal briefly only with the two groups that may be regarded as *dhammā* in the sense of mental factors. We already touched on both of these in relation to right effort (Chapter V); now we shall consider them in specific connection with the practice of right mindfulness. We shall discuss the other types of *dhammā*—the five aggregates and the six senses—in the final chapter, in relation to the development of wisdom.

The five hindrances and seven factors of enlightenment require special attention because they are the principal impediments and aids to liberation. The hindrances—sensual desire, ill will, dullness and drowsiness, restlessness and worry, and doubt—generally become manifest in an early stage of practice, soon after the initial expectations and gross disturbances subside and the subtle tendencies find the opportunity to surface. Whenever one of the hindrances crops up, its presence should be noted; then, when it fades away, a note should be made of its disappearance. To ensure that the hindrances are kept under control an element of comprehension is needed: we have to understand how the hindrances arise, how they can be removed, and how they can be prevented from arising in the future.[59]

A similar mode of contemplation is to be applied to the seven factors of enlightenment: mindfulness, investigation, energy, rapture, tranquillity, concentration, and equanimity. When any one of these factors arises, its presence should be noted. Then, after noting its presence, one has to investigate to discover how it arises and how it can be matured.[60] When they first spring up, the enlightenment factors are weak, but with consistent cultivation they accumulate strength. Mindfulness initiates the contemplative process. When it becomes well-established, it arouses investigation,

---

59. For a full account, see Soma Thera, *The Way of Mindfulness*, pp. 116–127.
60. Ibid., pp. 131–146.

the probing quality of intelligence. Investigation in turn calls forth energy, energy gives rise to rapture, rapture leads to tranquillity, tranquillity to one-pointed concentration, and concentration to equanimity. Thus the whole evolving course of practice leading to enlightenment begins with mindfulness, which remains throughout as the regulating power ensuring that the mind is clear, cognizant, and balanced.

VII. Right Concentration
(*Sammā Samādhi*)

The eighth factor of the path is right concentration, in Pāli *sammā samādhi.* Concentration represents an intensification of a mental factor present in every state of consciousness. This factor, one-pointedness of mind (*citt'ekaggatā*), has the function of unifying the other mental factors in the task of cognition. It is the factor responsible for the individuating aspect of consciousness, ensuring that every *citta* or act of mind remains centred on its object. At any given moment the mind must be cognizant of something—a sight, a sound, a smell, a taste, a touch, or a mental object. The factor of one-pointedness unifies the mind and its other concomitants in the task of cognizing the object, while it simultaneously exercises the function of centring all the constituents of the cognitive act on the object. One-pointedness of mind explains the fact that in any act of consciousness there is a central point of focus, towards which the entire objective datum points from its outer peripheries to its inner nucleus.

However, *samādhi* is only a particular kind of one-pointedness; it is not equivalent to one-pointedness in its entirety. A gourmet sitting down to a meal, an assassin about to slay his victim, a soldier on the battlefield—these all act with a concentrated mind, but their concentration cannot be characterized as *samādhi. Samādhi* is exclusively wholesome one-pointedness, the concentration in a wholesome state of mind. Even then its range is still narrower: it does not signify every form of wholesome concentration, but only the intensified concentration that results from a deliberate attempt to raise the mind to a higher, more purified level of awareness.

The commentaries define *samādhi* as the centring of the mind and mental factors rightly and evenly on an object. *Samādhi*, as wholesome concentration, collects together the ordinarily dispersed and dissipated stream of mental states to induce an inner unification. The two salient features of a concentrated mind are unbroken attentiveness to an object and the consequent tranquillity of the mental functions, qualities which distinguish it from the unconcentrated mind. The mind untrained in concentration moves in a scattered manner which the Buddha compares to the flapping about of a fish taken from the water and thrown onto dry land. It cannot stay fixed but rushes from idea to idea, from thought to thought, without inner control. Such a distracted mind is also a deluded mind. Overwhelmed by worries and concerns, a constant prey to the defilements, it sees things only in fragments, distorted by the ripples of random thoughts. But the mind that has been trained in concentration, in contrast, can remain focused on its object without distraction. This freedom from distraction further induces a softness and serenity which make the mind an effective instrument for penetration. Like a lake unruffled by any breeze, the concentrated mind is a faithful reflector that mirrors whatever is placed before it exactly as it is.

The Development of Concentration

Concentration can be developed through either of two methods—either as the goal of a system of practice directed expressly towards the attainment of deep concentration at the level of absorption or as the incidental accompaniment of the path intended to generate insight. The former method is called the development of serenity (*samatha-bhāvanā*), the second the development of insight (*vipassanā-bhāvanā*). Both paths share certain preliminary requirements. For both, moral discipline must be purified, the various impediments must be severed, the meditator must seek out suitable instruction (preferably from a personal teacher), and must resort to a dwelling conducive to practice. Once these preliminaries have been dispensed with, the meditator on the path of serenity has to obtain an object of meditation, something to be used as a focal point for developing concentration.[61]

61. In what follows I have to restrict myself to a brief overview. For a full

If the meditator has a qualified teacher, the teacher will probably assign him an object judged to be appropriate for his temperament. If he doesn't have a teacher, he will have to select an object himself, perhaps after some experimentation. The meditation manuals collect the subjects of serenity meditation into a set of forty, called "places of work" (*kammaṭṭhāna*) since they are the places where the meditator does the work of practice. The forty may be listed as follows:

ten *kasiṇas*
ten unattractive objects (*dasa asubhā*)
ten recollections (*dasa anussatiyo*)
four sublime states (*cattāro brahmavihārā*)
four immaterial states (*cattāro āruppā*)
one perception (*eka saññā*)
one analysis (*eka vavaṭṭhāna*).

The *kasiṇas* are devices representing certain primordial qualities. Four represent the primary elements—the earth, water, fire, and air *kasiṇas*; four represent colors—the blue, yellow, red, and white *kasiṇas*; the other two are the light and the space *kasiṇas*. Each *kasiṇa* is a concrete object representative of the universal quality it signifies. Thus an earth *kasiṇa* would be a circular disk filled with clay. To develop concentration on the earth *kasiṇa* the meditator sets the disk in front of him, fixes his gaze on it, and contemplates "earth, earth." A similar method is used for the other *kasiṇas*, with appropriate changes to fit the case.

The ten "unattractive objects" are corpses in different stages of decomposition. This subject appears similar to the contemplation of bodily decay in the mindfulness of the body, and in fact in olden times the cremation ground was recommended as the most appropriate place for both. But the two meditations differ in emphasis. In the mindfulness exercise stress falls on the application of reflective thought, the sight of the decaying corpse serving as a stimulus for consideration of one's own eventual death and disintegration. In this exercise the use of reflective thought is discouraged. The stress instead falls on one-pointed mental fixation on the object, the less thought the better.

exposition, see Vism, Chapters III–XI.

The ten recollections form a miscellaneous collection. The first three are devotional meditations on the qualities of the Triple Gem—the Buddha, the Dhamma, and the Sangha; they use as their basis standard formulas that have come down in the Suttas. The next three recollections also rely on ancient formulas: the meditations on morality, generosity, and the potential for divine-like qualities in oneself. Then come mindfulness of death, the contemplation of the unattractive nature of the body, mindfulness of breathing, and lastly, the recollection of peace, a discursive meditation on *Nibbāna*.

The four sublime states or "divine abodes" are the outwardly directed social attitudes—loving kindness, compassion, sympathetic joy, and equanimity—developed into universal radiations which are gradually extended in range until they encompass all living beings. The four immaterial states are the objective bases for certain deep levels of absorption: the base of infinite space, the base of infinite consciousness, the base of nothingness, and the base of neither-perception-nor-non-perception. These become accessible as objects only to those who are already adept in concentration. The "one perception" is the perception of the repulsiveness of food, a discursive topic intended to reduce attachment to the pleasures of the palate. The "one analysis" is the contemplation of the body in terms of the four primary elements, already discussed in the chapter on right mindfulness.

When such a variety of meditation subjects is presented, the aspiring meditator without a teacher might be perplexed as to which to choose. The manuals divide the forty subjects according to their suitability for different personality types. Thus the unattractive objects and the contemplation of the parts of the body are judged to be most suitable for a lustful type, the meditation on loving kindness to be best for a hating type, the meditation on the qualities of the Triple Gem to be most effective for a devotional type, etc. But for practical purposes the beginner in meditation can generally be advised to start with a simple subject that helps reduce discursive thinking. Mental distraction caused by restlessness and scattered thoughts is a common problem faced by persons of all different character types; thus a meditator of any temperament can benefit from a subject which promotes a slowing down and stilling of the thought process. The subject generally recommended for its effectiveness in clearing the mind of stray thoughts is mindfulness of breathing, which can therefore be suggested as the subject most suitable for beginners as well as veterans seeking a direct approach to deep concentration. Once the mind settles down and one's thought patterns become easier to notice, one might then make use of other subjects to deal with special problems that arise: the meditation on loving kindness may be used to counteract anger and ill will, mindfulness of the bodily parts to weaken sensual lust, the recollection of the Buddha to inspire faith and devotion, the meditation on death to arouse a sense of urgency. The ability to select the subject appropriate to the situation requires skill, but this skill evolves through practice, often through simple trial-and-error experimentation.

The Stages of Concentration

Concentration is not attained all at once but develops in stages. To enable our exposition to cover all the stages of concentration, we will consider the case of a meditator who follows the entire path of serenity meditation from start to finish, and who will make much faster progress than the typical meditator is likely to make.

After receiving his meditation subject from a teacher, or selecting it on his own, the meditator retires to a quiet place. There he assumes the correct meditation posture—the legs crossed comfortably, the upper part of the body held straight and erect, hands placed one above the other on the lap, the head kept steady, the mouth and eyes closed (unless a *kasiṇa* or other visual object is used), the breath flowing naturally and regularly through the nostrils. He then focuses his mind on the object and tries to keep it there, fixed and alert. If the mind strays, he notices this quickly, catches it, and brings it back gently but firmly to the object, doing this over and over as often as is necessary. This initial stage is called preliminary concentration (*parikkamma-samādhi*) and the object the preliminary sign (*parikkamma-nimitta*).

Once the initial excitement subsides and the mind begins to settle into the practice, the five hindrances are likely to arise, bubbling up from the depths. Sometimes they appear as thoughts, sometimes as images, sometimes as obsessive emotions: surges of desire, anger and resentment, heaviness of mind, agitation, doubts. The hindrances pose a formidable barrier, but with patience and sustained effort they can be overcome. To conquer them the meditator will have to be adroit. At times, when a particular hindrance becomes strong, he may have to lay aside his primary subject of meditation and take up another subject expressly opposed to the hindrance. At other times he will have to persist with his primary subject despite the bumps along the road, bringing his mind back to it again and again.

As he goes on striving along the path of concentration, his exertion activates five mental factors which come to his aid. These factors are intermittently present in ordinary undirected consciousness, but there they lack a unifying bond and thus do not play any special role. However, when activated by the work of meditation, these five factors pick up power, link up with one another, and steer the mind towards *samādhi*, which they will govern as the "*jhāna* factors," the factors of absorption (*jhānaṅga*). Stated in their usual order the five are: initial application of mind (*vitakka*), sustained application of mind (*vicāra*), rapture (*pīti*), happiness (*sukha*), and one-pointedness (*ekaggatā*).

Initial application of mind does the work of directing the mind to the object. It takes the mind, lifts it up, and drives it into the object the way one drives a nail through a block of wood. This done, *sustained application of mind* anchors the mind on the object, keeping it there through its function of examination. To clarify the difference between these two factors, initial application is compared to the striking of a bell, sustained application to the bell's reverberations. *Rapture*, the third factor, is the delight and joy that accompany a favorable interest in the object, while *happiness*, the fourth factor, is the pleasant feeling that accompanies successful concentration. Since rapture and happiness share similar qualities they tend to be confused with each other, but the two are not identical. The difference between them is illustrated by comparing rapture to the joy of a weary desert-farer who sees an oasis in the distance, happiness to his pleasure when drinking from the pond and resting in the shade. The fifth and final factor of absorption is *one-pointedness*, which has the pivotal function of unifying the mind on the object.[62]

When concentration is developed, these five factors spring up and counteract the five hindrances. Each absorption factor opposes

62. See Vism IV, 88–109.

a particular hindrance. Initial application of mind, through its work of lifting the mind up to the object, counters dullness and drowsiness. Sustained application, by anchoring the mind on the object, drives away doubt. Rapture shuts out ill will, happiness excludes restlessness and worry, and one-pointedness counters sensual desire, the most alluring inducement to distraction. Thus, with the strengthening of the absorption factors, the hindrances fade out and subside. They are not yet eradicated—eradication can only be effected by wisdom, the third division of the path—but they have been reduced to a state of quiescence where they cannot disrupt the forward movement of concentration.

At the same time that the hindrances are being overpowered by the *jhāna* factors inwardly, on the side of the object too certain changes are taking place. The original object of concentration, the preliminary sign, is a gross physical object; in the case of a *kasiṇa*, it is a disk representing the chosen element or color, in the case of mindfulness of breathing the touch sensation of the breath, etc. But with the strengthening of concentration the original object gives rise to another object called the "learning sign" (*uggaha-nimitta*). For a *kasiṇa* this will be a mental image of the disk seen as clearly in the mind as the original object was with the eyes; for the breath it will be a reflex image arisen from the touch sensation of the air currents moving around the nostrils.

When the learning sign appears, the meditator leaves off the preliminary sign and fixes his attention on the new object. In due time still another object will emerge out of the learning sign. This object, called the "counterpart sign" (*paṭibhāga-nimitta*), is a purified mental image many times brighter and clearer than the learning sign. The learning sign is compared to the moon seen behind a cloud, the counterpart sign to the moon freed from the cloud. Simultaneously with the appearance of the counterpart sign, the five absorption factors suppress the five hindrances, and the mind enters the stage of concentration called *upacāra-samādhi*, "access concentration." Here, in access concentration, the mind is drawing close to absorption. It has entered the "neighborhood" (a possible meaning of *upacāra*) of absorption, but more work is still needed for it to become fully immersed in the object, the defining mark of absorption.

With further practice the factors of concentration gain in strength and bring the mind to absorption (*appanā-samādhi*). Like access concentration, absorption takes the counterpart sign as object. The two stages of concentration are differentiated neither by the absence of the hindrances nor by the counterpart sign as object; these are common to both. What differentiates them is the strength of the *jhāna* factors. In access concentration the *jhāna* factors are present, but they lack strength and steadiness. Thus the mind in this stage is compared to a child who has just learned to walk: he takes a few steps, falls down, gets up, walks some more, and again falls down. But the mind in absorption is like a man who wants to walk: he just gets up and walks straight ahead without hesitation.

Concentration in the stage of absorption is divided into eight levels, each marked by greater depth, purity, and subtlety than its predecessor. The first four form a set called the four *jhānas*, a word best left untranslated for lack of a suitable equivalent, though it can be loosely rendered "meditative absorption."[63] The second four also form a set, the four immaterial states (*ārupā*). The eight have to be attained in progressive order, the achievement of any later level being dependent on the mastery of the immediately preceding level.

The four jhānas make up the usual textual definition of right concentration. Thus the Buddha says:

> And what, monks, is right concentration? Herein, secluded from sense pleasures, secluded from unwholesome states, a monk enters and dwells in the first *jhāna*, which is accompanied by initial and sustained application of mind and filled with rapture and happiness born of seclusion.
>
> Then, with the subsiding of initial and sustained application of mind, by gaining inner confidence and mental unification, he enters and dwells in the second *jhāna*, which is free from initial and sustained application but is filled with rapture and happiness born of concentration.
>
> With the fading out of rapture, he dwells in equanimity, mindful and clearly comprehending; and he experiences in his

63. Some common renderings such as "trance," "musing," etc., are altogether misleading and should be discarded.

> own person that bliss of which the noble ones say: "Happily lives he who is equanimous and mindful"—thus he enters and dwells in the third *jhāna*.
>
> With the abandoning of pleasure and pain and with the previous disappearance of joy and grief, he enters and dwells in the fourth *jhāna*, which has neither-pleasure-nor-pain and purity of mindfulness due to equanimity.
>
> This, monks, is right concentration.[64]

The jhānas are distinguished by way of their component factors. The first *jhāna* is constituted by the original set of five absorption factors: initial application, sustained application, rapture, happiness, and one-pointedness. After attaining the first *jhāna* the meditator is advised to master it. On the one hand he should not fall into complacency over his achievement and neglect sustained practice; on the other, he should not become over-confident and rush ahead to attain the next *jhāna*. To master the *jhāna* he should enter it repeatedly and perfect his skill in it, until he can attain it, remain in it, emerge from it, and review it without any trouble or difficulty.

After mastering the first *jhāna*, the meditator then considers that his attainment has certain defects. Though the *jhāna* is certainly far superior to ordinary sense consciousness, more peaceful and blissful, it still stands close to sense consciousness and is not far removed from the hindrances. Moreover, two of its factors, initial application and sustained application, appear in time to be rather coarse, not as refined as the other factors. Then the meditator renews his practice of concentration intent on overcoming initial and sustained application. When his faculties mature, these two factors subside and he enters the second *jhāna*. This *jhāna* contains only three component factors: rapture, happiness, and one-pointedness. It also contains a multiplicity of other constituents, the most prominent of which is confidence of mind.

In the second *jhāna* the mind becomes more tranquil and more thoroughly unified, but when mastered even this state seems gross, as it includes rapture, an exhilarating factor that inclines to excitation. So the meditator sets out again on his course of

64. DN 22; *Word of the Buddha*, pp. 80–81.

training, this time resolved on overcoming rapture. When rapture fades out, he enters the third *jhāna*. Here there are only two absorption factors, happiness and one-pointedness, while some other auxiliary states come into ascendancy, most notably mindfulness, clear comprehension, and equanimity. But still, the meditator sees, this attainment is defective in that it contains the feeling of happiness, which is gross compared to neutral feeling, feeling that is neither pleasant not painful. Thus he strives to get beyond even the sublime happiness of the third *jhāna*. When he succeeds, he enters the fourth *jhāna*, which is defined by two factors—one-pointedness and neutral feeling—and has a special purity of mindfulness due to the high level of equanimity.

Beyond the four jhānas lie the four immaterial states, levels of absorption in which the mind transcends even the subtlest perception of visualized images still sometimes persisting in the jhānas. The immaterial states are attained, not by refining mental factors as are the jhānas, but by refining objects, by replacing a relatively gross object with a subtler one. The four attainments are named after their respective objects: the base of infinite space, the base of infinite consciousness, the base of nothingness, and the base of neither-perception-nor-non-perception.[65] These states represent levels of concentration so subtle and remote as to elude clear verbal explanation. The last of the four stands at the apex of mental concentration; it is the absolute, maximum degree of unification possible for consciousness. But even so, these absorptions reached by the path of serenity meditation, as exalted as they are, still lack the wisdom of insight, and so are not yet sufficient for gaining deliverance.

The kinds of concentration discussed so far arise by fixing the mind upon a single object to the exclusion of other objects. But apart from these there is another kind of concentration which does not depend upon restricting the range of awareness. This is called "momentary concentration" (*khaṇika-samādhi*). To develop momentary concentration the meditator does not deliberately attempt to exclude the multiplicity of phenomena from his field of attention. Instead, he simply directs mindfulness

---

65. In Pāli: *ākāsānañcāyatana, viññāṇañcāyatana, ākiñcaññāyatana, n'eva-saññā-nāsaññāyatana.*

to the changing states of mind and body, noting any phenomenon that presents itself; the task is to maintain a continuous awareness of whatever enters the range of perception, clinging to nothing. As he goes on with his noting, concentration becomes stronger moment after moment until it becomes established one-pointedly on the constantly changing stream of events. Despite the change in the object, the mental unification remains steady, and in time acquires a force capable of suppressing the hindrances to a degree equal to that of access concentration. This fluid, mobile concentration is developed by the practice of the four foundations of mindfulness, taken up along the path of insight; when sufficiently strong it issues in the breakthrough to the last stage of the path, the arising of wisdom.

VIII. The Development of Wisdom

Though right concentration claims the last place among the factors of the Noble Eightfold Path, concentration itself does not mark the path's culmination. The attainment of concentration makes the mind still and steady, unifies its concomitants, opens vast vistas of bliss, serenity, and power. But by itself it does not suffice to reach the highest accomplishment, release from the bonds of suffering. To reach the end of suffering demands that the Eightfold Path be turned into an instrument of discovery, that it be used to generate the insights unveiling the ultimate truth of things. This requires the combined contributions of all eight factors, and thus a new mobilization of right view and right intention. Up to the present point these first two path factors have performed only a preliminary function. Now they have to be taken up again and raised to a higher level. Right view is to become a direct seeing into the real nature of phenomena, previously grasped only conceptually; right intention, to become a true renunciation of defilements born out of deep understanding.

Before we turn to the development of wisdom, it will be helpful to inquire why concentration is not adequate to the attainment of liberation. Concentration does not suffice to bring liberation because it fails to touch the defilements at their fundamental level.

The Buddha teaches that the defilements are stratified into three layers: the stage of latent tendency, the stage of manifestation, and the stage of transgression. The most deeply grounded is the level of latent tendency (*anusaya*), where a defilement merely lies dormant without displaying any activity. The second level is the stage of manifestation (*pariyuṭṭhāna*), where a defilement, through the impact of some stimulus, surges up in the form of unwholesome thoughts, emotions, and volitions. Then, at the third level, the defilement passes beyond a purely mental manifestation to motivate some unwholesome action of body or speech. Hence this level is called the stage of transgression (*vītikkama*).

The three divisions of the Noble Eightfold Path provide the check against this threefold layering of the defilements. The first, the training in moral discipline, restrains unwholesome bodily and verbal activity and thus prevents defilements from reaching the stage of transgression. The training in concentration provides the safeguard against the stage of manifestation. It removes already manifest defilements and protects the mind from their continued influx. But even though concentration may be pursued to the depths of full absorption, it cannot touch the basic source of affliction—the latent tendencies lying dormant in the mental continuum. Against these concentration is powerless, since to root them out calls for more than mental calm. What it calls for, beyond the composure and serenity of the unified mind, is wisdom (*paññā*), a penetrating vision of phenomena in their fundamental mode of being.

Wisdom alone can cut off the latent tendencies at their root because the most fundamental member of the set, the one which nurtures the others and holds them in place, is ignorance (*avijjā*), and wisdom is the remedy for ignorance. Though verbally a negative, "unknowing," ignorance is not a factual negative, a mere privation of right knowledge. It is, rather, an insidious and volatile mental factor incessantly at work inserting itself into every compartment of our inner life. It distorts cognition, dominates volition, and determines the entire tone of our existence. As the Buddha says: "The element of ignorance is indeed a powerful element" (SN14:13).

At the cognitive level, which is its most basic sphere of operation, ignorance infiltrates our perceptions, thoughts, and views, so that we come to misconstrue our experience, overlaying it with multiple strata of delusions. The most important of these delusions are three: the delusions of seeing permanence in the impermanent, of seeing satisfaction in the unsatisfactory, and of seeing a self in the selfless.[66] Thus we take ourselves and our world to be solid, stable, enduring entities, despite the ubiquitous reminders that everything is subject to change and destruction. We assume we have an innate right to pleasure, and direct our efforts to increasing and intensifying our enjoyment with an anticipatory fervor undaunted by repeated encounters with pain, disappointment, and frustration. And we perceive ourselves as self-contained egos, clinging to the various ideas and images we form of ourselves as the irrefragable truth of our identity.

Whereas ignorance obscures the true nature of things, wisdom removes the veils of distortion, enabling us to see phenomena in their fundamental mode of being with the vivacity of direct perception. The training in wisdom centres on the development of insight (*vipassanā-bhāvanā*), a deep and comprehensive seeing into the nature of existence which fathoms the truth of our being in the only sphere where it is directly accessible to us, namely, in our own experience. Normally we are immersed in our experience, identified with it so completely that we do not comprehend it. We live it but fail to understand its nature. Due to this blindness experience comes to be misconstrued, worked upon by the delusions of permanence, pleasure, and self. Of these cognitive distortions, the most deeply grounded and resistant is the delusion of self, the idea that at the core of our being there exists a truly established "I" with which we are essentially identified. This notion of self, the Buddha teaches, is an error, a mere presupposition lacking a real referent. Yet, though a mere presupposition, the idea of self is not inconsequential. To the contrary, it entails consequences that can be calamitous. Because we make the view of self the lookout point from which we survey the world, our minds divide everything up into the dualities of "I" and "not I," what is "mine" and what is "not mine." Then, trapped in these dichotomies, we fall victim to the defilements

66. *Anicce niccavipallāsa, dukkhe sukhavipallāsa, anattani atta-vipallāsa* (AN 4:49).

they breed, the urges to grasp and destroy, and finally to the suffering that inevitably follows.

To free ourselves from all defilements and suffering, the illusion of selfhood that sustains them has to be dispelled, exploded by the realization of selflessness. Precisely this is the task set for the development of wisdom. The first step along the path of development is an analytical one. In order to uproot the view of self, the field of experience has to be laid out in certain sets of factors, which are then methodically investigated to ascertain that none of them singly or in combination can be taken as a self. This analytical treatment of experience, so characteristic of the higher reaches of Buddhist philosophical psychology, is not intended to suggest that experience, like a watch or car, can be reduced to an accidental conglomeration of separable parts. Experience does have an irreducible unity, but this unity is functional rather than substantial; it does not require the postulate of a unifying self separate from the factors, retaining its identity as a constant amidst the ceaseless flux.

The method of analysis applied most often is that of the five aggregates of clinging (*pañc'upādānakkhandhā*): material form, feeling, perception, mental formations, and consciousness.[67]

Material form constitutes the material side of existence: the bodily organism with its sense faculties and the outer objects of cognition. The other four aggregates constitute the mental side. Feeling provides the affective tone, perception the factor of noting and identifying, the mental formations the volitional and emotive elements, and consciousness the basic awareness essential to the whole occasion of experience. The analysis by way of the five aggregates paves the way for an attempt to see experience solely in terms of its constituting factors, without slipping in implicit references to an unfindable self. To gain this perspective requires the development of intensive mindfulness, now applied to the fourth foundation, the contemplation of the factors of existence (*dhammānupassanā*). The disciple will dwell contemplating the five aggregates, their arising and passing:

---

67. In Pāli: *rūpakkhandha, vedanākkhandha, saññākkhandha, saṅkhārakkhandha, viññāṇakkhandha.*

> The disciple dwells in contemplation of phenomena, namely, of the five aggregates of clinging. He knows what material form is, how it arises, how it passes away; knows what feeling is, how it arises, how it passes away; knows what perception is, how it arises, how it passes away; knows what mental formations are, how they arise, how they pass away; knows what consciousness is, how it arises, how it passes away.[68]

Or the disciple may instead base his contemplation on the six internal and external spheres of sense experience, that is, the six sense faculties and their corresponding objects, also taking note of the "fetters" or defilements that arise from such sensory contacts:

> The disciple dwells in contemplation of phenomena, namely, of the six internal and external sense bases. He knows the eye and forms, the ear and sounds, the nose and odours, the tongue and tastes, the body and tangibles, the mind and mental objects; and he knows as well the fetter that arises in dependence on them. He understands how the unarisen fetter arises, how the arisen fetter is abandoned, and how the abandoned fetter does not arise again in the future.[69]

The view of self is further attenuated by examining the factors of existence, not analytically, but in terms of their relational structure. Inspection reveals that the aggregates exist solely in dependence on conditions. Nothing in the set enjoys the absolute self-sufficiency of being attributed to the assumed "I." Whatever factors in the body-mind complex be looked at, they are found to be dependently arisen, tied to the vast net of events extending beyond themselves temporally and spatially. The body, for example, has arisen through the union of sperm and egg and subsists in dependence on food, water, and air. Feeling, perception, and mental formations occur in dependence on the body with its sense faculties. They require an object, the corresponding consciousness, and the contact of the object with the consciousness through the media of the sense faculties. Consciousness in its turn depends on the sentient organism and the entire assemblage of co-arisen mental factors. This whole process of becoming, moreover,

68. DN 22; *Word of the Buddha*, pp. 71–72.

69. Ibid.; *Word of the Buddha*, p. 73.

has arisen from the previous lives in this particular chain of existences and inherits all the accumulated *kamma* of the earlier existences. Thus nothing possesses a self-sufficient mode of being. All conditioned phenomena exist relationally, contingent and dependent on other things.

The above two steps—the factorial analysis and the discernment of relations—help cut away the intellectual adherence to the idea of self, but they lack sufficient power to destroy the ingrained clinging to the ego sustained by erroneous perception. To uproot this subtle form of ego-clinging requires a counteractive perception: direct insight into the empty, coreless nature of phenomena. Such an insight is generated by contemplating the factors of existence in terms of their three universal marks—impermanence (*aniccatā*), unsatisfactoriness (*dukkhatā*), and selflessness (*anattatā*). Generally, the first of the three marks to be discerned is impermanence, which at the level of insight does not mean merely that everything eventually comes to an end. At this level it means something deeper and more pervasive, namely, that conditioned phenomena are in constant process, happenings which break up and perish almost as soon as they arise. The stable objects appearing to the senses reveal themselves to be strings of momentary formations (*saṅkhārā*); the person posited by common sense dissolves into a current made up of two intertwining streams—a stream of material events, the aggregate of material form, and a stream of mental events, the other four aggregates.

When impermanence is seen, insight into the other two marks closely follows. Since the aggregates are constantly breaking up, we cannot pin our hopes on them for any lasting satisfaction. Whatever expectations we lay on them are bound to be dashed to pieces by their inevitable change. Thus when seen with insight they are *dukkha*, suffering, in the deepest sense. Then, as the aggregates are impermanent and unsatisfactory, they cannot be taken as self. If they were self, or the belongings of a self, we would be able to control them and bend them to our will, to make them everlasting sources of bliss. But far from being able to exercise such mastery, we find them to be grounds of pain and disappointment. Since they cannot be subjected to control, these very factors of our being are *anattā:* not a self, not the belongings of a self, just empty, ownerless phenomena occurring in dependence on conditions.

When the course of insight practice is entered, the eight path factors become charged with an intensity previously unknown. They gain in force and fuse together into the unity of a single cohesive path heading towards the goal. In the practice of insight all eight factors and three trainings co-exist; each is there supporting all the others; each makes its own unique contribution to the work. The factors of moral discipline hold the tendencies to transgression in check with such care that even the thought of unethical conduct does not arise. The factors of the concentration group keep the mind firmly fixed upon the stream of phenomena, contemplating whatever arises with impeccable precision, free from forgetfulness and distraction. Right view, as the wisdom of insight, grows continually sharper and deeper; right intention shows itself in a detachment and steadiness of purpose bringing an unruffled poise to the entire process of contemplation.

Insight meditation takes as its objective sphere the "conditioned formations" (*saṅkhārā*) comprised in the five aggregates. Its task is to uncover their essential characteristics: the three marks of impermanence, unsatisfactoriness, and selflessness. Because it still deals with the world of conditioned events, the Eightfold Path in the stage of insight is called the mundane path (*lokiyamagga*). This designation in no way implies that the path of insight is concerned with mundane goals, with achievements falling in the range of saṃsāra. It aspires to transcendence, it leads to liberation, but its objective domain of contemplation still lies within the conditioned world. However, this mundane contemplation of the conditioned serves as the vehicle for reaching the unconditioned, for attaining the supramundane. When insight meditation reaches its climax, when it fully comprehends the impermanence, unsatisfactoriness, and selflessness of everything formed, the mind breaks through the conditioned and realizes the unconditioned, *Nibbāna*. It sees *Nibbāna* with direct vision, makes it an object of immediate realization.

The breakthrough to the unconditioned is achieved by a type of consciousness or mental event called the supramundane path (*lokuttaramagga*). The supramundane path occurs in four stages, four "supramundane paths," each marking a deeper level of realization and issuing in a fuller degree of liberation, the fourth and last in complete liberation. The four paths can be achieved in close proximity to one another—for those with extraordinarily sharp faculties even in the same sitting—or (as is more typically the case) they can be spread out over time, even over several lifetimes.[70] The supramundane paths share in common the penetration of the Four Noble Truths. They understand them, not conceptually, but intuitively. They grasp them through vision, seeing them with self-validating certainty to be the invariable truths of existence. The vision of the truths which they present is complete at one moment. The four truths are not understood sequentially, as in the stage of reflection when thought is the instrument of understanding. They are seen simultaneously: to see one truth with the path is to see them all.

As the path penetrates the four truths, the mind exercises four simultaneous functions, one regarding each truth. It fully comprehends the truth of suffering, seeing all conditioned existence as stamped with the mark of unsatisfactoriness. At the same time it abandons craving, cuts through the mass of egotism and desire that repeatedly gives birth to suffering. Again, the mind realizes cessation, the deathless element *Nibbāna*, now directly present to the inner eye. And fourthly, the mind develops the Noble Eightfold Path, whose eight factors spring up endowed with tremendous power, attained to supramundane stature: right view as the direct seeing of *Nibbāna*, right intention as the mind's application to *Nibbāna*, the triad of ethical factors as the checks on moral transgression, right effort as the energy in the path-consciousness, right mindfulness as the factor of awareness, and right concentration as the mind's one-pointed focus. This ability of the mind to perform four functions at the same moment is

70. In the first edition of this book I stated here that the four paths have to be passed through sequentially, such that there is no attainment of a higher path without first having reached the paths below it. This certainly seems to be the position of the Commentaries. However, the Suttas sometimes show individuals proceeding directly from the stage of worldling to the third or even the fourth path and fruit. Though the commentator explains that they passed through each preceding path and fruit in rapid succession, the canonical texts themselves give no indication that this has transpired but suggest an immediate realization of the higher stages without the intermediate attainment of the lower stages.

compared to a candle's ability to simultaneously burn the wick, consume the wax, dispel darkness, and give light.[71]

The supramundane paths have the special task of eradicating the defilements. Prior to the attainment of the paths, in the stages of concentration and even insight meditation, the defilements were not cut off but were only debilitated, checked and suppressed by the training of the higher mental faculties. Beneath the surface they continued to linger in the form of latent tendencies. But when the supramundane paths are reached, the work of eradication begins.

Insofar as they bind us to the round of becoming, the defilements are classified into a set of ten "fetters" (*saṃyojana*) as follows: (1) personality view, (2) doubt, (3) clinging to rules and rituals, (4) sensual desire, (5) aversion, (6) desire for fine-material existence, (7) desire for immaterial existence, (8) conceit, (9) restlessness, and (10) ignorance. The four supramundane paths each eliminate a certain layer of defilements. The first, the path of stream-entry (*sotāpatti-magga*), cuts off the first three fetters, the coarsest of the set, eliminates them so they can never arise again. "Personality view" (*sakkāya-diṭṭhi*), the view of a truly existent self in the five aggregates, is cut off since one sees the selfless nature of all phenomena. Doubt is eliminated because one has grasped the truth proclaimed by the Buddha, seen it for oneself, and so can never again hang back due to uncertainty. And clinging to rules and rites is removed since one knows that deliverance can be won only through the practice of the Eightfold Path, not through rigid moralism or ceremonial observances.

The path is followed immediately by another state of supramundane consciousness known as the fruit (*phala*), which results from the path's work of cutting off defilements. Each path is followed by its own fruit, wherein for a few moments the mind enjoys the blissful peace of *Nibbāna* before descending again to the level of mundane consciousness. The first fruit is the fruit of stream-entry, and a person who has gone through the experience of this fruit becomes a "stream-enterer" (*sotāpanna*). He has entered the stream of the Dhamma carrying him to final deliverance. He is bound for liberation and can no longer fall back into the ways of an unenlightened worldling. He still has certain

71. See Vism XXII, 92–103.

defilements remaining in his mental makeup, and it may take him as long as seven more lives to arrive at the final goal, but he has acquired the essential realization needed to reach it, and there is no way he can fall away.

An enthusiastic practitioner with sharp faculties, after reaching stream-entry, does not relax his striving but puts forth energy to complete the entire path as swiftly as possible. He resumes his practice of insight contemplation, passes through the ascending stages of insight-knowledge, and in time reaches the second path, the path of the once-returner (*sakadāgāmi-magga*). This supramundane path does not totally eradicate any of the fetters, but it attenuates the roots of greed, aversion, and delusion. Following the path the meditator experiences its fruit, then emerges as a "once-returner" who will return to this world at most only one more time before attaining full liberation.

But our practitioner again takes up the task of contemplation. At the next stage of supramundane realization he attains the third path, the path of the non-returner (*anāgāmi-magga*), with which he cuts off the two fetters of sensual desire and ill will. From that point on he can never again fall into the grip of any desire for sense pleasure, and can never be aroused to anger, aversion, or discontent. As a non-returner he will not return to the human state of existence in any future life. If he does not reach the last path in this very life, then after death he will be reborn in a higher sphere in the fine-material world (*rūpaloka*) and there reach deliverance.

But our meditator again puts forth effort, develops insight, and at its climax enters the fourth path, the path of arahatship (*arahatta-magga*). With this path he cuts off the five remaining fetters—desire for fine-material existence and desire for immaterial existence, conceit, restlessness, and ignorance. The first is the desire for rebirth into the celestial planes made accessible by the four jhānas, the planes commonly subsumed under the name "the Brahma-world." The second is the desire for rebirth into the four immaterial planes made accessible by the achievement of the four immaterial attainments. Conceit (*māna*) is not the coarse type of pride to which we become disposed through an over-estimation of our virtues and talents, but the subtle residue of the notion of an ego which subsists even after conceptually explicit views of self have been eradicated. The texts refer to this type of conceit as the conceit "I am" (*asmimāna*). Restlessness (*uddhacca*) is the subtle excitement which persists in any mind not yet completely enlightened, and ignorance (*avijjā*) is the fundamental cognitive obscuration which prevents full understanding of the Four Noble Truths. Although the grosser grades of ignorance have been scoured from the mind by the wisdom faculty in the first three paths, a thin veil of ignorance overlays the truths even in the non-returner.

The path of arahatship strips away this last veil of ignorance and, with it, all the residual mental defilements. This path issues in perfect comprehension of the Four Noble Truths. It fully fathoms the truth of suffering; eradicates the craving from which suffering springs; realizes with complete clarity the unconditioned element, *Nibbāna*, as the cessation of suffering; and consummates the development of the eight factors of the Noble Eightfold Path.

With the attainment of the fourth path and fruit the disciple emerges as an *arahat*, one who in this very life has been liberated from all bonds. The *arahat* has walked the Noble Eightfold Path to its end and lives in the assurance stated so often in the formula from the Pāli Canon: "Destroyed is birth; the holy life has been lived; what had to be done has been done; there is no coming back to any state of being." The *arahat* is no longer a practitioner of the path but its living embodiment. Having developed the eight factors of the path to their consummation, the Liberated One lives in the enjoyment of their fruits, enlightenment and final deliverance.

Epilogue

This completes our survey of the Noble Eightfold Path, the way to deliverance from suffering taught by the Buddha. The higher reaches of the path may seem remote from us in our present position, the demands of practice may appear difficult to fulfil. But even if the heights of realization are now distant, all that we need to reach them lies just beneath our feet. The eight factors of the path are always accessible to us; they are mental components which can be established in the mind simply through determination and effort. We have to begin by straightening out our views and clarifying our intentions. Then we have to purify our conduct—our speech, action, and livelihood. Taking these measures as our foundation, we have to apply ourselves with energy and mindfulness to the cultivation of concentration and insight. The rest is a matter of gradual practice and gradual progress, without expecting quick results. For some progress may be rapid, for others it may be slow, but the rate at which progress occurs should not cause elation or discouragement. Liberation is the inevitable fruit of the path and is bound to blossom forth when there is steady and persistent practice. The only requirements for reaching the final goal are two: to start and to continue. If these requirements are met there is no doubt the goal will be attained. This is the Dhamma, the undeviating law.

Appendix

A Factorial Analysis of the Noble Eightfold Path
(Pāli and English)

(i)	*Sammā diṭṭhi*	Right view
	• *dukkhe ñāṇa*	• understanding suffering
	• *dukkhasamudaye ñāṇa*	• understanding its origin
	• *dukkha-nirodhe ñaṇa*	• understanding its cessation
	• *dukkha-nirodha-gāminī-paṭipadāya ñāṇa*	• understanding the way leading to its cessation
(ii)	*Sammā saṅkappa*	Right intention
	• *nekkhamma-saṅkappa*	• intention of renunciation
	• *abyāpāda-saṅkappa*	• intention of good will
	• *avihiṃsā-saṅkappa*	• intention of harmlessness
(iii)	*Sammā vācā*	Right speech
	• *musāvādā veramaṇī*	• abstaining from false speech
	• *pisuṇāya vācāya veramaṇī*	• abstaining from slanderous speech
	• *pharusāya vācāya veramaṇī*	• abstaining from harsh speech
	• *samphappalāpā veramaṇī*	• abstaining from idle chatter
(iv)	*Sammā kammanta*	Right action
	• *pāṇātipātā veramaṇī*	• abstaining from taking life
	• *adinnādānā veramaṇī*	• abstaining from stealing
	• *kāmesu micchā-cārā veramaṇī*	• abstaining from sexual misconduct
(v)	*Sammā ājīva*	Right livelihood
	• *micchā ājīvaṃ pahāya sammā ājīvena jīvitaṃ kappeti*	• giving up wrong livelihood, one earns one's living by a right form of livelihood
(vi)	*Sammā vāyāma*	Right effort
	• *saṃvarappadhāna*	• effort to restrain defilements
	• *pahānappadhāna*	• effort to abandon defilements
	• *bhāvanāppadhāna*	• effort to develop wholesome states

	• *anurakkhaṇappa-dhāna*	• effort to maintain wholesome states
(vii)	*Sammā sati*	Right mindfulness
	• *kāyānupassanā*	• mindful contemplation of the body
	• *vedanānupassanā*	• mindful contemplation of feelings
	• *cittānupassanā*	• mindful contemplation of the mind
	• *dhammānupassanā*	• mindful contemplation of phenomena
(viii)	*Sammā samādhi*	Right concentration
	• *paṭhamajjhāna*	• the first *jhāna*
	• *dutiyajjhāna*	• the second *jhāna*
	• *tatiyajjhāna*	• the third *jhāna*
	• *catutthajjhāna*	• the fourth *jhāna*

Recommended Reading

I. General treatments of the Noble Eightfold Path

Ledi Sayadaw. *The Noble Eightfold Path and Its Factors Explained.* (Wheel 245/247).
Nyanatiloka Thera. *The Word of the Buddha.* (BPS, 2011).
Piyadassi Thera. *The Buddha's Ancient Path.* (BPS, 2003).

II. Right View

Ñāṇamoli, Bhikkhu. *The Discourse on Right View.* (Wheel 377/379).
Nyanatiloka Thera. *Karma and Rebirth.* (see Wheel 394/396).
Story, Francis. *The Four Noble Truths.* (Wheel 34/35).
Wijesekera, O.H. de A. *The Three Signata.* (Wheel 20).

III. Right Intention

Ñāṇamoli Thera. *The Practice of Loving Kindness.* (Wheel 7).
Nyanaponika Thera. *The Four Sublime States.* (Wheel 6).
Prince, T. *Renunciation.* (Bodhi Leaf 36).

IV. Right Speech, Right Action, & Right Livelihood

Bodhi, Bhikkhu. *Going for Refuge and Taking the Precepts.* (Wheel 282/284).
Nārada Thera. *Everyman's Ethics.* (Wheel 14).
Vajirañāṇavarorasa. *The Five Precepts and the Five Ennoblers.* (Bangkok: Mahāmakuṭa, 1975).

V. Right Effort

Nyanaponika Thera. *The Five Mental Hindrances and Their Conquest.* (Wheel 26).
Piyadassi Thera. *The Seven Factors of Enlightenment.* (Wheel 1).
Soma Thera. *The Removal of Distracting Thoughts.* (Wheel 21).

VI. Right Mindfulness

Nyanaponika Thera. *The Heart of Buddhist Meditation.* (BPS, 2012).
Nyanaponika Thera. *The Power of Mindfulness.* (Wheel 121/122).
Nyanasatta Thera. *The Foundations of Mindfulness* (Satipaṭṭhāna Sutta). (Wheel 19, reissued as bookshop item BP522).
Soma Thera. *The Way of Mindfulness.* (BPS, 2003).

VII. Right Concentration & The Development of Wisdom

Buddhaghosa, Bhadantacariya. *The Path of Purification* (*Visuddhi-magga*). Translated by Bhikkhu Ñāṇamoli, 4th ed. (BPS, 2011).
Khantipālo, Bhikkhu. *Calm and Insight.* (London: Curzon, 1980).
Ledi Sayadaw. *A Manual of Insight.* (Wheel 31/32).
Nyanatiloka Thera. *The Buddha's Path to Deliverance.* (BPS, 2010).
Solé-Leris, Amadeo. *Tranquillity and Insight.* (London: Rider, 1986; BPS, 1992; BPS Pariyatti Edition, 2023).
Vajirañāṇa, Paravahera. *Buddhist Meditation in Theory and Practice.* 2nd ed. (Kuala Lumpur, Malaysia: Buddhist Missionary Society, 1975).

All Wheel Publications and Bodhi Leaves referred to above were published by the Buddhist Publication Society, and republished by Pariyatti (pariyatti.org) and available worldwide (store.pariyatti.org).

ABOUT PARIYATTI

Pariyatti is dedicated to providing affordable access to authentic teachings of the Buddha about the Dhamma theory (*pariyatti*) and practice (*paṭipatti*) of Vipassana meditation. A 501(c)(3) nonprofit charitable organization since 2002, Pariyatti is sustained by contributions from individuals who appreciate and want to share the incalculable value of the Dhamma teachings. We invite you to visit www.pariyatti.org to learn about our programs, services, and ways to support publishing and other undertakings.

Pariyatti Publishing Imprints

Vipassana Research Publications (focus on Vipassana as taught by S.N. Goenka in the tradition of Sayagyi U Ba Khin)

BPS Pariyatti Editions (selected titles from the Buddhist Publication Society, copublished by Pariyatti)

MPA Pariyatti Editions (selected titles from the Myanmar Pitaka Association, copublished by Pariyatti)

Pariyatti Digital Editions (audio and video titles, including discourses)

Pariyatti Press (classic titles returned to print and inspirational writing by contemporary authors)

Pariyatti enriches the world by

- disseminating the words of the Buddha,
- providing sustenance for the seeker's journey,
- illuminating the meditator's path.

www.ingramcontent.com/pod-product-compliance
Lightning Source LLC
Chambersburg PA
CBHW020349170426
43200CB00005B/104
* 9 7 8 1 6 8 1 7 2 2 0 0 9 *